Secret Societies in America:
Foundational Studies of Fraternalism

Selected and Edited by
William D. Moore and Mark A. Tabbert

Secret Societies in America:
Foundational Studies of Fraternalism

A Cornerstone Book
Published by Cornerstone Book Publishers
An Imprint of Michael Poll Publishing
Copyright © 2011 by William D. Moore and Mark A. Tabbert

Cornerstone Book Publishers
New Orleans, LA

Cover Images:
Officers of the Grand Lodge, Ancient Free & Accepted Masons, of Idaho, 1876. Courtesy of the Grand Lodge of Idaho, Ancient Free & Accepted Masons.

John C. H. Grabill, Photograph of Grand Lodge I. O. O. F. of Dakotas, Street Parade, May 21, 1890. Courtesy of the Library of Congress, Prints & Photographs. LOT 3076-5, no. 3175.

Photo editing by Arthur W. Pierson Photography, Falls Church, Virginia (www.piersonphoto.com)

First Cornerstone Edition - 2011
www.cornerstonepublishers.com

ISBN: 1-613420-24-2
ISBN 13: 978-1-61342-024-9

MADE IN THE USA

The American has dwindled into an Odd-Fellow, - one who may be known by the development of his organ of gregariousness . . . who . . . ventures to live. . . by the aid of the mutual insurance company, which has promised to bury him decently . . .

- Henry David Thoreau

Introduction
by William D. Moore

FRATERNAL organizations were a characteristic feature of American society during the decades surrounding the turn of the twentieth century. Throughout the nineteenth century Americans had organized and joined voluntary ritualistic groups, basing their activities upon a model established by Freemasons in North America as early as the 1730s. In 1897, W.S. Harwood, writing in the *North American Review*, dubbed the post-bellum period the "Golden Age of Fraternalism."[1] He noted that fraternal organizations, then commonly called "secret societies," claimed 5.5 million members while the total U. S. adult population was approximately 19 million. At the time, the five largest fraternal groups – Freemasons, Odd Fellows, Knights of Pythias, Ancient Order of United Workmen, and Knights of the Maccabees – had a combined membership of more than 2.5 million. Albert C. Stevens, compiler of the invaluable *Cyclopedia of Fraternities*, estimated that 40 percent of all adult males held membership in at least one fraternal order.[2]

By bringing together foundational studies of American fraternalism, this volume seeks to assist and promote the burgeoning scholarship on this aspect of American life. Throughout most of the twentieth century, American scholars largely ignored groups like the Modern Woodmen of America, the Knights of Columbus, the Patriotic Order of Sons of America, the Fraternal Order of Eagles, the Benevolent and Protective Order of Elks, the Ancient Order of Foresters, and even the Freemasons. Individuals who sought to examine and explain the American experience disregarded the fraternal affiliations of prominent figures, including presidents and captains of industry, or treated these biographical details as peculiar and inconsequential. Ritual-based orders, and their millions of members, were largely perceived to be unworthy of scholarly investigation.

Fraternal Studies
Following the celebration of the American bicentennial in 1976, however, a cohort of scholars forged a new and vital literature which has demonstrated the significance of these groups to

American society. Founded by the Supreme Council, 33°, Ancient Accepted Scottish Rite of Freemasonry, Northern Masonic Jurisdiction, USA, as a patriotic gift to the American people, the Museum of Our National Heritage, in Lexington, Massachusetts, generated the earliest contributions to this scholarship. Under the leadership of Clement M. Silvestro, an accomplished and respected museum professional who previously had served as director of the American Association for State and Local History and associate director of the Chicago Historical Society, this institution established a mission of collecting and analyzing the material culture of American fraternalism.[3] Barbara Franco, a graduate of the Cooperstown Graduate Program in museum studies, mounted a series of innovative and influential exhibitions, with accompanying catalogues, which insightfully examined the fascinating, but underappreciated, physical manifestations of America's culture of voluntarism.[4]

While Franco and the Museum of Our National Heritage were exhibiting fraternal materials, other scholars also became interested in the subject. In 1982, Harper & Row published Christopher J. Kaufman's *Faith & Fraternalism: The History of the Knights of Columbus, 1882-1982*.[5] Although in many ways his work is a conservative organizationally commissioned institutional history, Kaufman successfully demonstrated that the Knights of Columbus had played a significant role in the development of the American Catholic church and within American society as a whole. Princeton University Press in 1984 published Lynn Dumenil's *Freemasonry and American Culture, 1880 – 1930* which originated as her doctoral dissertation at the University of California Berkeley.[6] This seminal work sought to understand the role of voluntary associations within the industrializing United States and focused upon issues related to the secularization of the fraternity. Dumenil argued that Freemasonry mirrored American society, and thus an analysis of the group could provide insight into middle-class attitudes towards work, leisure, success, morality, and religion during a period of profound change resulting from industrialization, urbanization, and modernization.[7]

Both Kaufman and Dumenil examined groups with exclusively male memberships, but neither utilized gender as a mode of analysis. Kaufman viewed the Knights as Catholics; Dumenil understood the Masons as bourgeois. Neither author focused upon these groups as representing men purposefully gathering with other men. In the early eighties, gender studies were still largely concerned with the social construction of femininity. Scholars were not yet investigating how American manhood was defined historically.

In 1989, two monographs propelled the study of masculinity to the forefront of scholarly discussions of American fraternalism. Mary Ann Clawson's *Constructing Brotherhood: Class, Gender, and Fraternalism* offered a sociological argument which posited that fraternalism was a resource with which Americans constructed power relations in a manner that emphasized gender identity while camouflaging class distinctions.[8] Grounded in social history, Clawson's study is rich in numerical details concerning membership demographics and financial relationships. The same year, Mark Carnes' *Secret Ritual and Manhood in Victorian America* proffered a psychosexual analysis of American fraternal rituals.[9] Carnes built upon Dumenil, but examined what the rituals performed by fraternalists revealed about how participants situated themselves within the world and in relation to existential human issues such as death, kinship, and interpersonal responsibility. Carnes' impact upon the field is visible in Franco's subsequent article "The Ritualization of Male Friendship and Virtue in Nineteenth-Century Fraternal Organizations" which appeared in 1997.[10]

During this period, the American historical establishment encouraged scholarship that investigated how institutions have structured culture and society. Carnes, Clawson, and Dumenil participated in this discourse. Subsequent scholars, seeking to further illuminate these issues, continued to scrutinize the history and practices of fraternal groups. In *Service Clubs in American Society: Rotary, Kiwanis, and Lions*, Jeffrey Charles provided the first serious analysis of the twentieth-century groups which evolved out of the nineteenth-century secret orders.[11] Similarly, in his volume entitled *From Mutual Aid to the Welfare State: Fraternal Societies and Social Services, 1890-1967*, David Beito examined the social, medical and financial benefits provided by fraternal organizations.[12] Steven C. Bullock's *Revolutionary Brotherhood: Freemasonry and the Transformation of the American Social Order, 1730-1840* will be, for the foreseeable future, the most essential resource for individuals examining the first century of Masonry in the United States.[13]

In the new century, scholars have used fraternal organizations to examine the bonds which link individuals together to form society. Robert Putnam's much-cited *Bowling Alone: The Collapse and Revival of American Community* made the term "social capital" part of our common American vocabulary.[14] Putnam suggests that the decline of secret societies in the twentieth century is one manifestation of a larger decay of American social institutions which has left individuals alienated and disconnected from their families, friends, and neighbors. Reacting to Putnam's work, Theda Skocpol, a sociologist at Harvard, led a group of scholars to examine the influence of fraternal groups upon black Americans. This work culminated in *"What a Mighty Power We Can Be": African American Fraternal Groups and the Struggle for Racial Equality* published by Princeton University Press.[15] In contrast to Putnam and Skocpol, Jason Kaufman has argued, in his *For the Common Good? American Civic Life and the Golden Age of Fraternity*, that fraternal societies were corrosive, rather than beneficial, and that they exacerbated ethnic, race, religious, and class distinctions.[16]

Recent increased scholarly attention to fraternalism has resulted in conferences and academic fellowships. Established in 2007 in Edinburgh, Scotland, the International Conference on the History of Freemasonry provides a forum for scholars from around the world to discuss Freemasonry and fraternalism.[17] This biannual conference has featured work on American fraternal organizations at each of its gatherings. Similarly, in January of 2010, the National Heritage Museum, in Lexington, Massachusetts, sponsored a symposium entitled "New Perspectives on American Freemasonry and Fraternalism" which drew participants from across the United States.[18] The papers from this conference subsequently were published in a special issue of the new *Journal for Research into Freemasonry and Fraternalism.*[19]

Following a model implemented at a number of European universities, the University of California at Los Angeles, under the leadership of Margaret Jacob, an eminent scholar of European Freemasonry, has established a program in Freemasonry and Civil Society, which hosts a postdoctoral fellowship. With the support of the Masonic Grand Lodge of California, this fellowship assists emerging scholars with doctorates in pursuing research, while also providing opportunities for students to study the impact of fraternalism upon the United States and other nations.[20] Similarly, in 2008 the Oklahoma Masonic Charity Foundation contributed funds to endow a faculty chair in gender studies at Oklahoma State University, in Stillwater, Oklahoma. Administered through the Center for Gender Studies within the OSU College of Arts and Sciences, this interdisciplinary chair promotes scholarship concerning masculine ideals, social networks, and moral attitudes.[21]

This Volume

Bringing together nineteen essays about American secret societies published before the current blossoming of scholarly interest in fraternalism, this collection presents the foundation which underpins the later historiography. Some of these contributions appear regularly in the bibliographies of the books previously addressed. Others, although less regularly acknowledged in footnotes, are included because of the important insights their authors provide and the perspectives they offer into periods of fraternal growth and decline.

The articles are organized into four categories. The first, entitled "Journalistic Studies," documents how fraternalism has been portrayed in the American periodical press. These sources reveal transformations in the clubs and orders, but also demonstrate changing styles in popular prose. The section called "Historical Studies" presents two important articles from the middle decades of the twentieth century. These works by Schlesinger and Davis are noteworthy for their early recognition of fraternalism's relevance. Essays by Georg Simmel and Noel Gist comprise the category termed "Sociological Studies." These writings provide perspectives which have informed the work of subsequent authors. Finally, the last division gathers six essays concerning the insurance functions of America's secret societies. Although fraternal benefit programs have been examined by authors including Clawson and Beito, this aspect of the phenomenon has yet to receive adequate attention. Period commentary on the virtues and drawbacks of systems developed to provide financial stability to the groups' members during industrialization's economic turmoil is central to this division.

By gathering into one volume these essays, which otherwise can prove complicated to locate and difficult to access, we hope to foster further intellectual investigation and scholarly discourse. We are optimistic that this collection will attract and inspire readers who will, in turn, contribute to our understanding of America's "secret societies" and the numerous individuals who promoted, reshaped, and belonged to them over their centuries of existence.

Notes

1. Harwood's essay is reprinted in this volume.
2. Albert C. Stevens, *Cyclopedia of Fraternities* (New York: Hamilton Printing and Publishing, 1899).
3. Clement M. Silvestro, "Preface," in Barbara Franco, *Fraternally Yours: A Decade of Collecting* (Lexington, MA: Scottish Rite Masonic Museum of Our National Heritage, 1986), 4-5; "Silvestro, Clement Mario," in *Who's Who in America 2010* 64th ed. Vol. 2 (New Providence, NJ: Marquis Who's Who, 2010), 4342. In 2004, the Museum changed its name to the National Heritage Museum. See http://nationalheritagemuseum.org (Accessed August 8, 2011).
4. Scottish Rite Masonic Museum of Our National Heritage, *Masonic Symbols in American Decorative Arts*, (Lexington, MA: Scottish Rite Masonic Museum of Our National Heritage, 1976); *The Masonic Tradition in the Decorative Arts* (Utica, NY: Munson-Williams-Proctor Institute, 1980); Scottish Rite Masonic Museum of Our National Heritage, *Bespangled, Painted, & Embroidered: Decorated Masonic Aprons in America, 1790-1850* (Lexington, MA : Scottish Rite Masonic Museum of Our National Heritage, 1980); Barbara Franco, *Fraternally Yours: A Decade of Collecting*. (Lexington, MA: Scottish Rite Masonic Museum of Our National Heritage, 1986).
5. Christopher J. Kaufman, *Faith & Fraternalism: The History of the Knights of Columbus, 1882-1982* (New York: Harper & Row, 1982).
6. Lynn Dumenil, *Freemasonry and American Culture, 1880-1930* (Princeton, New Jersey: Princeton University Press, 1984).
7. Dumenil, *xiv*.
8. Mary Ann Clawson, *Constructing Brotherhood: Class, Gender, and Fraternalism* (Princeton, NJ: Princeton University Press, 1989).
9. Mark C. Carnes, *Secret Ritual and Manhood in Victorian America* (New Haven: Yale University Press, 1989). Carnes's thesis was presented to a popular audience in Mark Carnes, "Iron John in the Gilded Age," *American Heritage* 44(5)(September 1993): 37-45.
10. Barbara Franco, "The Ritualization of Male Friendship and Virtue in Nineteenth-Century Fraternal Organizations," in Katherine Martinez and

Kenneth L. Ames, eds. *The Material Culture of Gender; The Gender of Material Culture.* (Winterthur, DE: Henry Francis du Pont Winterthur Museum, 1997), 281-297.

11. Jeffrey A. Charles, *Service Clubs in American Society: Rotary, Kiwanis, and Lions* (Urbana: University of Illinois Press, 1993).

12. David T. Beito, *From Mutual Aid to the Welfare State: Fraternal Societies and Social Services, 1890-1967* (Chapel Hill: University of North Carolina Press, 2000).

13. Steven C. Bullock, *Revolutionary Brotherhood: Freemasonry and the Transformation of the American Social Order, 1730-1840* (Chapel Hill: University of North Carolina Press, 1996).

14. Robert D. Putnam, *Bowling Alone: The Collapse and Revival of American Community* (New York: Simon & Schuster, 2000).

15. Theda Skocpol, *What a Mighty Power We Can Be: African American Fraternal Groups and the Struggle for Racial Equality* (Princeton: Princeton University Press, 2006).

16. Jason Kaufman, *For the Common Good? American Civic Life and the Golden Age of Fraternity* (New York: Oxford University Press, 2002).

17. Supersonic Events Ltd., "The History of the International Conference on the History of Freemasonry," *ICHF*, http://ichf2011.org/index.php?option=com_content&view=category&layout=blog&id=3&Itemid=26 (Accessed December 23, 2010).

18. National Heritage Museum, "Symposium Registration," *National Heritage Museum*, http://www.nationalheritagemuseum.org/Default.aspx?tabid=589 (Accessed December 23, 2010).

19. *Journal For Research into Freemasonry and Fraternalism* 2(1)(2011). See http://www.equinoxpub.com/jrff (Accessed August 8, 2011).

20. "Freemasonry and Civil Society," Freemasonry and Civil Society Program at UCLA, http://www.freemasonryandcivilsociety.ucla.edu/index.htm (Accessed December 23, 2010).

21. Robert G. Davis, "Masonic Charity Foundation Gift a Strategic Move for Freemasonry!" *Masonic Charity Foundation of Oklahoma.* http://www.mcfok.org/successes/success_osu_chair.shtml (Accessed January 7, 2011).

Table of Contents

Secret Societies in America:
Foundational Studies of Fraternalism

W. S. Harwood has been widely recognized for identifying the final decades of the nineteenth century as the "Golden Age of Fraternity." This essay provides a balanced contemporary overview of the fraternal organizations which swelled to importance in the years following the Civil War. Harwood celebrates the role that the societies played in providing economic relief and fostering reverence while recognizing that they simultaneously could harm their members by tempting men to squander resources on frivolous adornments while luring them away from their families and business endeavors.

SECRET SOCIETIES IN AMERICA
W.S. Harwood
1897
North American Review 164 (May 1897), 617-624.

THE membership of the secret fraternal orders of the United States in the month of December, 1896, was, in round numbers, 6,400,000. Taking the adult male population of the nation at the present time to be nineteen millions, and allowing that some men belong to more than one order, it will be seen that, broadly speaking, every fifth, or possibly every eighth, man you meet is identified with some fraternal organization, for the preservation of whose secrets he has given a solemn oath, a pledge more binding in its nature than perhaps any other known among men. In this vast number have not been included the many thousands who are members of the various labor organizations, though they, to a greater or lesser extent, are knit together by secret threads; nor about 500,000 members of the secret military orders, as the G. A. R.; nor has any account been taken of the many other thousands who are identified with the fraternities of the colleges.

Perhaps even more significant than the fact that there are so many millions of oath-bound men in the United States is the further fact that auxiliary to and a part of these orders are military branches, having at the present time about two hundred and fifty thousand members in the prime of life, who are trained in military tactics and who know the sword and musket manual as well as does the cleverest "regular," many of them thoroughly informed as to the history, the present needs, and the possibilities of military life.

Some of these organizations are of quite recent date. Indeed, since the closing of the War of the Rebellion there has been a remarkable increase in their number in this country. And in the last two decades, especially, there has been a strong growth. The beneficiary nature of some of the orders, combined with the secret work and the fraternal element, has no doubt attracted many men to seek entrance.

It is far beyond reasonable computation to attempt to indicate the amount of money given by these fraternal orders in a single year in aid of their members. Many of the benefactions do not come into consideration in the making up of reports, and many are the result of purely fraternal generosity. Some idea, perhaps, may be gleaned from the formally announced amount which is given every year in benefits of one kind and another — money paid for caring for the sick, burying the dead, supporting the widows and orphans of deceased members, and in sums paid out to the widows of deceased members in the form of insurance.

These amounts range in size from ten to twenty thousands of dollars per annum, to seven million five hundred thousand for a single organization. Many of the organizations pay out over a million dollars per year in this way. While it is difficult to arrive at positive figures as to the amount which has been paid out by the fraternal orders in the United States since their establishment, yet, allowing for the amount paid out in the year 1896 and not included in the annual reports of the grand secretaries of the various bodies, the enormous total of $475,000,000 has been given by these organizations in beneficences. It should be stated, also, that this is exclusive of the three larger orders, the Masonic, the Odd Fellows, and the Knights of Pythias. As nearly as can be computed these three orders have paid out in the same line one hundred and seventy-six millions more, making all told the vast sum of nearly six hundred and fifty millions of dollars.

A tabular statement follows, but it should be clearly understood that the amount of money recorded as paid out in benevolences by the various orders does not include the private monetary gifts of the members. Did it include these private beneficences the sum must be immensely augmented. It is impossible to ascertain the amount which is given in this personal manner, for the significant reason that it is all given for the aid of those who would scorn such aid were the fact made public that they were to be made the recipients of it. In the period between the years 1892-93, and the close of the year 1896, many men holding responsible positions were compelled to relinquish these positions because of the prevailing hard times, and during this period thousands, indeed, tens of thousands, of dollars have been given by fellow-craftsmen to such of these unfortunates as were members of secret orders. It was not money given in charity, it was not a premium on mendicancy; it was not alms : it was the visible token of the great-heartedness which is one of the vital elements in fraternal life.

Take, for instance, one body, the Masonic, which may be considered typical of all. In connection with each lodge there is a relief committee whose duties are done with delicacy, whose acts are performed in tender and sympathetic secrecy. These committees ascertain the needs of those members who are facing hard fortune, aid them with money, with clothing, with provisions; or, if possible, secure positions for future bread-winning. No record is kept in any form for the public eye of these private beneficences. Indeed, in some cases, not even the names of the members of the committee itself are known to the other members of the lodge to which they belong.

So in all these orders there are like acts. The sum which the members of the fraternal orders give to such of their members as are in need would amount to several millions of dollars per year, were only one dollar per capita given; it is undoubtedly largely in excess of such an amount. There are large and well-equipped homes for orphans of deceased members, too, and for aged and indigent members, for which many thousands of dollars are expended annually.

The figures hereinafter given were secured by the writer in the month of December, 1896. In some instances the general secretaries of the organizations — from whom, in the main, the data were secured — estimated the membership and the revenue for several months past, dating from the annual meeting of the orders held in the summer or spring of 1896. The close contact of these officers with the subordinate lodges, the frequency of reports from the lodges and the intimate relationship between the general secretaries and the subordinate lodges give the general officers unusual avenues of information and make the figures practically complete to the month of January, 1897. It should be stated that, as there is no general grand lodge of the Masonic order, and as no reports are made from the lodges to any superior body, the amount of money contributed in public beneficences by this order has been in some measure estimated from the best general information obtainable.

Here is the table itself :

Name of order.	Membership.	Amount paid in beneficences.
Masonic	750,000	$90,000,000
Odd Fellows	810,000	74,600,000
Knights of Pythias	475,000	10,362,000
Ancient Order United Workmen	361,301	71,729,180
Royal Arcanum	189,161	38,206,422
Modern Woodmen of America	204,332	7,229,985
Knights and Ladies of Honor	85,000	12,000,000
United American Mechanics	· 56,000	3,000,000
Catholic Knights of America	26,000	7,007,133
Order United Friends	15,000	4,931,700
Benevolent Protective Order Elks	32,500	500,000
Equitable Aid Union	16,610	7,742,748
United Order Pilgrim Fathers	22,000	2,321,030
National Provident Union	6,300	1,293,450
Improved Order Red Men	165,000	14,200,000
Ancient Order Foresters	36,825	80,000,000
Royal Templars	168,000	4,573,025
Tribe of Ben Hur	11,294	49,250
Catholic Benevolent Union	45,250	7,031,481
Knights of the Maccabees	244,704	7,233,930
American Legion of Honor	52,100	33,672,676
Order Scottish Clans	4,000	575,000
National Union	47,791	7,539,948
Knights of the Golden Eagle	60,000	1,811,186
Ancient Order of Hibernians	98,000	* 681,928
Order B'rith Abraham	11,785	1,121,500
Improved Order Heptasoths	31,118	2,114,000
B'nai B'rith Improved	2,700	132,550
B'nai B'rith Independent	34,925	43,175,000

Catholic Mutual Benefit Association	41,800	6,600,000
Order of Chosen Friends	29,413	11,617,000
Ancient Order Druids	16,500	3,806,697
Foresters of America	140,575	4,795,291
Independent Order Foresters	110,000	4,070,000
Order Golden Chain	11,550	2,228,221
Royal Society Good Fellows	13,164	3,124,154
Home Circle	8,140	1,650,000
Independent Order Free Sons Israel	14,300	4,860,900
Irish Catholic Benevolent Union	16,500	2,750,000
Knights of Honor	118,287	62,009,200
Knights of Malta	17,600	……..
Fraternal Mystic Circle	11,423	952,091
Knights of St. John and Malta	5,350	237,420
New England Order Protection	23,186	1,336,000
Independent Order Rechabites	3,520	……..
Woodmen of the World	76,962	1,370,107
Unt. Ord. of Odd Fellows (colored)	130,350	† 238,783
United Amrican Mechanics, Junor Order		187,000
2,725,485	Order Sons of St. George	
34,108	……..	
Masonic (colored)	224,000	……..
Sons of Temperance	25,474	……..
Independent Order Good Templars	281,600	……..
	5,454,329	$649,082,471

* For last two years only.   † For one year only.

Of course the table does not include anything of the expenditures of the orders for room rent, for uniforms, for banquets, for regalia, for lodge-room furnishings. There are about seventy thousand lodges in the United States, and, allowing them an average of fifty dollars per month for lodge-room rent—a low estimate, as many of the orders have expensive suites of rooms in great city buildings costing thousands of dollars in rental per annum—allowing but fifty dollars per month as the average throughout the towns and cities of the country, it will be seen that there is spent annually the sum of forty-two millions of dollars for the bare rental of lodge-rooms. The furnishings and decorations of some of the lodges are rare and costly. Many splendid buildings have been erected for lodge uses primarily, and much money is invested by the orders in property of various kinds.

But while these secret orders are a vast power for good in giving aid and comfort to their members, in caring for the sick and ministering to the distressed in mind, body, and estate; while they give vast sums in beneficence and afford wide opportunity for developing the social side of their members, yet they are not an unmixed blessing to the race. The newspaper paragraphers have a sound basis in fact for their threadbare joke about the man who cannot find his latch-key hole when he reaches home after the lodge banquet.

This is not the place to discuss the temperance question or to dwell upon the evils of inebriety, but one should note in a consideration of the vast influence of these fraternal organizations the inimical possibilities of conviviality.

Yet another danger must be considered in estimating the influence of secret societies. One does not trifle with truth in saying that no human gauge can measure the sorrow that comes to some families through the too close attention of husband and father to the lodge-room. There is a strange and powerful attraction for some men in the mysticism of the ritual. There is a peculiar fascination in the unreality of the initiation, an allurement about fine "team" work, a charm of deep potency in the unrestricted, out-of-the-world atmosphere which surrounds the scenes where men are knit together by the closest ties, bound by the most solemn obligations to maintain secrecy as to the events which transpire within their walls.

In the business life of the land instances are not wanting where men have become so infatuated with their secret society work that they have sacrificed position and even financial standing that they might satisfy their craving for greater knowledge of the secret workings of many of the leading organizations. In the commonplace vernacular of the lodge devotees, these were "jiners" — men found in every community who are more eager to be initiated into some new order than to be strengthened in business standing. I think it will not be denied by any fair-minded and conservative member of these organizations that a very large number, throughout the whole United States, suffer in pocket, and not infrequently in business position, in gratifying their desire to belong to, and take all the degrees in, all the secret societies that appeal to their love for novelty and mystery.

There are many elevating and ennobling elements in these fraternities, but the broad, rich acres of man's selfishness are nowhere more carefully fertilized, tended, tilled, and reaped than in the lodge-room. It would all but revolutionize a large section of American Society if the wives and growing-up daughters of the households of the men who belong to these organizations should insist on their right to spend for their own adornment or their own personal pleasure dollar for dollar spent by husband or brother for dues and initiations, for regalia and uniforms and swords, for plumes and banners and banquets. In the great majority of cases the amount of money paid out for the actual expenses of the lodge, as the dues of the order, is not great; it is in the field of personal gratification that the vast unaccounted-for sum is expended. It is probable that, for mere personal gratification, aside from any real or imaginary benefits, the members of the various secret organizations in the United States will spend annually in banquets, railroad and travelling expenses, costly gifts to retiring officers, testimonials, elaborate uniforms, and rare swords not less than two hundred and fifty millions of dollars, and this is allowing but fifty dollars a year as an average for the delightful, but probably wholly unnecessary, expenses connected with the fraternities. It is quite likely the sum is considerably more than this.

But the importance of these fraternal organizations and their tremendous power for good must not be overlooked if we would arrive at a just appreciation of their significance. So numerous, so powerful, have these orders become, that these closing years of the century might well be called the Golden Age of fraternity. So strong has their hold become upon so many millions of people that the occasions have not been infrequent where other ministers than the priests of the Church of Rome have inveighed against the lodge, and sought to show its pernicious activity in tearing down what the church would build up, or, to put it more mildly, they have protested against the usurping influence of the lodge, its tendency to induce men to accept it as their church, and to make its standards and forms and laws their guide of right conduct.

While the secret society has its peculiar dangers it has great elements of good. Its influence in making thoughtless men reverential, in increasing respect for government by law; its influence in maintaining and promoting allegiance to country, these are important elements of its service. While men with evil tendencies and deformed moral natures are known to be members of fraternal orders, and while, when so known, they are not always as promptly removed as might be wished, yet I think it is but fair to say that cases are exceedingly rare in reputable organizations where men of known badness are admitted. Indeed, one of the greatest powers of the secret fraternal orders of the present day is found in the element of selection. No other organization in the immediate hands of man, and unidentified with religion, so universally sets so high a standard of sobriety, integrity, and honesty; none other, when a seeker for admission appears, so sharply scrutinizes his past, so searchingly investigates his present. The prime essential in all secret organizations of this character is that the initiate shall be a manly man; after that a companionable man.

Nor should it be lost sight of that there is a demand upon these millions of oath-bound men in our land, whom we meet at every turn in the street, who touch elbows with us in business and in society, many of whom are leaders in the laity life of the church, and who are increasingly numerous in the ministerial ranks of the churches, it should not be forgotten that there is a most imperative demand upon the consciences of these men— the acknowledgment of a Supreme Being as ruler over all. To this should be added a rarely lacking, positive, unequivocal, and constant reverence for the Scriptures. Not that any test of religious belief is exacted, but I think it will be fair both to those who are inside and those who are outside of these organizations to say that the Bible, taken as the most sacred book of the Christian nations, is a work to which peculiar reverence is always given in fraternal organizations. No other organization of men in the world, with the single exception of the church, so universally, so consistently, and so insistently demands that recognition of divine authority which is at once the test and the evidence of the highest type of life.

It may be urged that the hidden power of the fraternal orders is used at times to influence the course of elections; that men who are members of these organizations band themselves too closely together even outside of their society; that they seek to aid a brother before one not bound by the same oath. While we may make some allowance for weaknesses in this regard upon the part of some, I do not think it follows that, because a man is a member of one of these organizations, he stands ready to stultify himself when he enters the polling booth or when he comes into social or commercial contact with those who are not members of his organization.

It is perhaps quite within bounds to say that these orders are increasing in membership in the United States at the rate of between two hundred and fifty and three hundred thousand members annually. Possibly the vast increase during the last twenty-five years may have been an abnormal one, but the indications all point to a constant augmentation of this enormous secret power. Perhaps in no other country in the world could these orders thrive so constantly and at the same time be so free from any suggestion of national censure. If all their secrets were paraded before the eyes of the world, we should find none directed against the best interests of our country.

In this essay from 1892, Walter Hill addresses the apparent contradiction of nineteenth-century Americans' love of magnificent titles and voluntary pomp while promoting national ideals of egalitarianism and democracy. He argues that the numerous voluntary organizations which differentiate American civic life from that of the Europeans fulfill the social function of providing a supposedly elevated status to every individual who desires the opportunity to be differentiated from their peers.

THE GREAT AMERICAN SAFETY-VALVE

Walter B Hill

1892

Century Magazine 44 (July 1892), 383-384.

THE Republic is opportunity. It is the birthright of every American boy to have the chance to be President, and of every American girl to have the chance to be the President's wife. The atmosphere is stimulating to ambition. The desire inspired by the genius of American institutions is " to be equal to our superiors and superior to our equals." But in the midst of universal suggestions prompting the citizen to high ambitions, the ugly fact remains that the positions of political distinction are relatively very few compared to the vast multitude of possible aspirants. The practical politician confesses this in the wail, "There ain't offices enough to go round among the boys."

The intelligent foreigner is much perplexed by this problem. He can understand why the undistinguished classes on the Continent submit contentedly to obscure conditions of life. It is the lot to which they are born. But here every school-boy is taught that the highest stations are open to him; and in a thousand papers, books, lectures, speeches, and sermons he is told that perseverance alone will put the highest prizes within his grasp. What, then, can explain the contentedness of the millions who, as the French say, never "pierce" the level of mediocrity? What is the great American safety-valve for these ambition's for precedence which our national life generates, fosters, and stimulates, without adequate provision for their gratification?

A friend from abroad, without the philosophic insight of Mr.

Bryce or the illuminating wit of Max O'Rell, was once presenting to me what seemed to him the serious phases of this problem. I thought myself competent to make the explanation; but I did not know how to take hold of the subject. We were standing in the office of a large hotel at the time, when an incident gave me the clue.

There walked up to the register a sturdy American citizen, who seized the pen as if he were about to sign some momentous document. Bending over the open page of the book, he scrawled his name, his mouth moving and writhing with every twist of the pen. It occurred to me to look at the record of this new arrival, and this is what I saw: " Hon. Sock Bruitt, Chairman of the Committee on Pumps, Whiskyville, Texas."

Seizing this thread, I proceeded to unravel as best I could the tangled skein of American life as it is organized into social, business, religious, and other associations, all of them elaborately officered.

Until I made the effort to explain the matter to "an alien to the commonwealth," I had never realized the full significance of the nonpolitical office-holding class in our country as a factor in the national life.

Take a city directory and examine the list of organizations usually printed in such a publication: you will see ample provision for the local ambitions of all the inhabitants. Take one of the books issued by a "live " church; examine the list of societies, devotional, missionary, temperance, young people's, Sunday-school, charitable, etc. The matter will be made clearer still if you study the subject in a small village where universal acquaintance is possible.

I made a test case of one small town, and found that every man, woman, and child (above ten years of age) in the place held an office — with the exception of a few scores of flabby, jellyfish characters, whose lack of ambition or enterprise removes them from consideration as elements of the problem.

But mere local precedence does not satisfy the more aspiring minds; hence, nearly all of the thousand and one societies have State and national organizations. Here is an enormous supply of official positions. Every trade, every profession, every benevolence, every sport, every church furnishes distinctions commensurate in territorial magnitude with our great country.

And still the full measure of American officialism is not attained. There must be international organization. The earth must be girdled;

and so, every society aims to plant a few lodges, or posts, or bands, or auxiliaries, or unions, or chapters (as they may be styled), beyond the seas. It little matters how few or scattered or insignificant these foreign plants may be. It is enough that "international organization has been accomplished" — and with it a new set of officials having world-wide jurisdiction.

The grandeur of all these distinctions suffers no diminution in their names. The chief officer is Ruler, Chancellor, Commander, Seigneur, President, Potentate, with many superlative and worshipful prefixes. And in the rituals of the numerous orders the Almighty is habitually referred to as the Supreme Commander, Ruler, Potentate, or otherwise, as the case may be. By this means the American imagination accomplishes an interuniversal as well as an international organization. A few years ago, in a little country village, there was instituted a chapter of a certain benevolent insurance order. The Chancellor was subsequently elected Grand Chancellor of the State. Afterward at a national convention he was made Supreme Grand Chancellor of the United States. The next year he was elected Most Supreme Grand Chancellor of the World; and it became his duty, the order paying his expenses, to make an international visitation to the three chapters in Australia, New Zealand, and England that composed the aforesaid "world."

When that triumphal tour was completed, his return home was heralded, and the chapter of his village arranged for a reception of the honorable dignitary. Never shall I forget the feeling of solemn awe that settled down upon the little community as the evening approached when the Most Supreme Grand Chancellor of the World was to arrive. This favored American was a "bigger man than old Grant."

Not only are there offices enough to "go round," but the really capable and pushing American is generally honored with a score. I have heard a busy and overworked man decline to be at the head of an organization because he was at the head of twenty-five already.

Here then we have the great American safety-valve — we are a nation of presidents.

Published at approximately the same time as W. S. Harwood's "Secret Societies in America, Foster's "Secret Societies and the State" adopts a distinctly different tone in arguing that the government of the United States should outlaw all oath-bound secret societies. Based upon a worldview in which the United States has inherited the Biblical Jews' status as God's chosen people, Foster argues that all secret societies, including such diverse groups as the Molly Maguires, the Ku Klux Klan, the Knights of the Golden Circle, and the Mafia, pollute society, corrupt morals, and threaten the nation's destiny. To support his position, Foster offers a specious history linking the Jesuits, the Illuminati, the Freemasons, and the English monarchy. At the time that it was published, the Masonic Grand Lodge of Iowa noted that Foster's article would "do credit as an anti-Masonic tract."

SECRET SOCIETIES AND THE STATE.
J. M. Foster
1898
The Arena 19 (99)(February 1898), 229-239.

IT has been authoritatively stated that "there are in the United States over fifty distinct secret orders, with over 70,000 lodges and 5,500,000 members. This does not include members of the various labor organizations, or the 500,000 members of secret military orders, such as the G. A. R., or those connected with college secret fraternities. These numbers will not include as many persons, since one man is often a member of two or more societies, but it is safe to say that in all there are fully 6,000,000 persons in this country held in the coils of Secretism."[1] Has the state any duty to perform with reference to this gigantic power, which is growing at the rate of 300,000 members per annum?

This leads to another inquiry: What is the nature and province of the state? I answer:

1. The state is not a voluntary association. A man may join a voluntary association or not, just as he elects. But has he this option in civil society? He is born into the state, and is by nature subject to its laws. The corporation and the nation differ as greatly as the artificial and the natural. The corporation is the creature of the state, is responsible to the state; and appeal can always be had from it to the state. But the state is the creature of God, accountable to none

but Him for the use it makes of the great powers with which He has invested it. "It is something monstrous," said Thomas Arnold of Rugby, "that the ultimate powers in human life should be destitute of the sense of right and wrong"; and that comes only from a sense of responsibility to God.

2. It is not a social compact. The atheist Hobbes of Malmesbury originated this idea. Denying the existence of any fixed standard of right, and consequently that there could be any such thing as virtue or vice, this speculative philosopher resolved all law into one, the will of the legislature. But who were his disciples? None but the godless, the dissipated, the scorners of all that is sacred. The heart of England was shocked at its blasphemy. It was stoutly resisted by the great thinkers of the seventeenth century as undermining the foundations of civil society and absorbing justice in the consciousness of power. After the Long Parliament, Hobbes fled to Paris to escape the evils of his own doctrines. The clearest assertion of this doctrine was in France, and its highest development was in the *Contrat Social* of Rousseau. But the dissemination of this doctrine cost that nation the Reign of Terror. There can be no doubt that this theory had its influence in the Convention which framed our national Constitution in 1787, for, as Franklin said, with three or four exceptions the members thought prayers unnecessary. Such a convention would be expected to give us a constitution that does not acknowledge Almighty God as the source of all authority and power, nor the Lord Jesus Christ as the divinely appointed Ruler of nations, nor the Bible as the fountain of all law. But the American people never have voted and never would vote to reject the higher law and Law-giver.

3. It is God's moral ordinance. It is that settled order of things which is manifestly in harmony with the divine will. It has its necessity in the constitution of our nature, and its authority in God's word: "The powers that be are ordained of God." It is clothed with authority and powers which transcend all human institutions, and thus becomes the heaven-ordained and heaven-commissioned agent representing the divine authority among men.

I. *The being of the state is from God.* The Creator has established divine institutions among men for specific purposes. The *family* is a divine institution. Marriage is an ordinance of God. It is God's appointed method of restraining vice, fostering virtue, multiplying the human race, and developing the better sentiments of the human

14

heart. It has its necessity in the very constitution of our nature, and its authority in God's word: "They twain shall be one flesh." The *Church is* a divine institution. It is "the kingdom of heaven" among men. Its organization is from God. "Upon this Rock I will build my church." Its authority is from God. "I will give to thee the keys of the kingdom of heaven." Its constitution is from God. "Unto them were committed the oracles of God." Its laws are from God. "Teaching them to observe all things whatsoever I have commanded you." Its commission is from God. "Go ye into all the world and preach the gospel to every creature." Its duties as the witness for the truth have been enjoined. "Ye are my witnesses, saith the Lord." The *state is* another divine institution. It is the arrangement, the appointment, the contrivance of heaven for man. It is the divinely appointed custodian of the rights of the people. It exists for the punishment of evil-doers and for the praise of them that do well. It guards the family. It protects the church.

God has appointed these three institutions in which the man is to be developed to the full girth and proportion of perfect manhood, to the measure of the stature of the fulness (sic) of a perfect man.

But the secret, oath-bound lodge is a mere human device. It lays upon its members obligations, with the solemnity of an oath oft repeated, that are inconsistent with loyalty to these divine ordinances. A man who performs all his duties properly in the home, the church, and civil society has no time or energy or means to devote to the secret lodge. It is a matter of unlimited experience that the good lodge member neglects his duties in one or other of these divine institutions. What is inconsistent with God's appointed order ought not to exist.

II. The powers of the state come from God. The state wields tremendous powers. It has the power to levy taxes, to institute a tariff, and to regulate that mighty factor in our commercial life — the currency. It has the power to organize schools, to enter the homes, take the children, place them in the schools and educate them, without asking the leave of the parents. It has the power to draw out all the physical, mental, and moral forces of the nation in self-defence, just as a sword is drawn from its sheath. It has the power of life and death. This does not reside in the individual. No man has a right to take away his own life, much less to employ another to do it for him. No company of men, even seventy millions, has the right to execute the criminal. And yet the state every day exercises a power which does not reside in the individual or the mass. Where does it get this power? The only answer is: "Power comes from Almighty God." As the Savior said to Pilate, "Thou could'st have no power over me at all except it were given to thee from above." In the 82nd Psalm rulers are called "gods," because they represent God on earth. In the 13th chapter of Romans rulers are called "God's ministers." They are clothed with authority from Him, and they administer His law. Civil government is the arm of Jehovah administering the affairs of His government among men. But secret oath-bound lodges are intruders upon this divine prerogative of the state.

The society of Jesus was organized by Ignatius Loyola in 1540. It is secret and oath-bound. The Encyclopaedia Britannica says: "Jesuitry is a naked sword, with its hilt at Rome and its point everywhere." Every Jesuit is bound by oath to poverty, chastity, and obedience. Coligny was brutally murdered by the Jesuits on the night of St. Bartholomew, Aug. 24, 1572. William the Silent, Prince of Orange, was struck down by Girard, a Spanish Jesuit, July 10, 1584. A Jesuit assassin, Ravaillac, stabbed Henry IV, May 14, 1610. The disloyal oaths caused the Jesuits to be expelled from Prussia, Italy, Austria, France. Many went to South America, a few to England. An old order of the masonic craft existed there, imported from Syria, whence it had come from the East. The Jesuits joined this order. They secured the protection of princes for the craft, and hence were called "Free." Charles I, Charles II, and James II joined the order, with many princes, though they never lifted a mason's tool. Hence the term "Accepted." The banishment of Charles II seems to have suggested to these Jesuits the first three degrees of apprentice, fellow-craft, and master mason. The grand lodge was not organized in London until June 24, 1717. But these Jesuits went with the banished King Charles II to France and organized lodges there.

From the members of these lodges who had taken the first three degrees, they organized another order called the Illuminati. This was nothing but a school of atheism and anarchy. It grew with wonderful rapidity. The French nation was honeycombed with it. The whole people were prepared for resisting authority. Mirabeau, the profligate and disappointed politician, and the Duke of Orleans, his silly tool, were at the head of this secret order. They issued the mandate. The dynamite exploded. France was deluged with blood.

The French Revolution was enacted. Anyone wishing to trace the steps of this tragedy, should read "The Conspiracy in Europe," by John Robinson [sic], A. M., Professor of Natural Philosophy, and secretary to the Royal Society of Edinburgh.[2]

What the Jesuits have done in France through the Masonic lodge, they may do in the United States. We know that Jesuits priests are in 100,000 confessionals in our country, and these are so many telephones, bringing them into speaking communication with our homes, offices, schools, churches, courts, and legislative halls. Many of our great cities are in the hands of the Jesuits. Some of our legislatures are under their power. The Jesuits at Washington have a way of bringing Senators and Representatives to their way of thinking. The daily press of our country is largely under their hand. They are making a deadly assault upon our public schools. The time is near when our government will be compelled to follow the example of the continent and expel the Jesuits.

The murder of William Morgan in 1826 by the Freemasons caused forty-five out of every fifty of the members to leave the order. In their indignation they exposed the oaths by which the lodge members are bound. This gave rise to the law which was passed by the Vermont Legislature in 1833.

> A person who administers to another an oath or affirmation, or obligation in the form of an oath, which is not required or authorized by law, or a person who suffers such an oath or obligation to be administered to him, or voluntarily takes the same, shall be fined not more than $100 and not less than $50; but this section shall not prohibit an oath or affidavit for the purpose of establishing a claim, petition, or application by an individual or corporation administered without intentional secrecy by a person authorized to administer oaths, or an oath or affidavit for the verification of commercial papers or documents relating to property, or which may be required by a public officer or tribunal of the United States, or of any State, or any other country, nor abridge the authority of the magistrate.

In 1839 the legislature increased the penalty to $200. Massachusetts and New Hampshire adopted this law. Daniel Webster, the great lawyer and statesman, said:

> All secret associations, the members of which take upon themselves extraordinary obligations to one another and are bound together by

secret oaths, are natural sources of jealousy and just alarm to others, and especially unfavorable to harmony and mutual confidence among men living together under public institutions; and are dangerous to the general cause of civil liberty and justice. Under the influence of this conviction I heartily approve the law lately enacted in the State of which I am a citizen, for abolishing all such oaths and obligations.

Massachusetts repealed this law in 1880. In 1893 the Masonic Lodge of Worcester, Mass., was incorporated under the general law of the State. But this was not deemed sufficient. And in 1896 the legislature passed an act authorizing the Masons to build a temple, have a library, hall, lectures, and a benevolent fund. This statute empowers them to accumulate property and do business to any extent they desire. Such powers in the hands of secret lodges are dangerous to any municipality.

In Hartford, Conn., in August, 1895, Dr. Griswold, a Mason, set fire to his buildings to get the insurance. He confided the facts to Dr. Jackson, a brother Mason. Dr. Jackson laid the facts before the civil authorities. The culprit was tried and sentenced to ten years in the penitentiary. Then the Hartford Lodge tried Dr. Jackson for unmasonic conduct in informing on that guilty brother, and expelled him. The lodge in that case was used against law and justice.

In Illinois, a judge refused to recognize the sign of distress given by a brother Mason, who was the criminal in the dock. He said: "I will not recognize those signs when I am on the bench." But his Masonic oath bound him to recognize them, and his lodge censured him for his unmasonic conduct. Thaddeus Stevens said: "By Freemasonry, trial by jury is transformed into an engine of despotism and Masonic fraud."

The government found it necessary to assail the "Knights of the Golden Circle" during the war, for they were plotting to destroy it. It became necessary to throttle the Molly Maguires and the Ku-Klux Klans as a means of self-protection. The Supreme Court of the United States has decided that anyone who has taken the Endowment-House oaths of the Mormon hierarchy should not be naturalized, and if he has been naturalized, should be disfranchised. Let it be proclaimed in trumpet tones, from the Atlantic to the Pacific, that the highest tribunal in our land has decreed that the secret oaths of that religious fraternity disqualify those taking them from becoming citizens; or if citizens, from exercising the privileges of citizenship. The murder of Dr. Cronin in Chicago led to the trial of the order of Clan-na-Gael. Their horrid oaths were exposed, just as the wicked oaths of the Endowment House in Salt Lake City were brought to light in the trial over the Idaho test-oaths disfranchising Mormons. The courts have decided that these disloyal oaths disqualify those taking them for citizenship.

The secret order of Mafia came over to us from Italy. They showed their true character in the murder of Chief of Police Hennessey, of New Orleans. That assassination was a crime which demanded retribution. Eleven members of the order were put on trial. Through fear of the order the jury acquitted them. A mob attacked the prison that very night and summarily despatched these guilty wretches. That massacre cannot be justified. It was mob law, and that is a danger and a symptom of a greater evil behind it. When justice breaks over its legal bounds, no one is safe, and the insidious disease of anarchy is underneath. But a secret order that is an oath-bound gang of ruffians and brigands cannot be tolerated here. That massacre is the handwriting on the walls of the secret dens of the Mafia.

The Highbinders of California have been imported hither from China. They are a secret, oath-bound, murderous order. The courts have dealt with them just as with the Mafia.

These facts lead us to the conclusion that the power of the government ought to be invoked in the destruction of all secret, oath-bound lodges. The Vermont law should be adopted by every State in the Union. Congress should crystallize it in a similar national law. That will drive these secret societies beyond our borders.

III. *The laws of the state come from God.* Law is the expression of the will of God. The phrase of Hooker is too sublime ever to become trite: "Law has its seat in the bosom of God, and its voice is the harmony of the world." Two thoughts filled the mind of Kant with ever-increasing admiration and delight: "The starry heavens above us, God's law within us." Cicero long ago declared that "those who fail to recognize the will of God as the basis of all law, lay the foundation of government *tanquam in aquis,* as it were in the waters." Blackstone said: "Any law that contravenes the law of God is no law at all." Man cannot make law. He may discover and interpret and apply God's law. God gave the ten commandments to the Jewish nation as their constitution. They are the basis of all moral legislation.

Justinian, the Roman emperor, made the decalogue the basis of his Tribonian Code. Charlemagne issued a code of laws based upon the ten commandments. Alfred the Good, King of England, gave his people a code founded upon the law of Sinai. The Magna Charta of King John was drawn from the law of Moses. John Calvin and the Reformers of Switzerland founded the Genevan Republic. They built upon the two tables of Sinai. William the Silent and the Reformers established the Dutch Republic. It was founded upon the ten commandments. Pym, Hampden, Sidney, Cromwell, and the Puritans gave England civil and religious liberty. Knox, Henderson, Melville, and the Covenanters gave Scotland civil and religious liberty. They gave what Moses had given them.

The Puritans of England, the Covenanters of Scotland, the Huguenots of France, and the Dutch Reformers from Holland brought civil and religious liberty to America. Plymouth Rock means the ten commandments. Our republic is the lineal descendant of the lawgiver of Sinai. The state is the divinely appointed keeper of both tables of the Decalogue. The majesty of law has been committed to the civil power. Here is the basis of moral legislation. Here we find the divine commission of the state to deal with the Secret Lodge System.

1. *The authority of the Lodge over its members is inimical to public justice.* Mackey's "Lexicon," page 8, says: "The Master is supreme in the Lodge. Such a thing as an appeal from the Master to the Lodge is unknown in Masonry. The power of the Master is supreme." Page 103: "The government of the Grand Lodge is completely despotic; its edict must be respected, obeyed without examination by its subordinate Lodges." The English nation could behead their king, and America could impeach their president, but the tyrant of the Lodge cannot be appealed from. "Should the Grand Lodge decree wrongfully or contrary to the ancient constitutions, there is no redress for its subordinates." "The Master is supreme arbiter in all questions of order. For no misdemeanor, however great, can he be tried by his Lodge, for as no one has a right to preside there in his presence except himself, it would be absurd to suppose that he could sit as judge in his own case." If there is any such thing as a dangerous

combination, the Lodge is one. An officer of a Grand Lodge in Missouri, in 1867, said:

> Not only do we know no North, no South, no East, no West, but we know no government save our own. To every government save that of Masonry, and to each and all alike, we are foreigners. We are a nation of men bound to each other only by Masonic ties, as citizens of the world, and that world the world of Masonry; brethren to each other all the world over; foreigners to all the world besides.

That is either pure bombast or the rankest treason. In either case those sentiments are unworthy and dangerous.

2. *The oaths of the Lodge are a menace to public rights.* Take the first three degrees of Masonry. The Entered Apprentice swears to keep the Lodge secrets, on the Bible, in the name of God, on the penalty of having his throat cut, his tongue torn out by the roots, and his body buried in the rough sands of the sea at low-water mark. The Fellow-Craft oath, besides secrecy, adds a promise to abide by all Lodge rules, obey signs and summonses, assist poor Fellow-Crafts, etc., under penalty of having his breast torn open and his heart plucked out and exposed, to be devoured by the vultures of the air, etc. The Master Mason's oath adds keeping of a brother Master Mason's secrets, murder and treason excepted, and they left to his own discretion, binding him under no less a penalty than that of having his body severed in twain, his bowels taken out and burned to ashes, and the ashes scattered on the rough sands of the sea, where the tide ebbs and flows twice every twenty-four hours. The Royal Arch degree amends the above thus: "Murder and treason *not* excepted." These oaths and imprecations increase in blasphemy and barbarity through all the thirty-three degrees.

These oaths are taken either in jest or in earnest. If the former, they should be prohibited, because they tend to break down the sacredness of the oath. If sincerely, who is to inflict these horrid penalties? Does the Lodge punish its guilty members thus? These oaths are dangerous and disloyal, and should be prohibited.

3. *The false religion of the Lodge corrupts society.* The Lodge is a religion. Mackey speaks of a Mason as "free from sin by living up to the rules of the order." "The white apron is by its symbolic purity to aid us to that purity of life and conduct which will enable us to present ourselves before the Grand Master of the Universe unstained

with sin." "Masonry consists in a knowledge of the great truths, that there is one God, and that the soul is immortal."

The Grand Sire of the Odd Fellows, in consecrating their cemetery near Chicago in 1868, said: "Our Grand Master will take all who are buried in this ground to Himself in the day when He makes up His jewels."

In the Lodge, Pagan, Mohammedan, Jew, and Christian unite in worship. But whom do they worship? Not the Christian's God, for it is not good Masonry to mention the name of Christ in the first three degrees. The worship in which all join without Christ is not the worship of the true God. It is the worship of Satan. They sacrifice to devils, not to God. As was said of the Samaritans, whose religion was a strange medley of the heathen nations with whom the King of Babylon colonized the land and the few Israelites left after the deportation of the ten tribes: "They feared Jehovah and served graven images."

The Tremont Temple Baptist congregation worshipped in Music Hall while the Temple was being rebuilt. On Easter Sabbath afternoon, 1896, some 2,500 knights marched into the hall in full uniform. The Boston Christian Endeavor choir occupied the platform. A Sire (sic) Knight presented the Baptist congregation with a lecture, a bronze pulpit, the figure of an angel whose uplifted hands supported an open Bible, the gift of the Lodge, valued at $1,500. Rev. George C. Lorimer, D. D., the pastor, accepted it on behalf of the congregation. Then the Endeavorers and Knights joined in singing hymns, and the congregation helped them. Was that not a repetition of the Samaritan compromise in God's worship? Dr. Lorimer was giving one hand to Christ and the other to the devil. Let our government remove this alluring tempter, the Lodge.

4. *The Lodge is the enemy of the home.* How often a Mason spends $300 for his uniform, while his wife wears a $1.50 calico dress. A writer in the *North American Review* for May last, says:

> For mere personal gratification, aside from any real or supposed benefits, the members of the various fraternities in the United States spend annually $250,000,000. It would all but revolutionize a large section of American society, if the wives and daughters of the households of the men who belong to these organizations should insist on their right to spend for their own adornment, or for their own personal pleasure, dollar for dollar spent by husband or brother

for initiation fees, dues, uniforms and regalia, swords, plumes, banners, and banquets.

The moral standard of the Lodge is shocking. Think of the Master Mason's oath. After the Jubula, Jubulo, Jubulum scenes, in which the candidate for the third degree has been struck in the throat by the first ruffian, Jubula, and on the left breast by the second ruffian, Jubulo, and in the bowels by Jubulum, the third ruffian, who kills him outright, and, at the end of fourteen days, he is raised from the grave, the following oath is administered, among others:

> I do promise and swear that I will not have carnal or illicit intercourse with the wife, mother, daughter, or sister of a brother of this degree, knowing her to be such, nor will I permit another brother of this degree to do so if in my power to prevent it.

The implication of that oath smells of the bottomless pit. Who would allow that standard of morals in society?

ENDNOTES

1. Report on Secret Societies in Reformed Presbyterian Synod, June, 1897.

2. He belonged to the lodge in Scotland. He took forty-five degrees in Paris. He was made the custodian of the papers of the French lodge. He travelled extensively in Europe and collected documentary evidence from many lodges. He clearly proved a "conspiracy against all the religions and governments of Europe, carried on in the secret meetings of Masons, Illuminati, and Reading Societies," and published these in a volume of 390 pages, in 1798. He divided the book into four chapters: 1. The Masonic Schism; 2. The Illuminati; 3. The German Union; 4. The French Revolution.

Harger provides an affectionate account of the role that lodges played in American communities in the first decade of the twentieth century. He celebrates the manner in which lodge membership secures transient Americans in webs of acquaintanceship and sociability, mentors them in self-improvement and oratory, and provides material security through mutual support and insurance. Harger also contends that fraternalism ameliorates the nation's class distinctions by enthralling individuals from "the president down to the humblest citizen."

THE LODGE
Charles Moreau Harger
1906
Atlantic Monthly 37 (April 1906), 488-494.

ENTER in the late evening a country town or a small city. Street lamps have become dim; store fronts are dark; the windows of the fifteen-cent restaurants are faintly outlined; here and there a weary horse whinnies in longing for its stable. It is a picture of lonesomeness, save for one inevitable bright spot. Over a stairway leading to a second story hall shines a triangular transparency sending its gleam far into the night. On its painted glass sides facing the main thoroughfares are pictured two hands clasped in token of brotherhood, and this message greets you: "Hiram Chapter No. 673, A. O. of T. K. Meets Wednesday evening. Visitors welcome."

If you possess the sign and password, and seek entrance to the haven of the followers of Trustful Knighthood, you will find gathered there above the hardware store most of the men of the village who do things. Doctors, lawyers, politicians, laborers, editors, teachers, farmers, railroad agents, are engaged in the exciting diversion of "work in the second degree," or are debating earnestly with keen argument the "good of the order," which may be almost anything from the fining of an absent-minded brother who at the last meeting wore home his official decorations, to a protest against an increase in the lodge dues.

If you wait long enough, there may come "an alarm at the door," and with much solemnity the outside watchman (a bank cashier) will inform the inside watchman (a lumberman), who will inform the Exalted Worthy Patron (a carpenter), that the members of the ladies' auxiliary of the Ancient Order of Trustful Knights are without, and the Exalted Worthy Patron will declare the lodge closed and the visitors given entrance. Headed by the Exalted Worthy Matron (the wife of the dry-goods merchant), the auxiliary will bring in baskets of sandwiches, pots of steaming coffee, and heaps of doughnuts and apples. The whole company will resolve itself into a merry social gathering; dancing will follow the feast; and when the Exalted Worthy Scribe sends a report to the lodge paper he will say that "all went home in the wee sma' hours, feeling that a good time had been had."

The lodge has become the social focus of many a town. It is so to a greater degree, perhaps, in the West than in the East. On the plains distances between population centres are greater; the ties of old family acquaintance are lacking; the fraternal order is the one thing that knows no barrier of wealth or position. The fact that many of the orders admit men and women to their membership on the same terms adds to the strength of the social claim, — it also brings about odd situations.

"I am going down town to-night," remarked a country town banker one evening to his wife. "The lodge meets this evening."

"That will leave me alone," was the response, "for Anna" (their one servant) "is going to lodge, too."

"Yes," agreed the husband. "We belong to the same lodge."

This very equality brings about a comradeship that in the newer communities makes easier the ways of life. You have an employee in your office or store. He works with his coat off, and through the day you consider him but little. You do not ask his opinion nor defer to his judgment. But on lodge night, when you enter the portals, — a lodge door, though it may admit only to the second floor of an unpainted frame building, is always a "portal," — you make your obeisance and mystic signs before a dignified potentate in robes of red and yellow whom you recognize as your employee.

You are surprised to see that he is completely master of the situation. To be sure, most of his work is written down in the ritual, but he rises to the occasion; and if you would sit in his place you must serve a long apprenticeship through the "chairs" until you are worthy. He gains thus a training, not possible elsewhere, in dealing with men. Somehow you have a greater respect for him the next day; he holds himself a little straighter. The democracy that politics does not give, that the church scarcely accomplishes to the same degree, comes through the mutual knowledge of the secret work of a fraternal order to whose tenets both have sworn allegiance.

What the old-fashioned "literary" or lyceum did in making its attendants ready debaters, capable of thinking on their feet, the lodge does in these days. The many matters of more or less moment that come before the order, the certainty of diversity of views, insure to all an opportunity for taking part in free and easy discussion under parliamentary rules. It is a school not to be despised, and for many it is the only one in which can be acquired this sort of knowledge.

Versatility is engendered by the rivalry of orders, and it is natural for the leader in one to take a commanding place in the management of others, for a broad similarity runs through the lodge ritualism, and there is a temptation to shine in many ceremonies that becomes often almost a passion. In every town are "joiners," who pride themselves on their many degrees and their multitude of grips and signs.

The candidate for a county office in a Western community who cannot wear a half-dozen different lodge pins on his waistcoat feels handicapped. The traveler who does not display on his lapel some fanciful design of dagger, scimiter (sic), or battle-axe is a rarity. The book agent comes into your office and gives you the hailing signal before asking your subscription for a new-fangled encyclopaedia in twenty-two volumes. The fellow passenger in the smoking-room of the Pullman glances meaningly at your emblem, which matches his own, and with "Where do you belong?" begins a friendly conversation.

Sometimes the recognition is merely preliminary to working a graft; sometimes the conductor is besought to pass the ticketless traveler because of a claim of brotherhood in the order, — but this is rare. The great mass of the lodge members hold their fraternal relations higher, and condemn the one who trades on knowledge thus obtained. It is a vast-knit sympathy that has grown to proportions unrealized save by those who know the people in the smaller communities and understand the comprehensiveness of the lodge membership network.

Take a typical Western town, a county-seat community of 4000 population, whose directory, issued a few months ago, lies before me. It has sixteen churches, with a membership of about 1500. But there are twenty-eight lodges, with a membership of 2400. There is, however, this difference: a person may belong to many lodges; he can join but one church. The lodges are in no sense rivals of the sanctuary; they inculcate similar principles of manliness and good citizenship and morality, but they do not undertake the regenerative work that is the province of the church. Yet many sects consider the lodge antagonistic to their ideals, and refuse to allow their members the privilege of belonging to secret orders.

In the minds of some the accomplishments of church and lodge are confused, perhaps naturally so. I remember an instance: a farmer living on a rather lonely road became ill, and after some weeks died, leaving his family with a mortgaged bit of land, many debts, barely furniture enough for its daily needs and a life insurance benefit due from one of the fraternal orders. An evangelist holding meetings in the neighboring schoolhouse, accompanied by two of his elders, came to the widow.

"It is unfortunate that your husband did not belong to the church instead of to the lodge," said the preacher.

The widow, loyal to her husband, and remembering the bitterness of long days of suffering and poverty, resented the insinuation.

"No, it is not," she declared. "We have lived in this neighborhood two years, but not an elder of the church came to help us when he was sick or offered me help when he was gone. The members of the lodge came here two at a time and stayed with him every night; they brought to me and the children things we needed, and they have paid me two thousand dollars, every cent I have in the world, and which will give me a little start to make a home for the children. I am glad he belonged to the lodge."

While she was perhaps not clear as to the ethics of the situation, and overlooked the business basis of the fraternal order, her view is shared by tens of thousands to whom the material welfare brought by the union of forces in secret affiliations brings a frank admiration of the outward expression of fraternity, shown in the friendliness engendered by association within lodge-room walls.

Indeed, the question often arises, might not some of the methods that make lodges successful be adapted to the needs of the church, to bring the material advantages of cooperation closer home to the members, holding them with firmer grasp? Even in orders that have no business basis, existing solely as promoters of the benefits of fraternity and for the care of those members to whom come affliction or penury, there is a loyalty that any church might envy. The privilege of fellowship is a strong incentive to every member to lead an upright life, — for not only is any other course certain to bring upon him the reprobation of his lodge brothers, but, if continued, it will end in disgraceful expulsion.

Assessment life insurance is the foundation of the larger number of fraternal orders. Be the members called knights, pilgrims, workmen, foresters, or patricians, they are engaged merely in a business venture, paying at given periods certain assessments to meet death claims as brother after brother is called away. The report of a "congress" of fraternal orders gives some startling statistics. For instance, ten years ago there were thirty-four societies in the organization; now there are over sixty. The insurance represented by the outstanding certificates is almost $5,600,000,000; the annual distribution of benefits $55,000,000. This is but one combination of orders. Another has as large a membership, and many orders are outside of both. Fraternal insurance includes something like one third of all that is written in this country, and at a cost not one twentieth of that necessary in the management of old-line companies, because it is so largely a freewill offering of time and effort on the part of the men and women in the union of cooperation.

Does the membership of the Trustful Knights show sign of lethargy, there comes an immediate response to the crisis. On some meeting night two brothers, standing at opposite stations in the hall, choose sides until the entire membership is divided into rival parties. Then begins a campaign for new members, and the community is ransacked for available material. A deputy from the grand lodge may assist in the work, utilizing his well-trained arts of persuasion and argument. Each member receives credit for the application cards on which his name is found, and a prize of worth is awarded to the one having the largest number of candidates on his record.

But the real fun comes when the harvest is ended and all the innocent joiners have been ridden on the lodge goat. Then it is that the Exalted Worthy Patron decides which group has made the greatest gains for the order, and assesses as the penalty of the opposition the furnishing of an oyster supper for the whole lodge. The entire gathering is at once transformed into a social company, wives and daughters and sweethearts appear, and there is merry-making long after the lamp in the triangular sign above the hallway has flickered and gone out.

What can stand against such effort as that? While such is the sentiment of sociability and loyalty, how can there come an end to the lodge as a typical American institution? Little wonder that it exerts so strong an influence. Here and there come failures because the assessments are not sufficient to meet the obligations, but new orders are all the time arising, and the spirit of the lodge survives with increasing strength.

While the death benefit to be received from a single order seldom exceeds $3000, hence making it the insurance of the moderately well-to-do, the multi-membership of the average citizen gives him a full complement of protection. Sagacious business men are found who carry large amounts of fraternal insurance, believing that in the end they are gainers over those who invest in old-line policies. Others make a judicious combination of both kinds, and so are preparing for their families along more than one line, as well as acquiring the social benefits that accrue from the possession of many secret signs and passwords.

A story is told of the most conspicuous joiner in a thriving Western city noted for its many lodge members. Indeed, it is said that everybody belongs to at least one lodge and nearly everybody to two or three. Recently a new family came to town, and located just across the street from the past master of all the organizations. One day, a week later, he caught the five-year-old son of the neighbor as the lad was passing, and with a few preliminary remarks led up to: —

"Say, my boy, is your father a Mason ?"

"No, sir," was the sharp reply. "Probably, then, he is an Odd Fellow?"

"No, sir, he ain't."

"Knight of Pythias? Woodman? Workman? Pyramid? Forester? Maccabee?"

The boy shook his head.

"Isn't your father a member of any lodge?" demanded the questioner in a puzzled tone.

"Not a one," replied the boy.

"Then why on earth does he make all those signs when he comes out in the front yard every morning?"

"Oh, that ain't lodge," cheerfully explained the lad. "Pa's got St. Vitus's dance."

The social influence of the lodge is by no means confined to the lodge room. It extends to the intimate life of the community in many of the recreative and serious affairs of mankind. Perhaps you would not care to have the Ancient Order of Trustful Knights storm your home some winter evening just as you had settled beside the fireplace with a good book ; but that sort of "surprise" is the height of enjoyment for the small town. The laughing, happy group of members, having gathered at Sir Knight Smith's, marches in close order to the door of the victim's home. If possible, the brother has been inveigled from the house, and is brought back to find his dwelling in the hands of his friends. It is probably a birthday or wedding anniversary, and a gaudy red plush rocker stands in the middle of the parlor, a mute testimonial of the esteem in which the members hold the host.

After the lunch brought by the callers has been served, the Exalted Worthy Patron makes a few appropriate remarks, extolling the virtues and standing of the recipient, and presents the chair, hoping for many prosperous returns of the day. And when they are gone, when the last "good-night" has died out, the honored brother rests in red plush luxury and is glad he joined the Trustful Knights.

Sometimes the venture is a larger one, and a whole lodge visits the castle of the order in a neighboring village. That is a gala occasion for both visitors and guests. Everybody turns out, and the hall is crowded. "Work" in the most hair-raising degree is "put on" by the team of the visiting lodge. Dignity and impressiveness mark the initiation, and the interested audience watches the proceedings closely, — part with pride and part with critical eyes. When the ability of the team has been exhibited in the exemplification of the "work," come speeches, recitations, and songs.

Perhaps one of the grand officers will be there. Now the Grand Exalted Worthy Patron may be when at home only a dry-goods clerk or a mender of shoes, but on his round of official visitation he takes on a prominence scarcely exceeded by the governor of the state. He is received with the honors of a potentate; salaams and genuflections mark his progress through the lodge room; and the robes he wears are dazzling in their beauty. But he brings something of the outside world to his fellows, and his address following the formal ceremonies is usually helpful both to the lodge life and to the individual.

Supper — or perhaps a banquet at the principal hotel of the town, with flurried waiters, many courses, and toast responses — follows, and dancing ends the evening. The gathering has done more to foster intercommunity friendliness than could a whole volume of resolutions by the respective city councils.

At stated times the grand lodge meets, and to it travel several delegates and Past Exalted Worthy Patrons from the various subordinate branches. The multiplicity of titles here becomes rather confusing, and the proceedings assume something of the nature of a conference on the Field of the Cloth of Gold. However, it gives the visitors a state-wide acquaintance that they otherwise might not attain, and introduces them into a broader life than they would find in their home towns. Then there is the supreme lodge. To the average lowly lodge member who does not hold official position this august body ranks with the United States Senate and the English Parliament. The titles dwarf the imagination. To members of the order the pomp is awe-inspiring; others are likely to smile a little at it all, — but that may be because they belong to a rival organization whose supreme lodge meets a month later.

Once a year, at least, in most lodges comes a pilgrimage to some church to listen to a sermon especially prepared for the order. It is impressive to see a hundred men, all good citizens, all carrying themselves with the feeling that they must do nothing to discredit the society, march into the meeting-house and take pews for the service.

So is it inspiring to see two members chosen by the lodge tramp sturdily to a sick brother's dwelling and remain with the family in its time of need; or to see the generous response when some one tells the assembly of trouble and want in any home. These good deeds do not reach the public; they are not enforced actions by the rules of the order; they are the outflowing of charity and everyday good will on the part of the members. No credit is claimed therefor; it is a mutual helpfulness in which all are united.

When death comes to a brother there arises a new opportunity for the lodge's kind offices. Many a family has met multiplied sadness in its new frontier home. Neighbors were few and acquaintances rare. But the father wore a tiny button or pin that told of his affiliation with a leading order, and more than one evidence of its significance came to them. There were offers of assistance, flowers, carriages. At the hour of the funeral, coming down the street two by two, each man with a band of crape on his coat sleeve, appears the entire membership. Like a guard of honor the lodge lines a pathway for the family as the home is left for the lonesome drive to the cemetery. Behind the hearse the members march to God's acre, and in solemn circle surround the open grave as the dead is laid to his final rest. They walk slowly past the gash in the green sod, with tender symbolism throwing upon the coffin sprigs of ever-green, that are for remembrance. As their ritual follows that of the church, it is difficult to see where in the relation of form to humanity's earthly needs one greatly surpasses the other.

And who shall say that grief is not assuaged when the family proudly reads in the country paper the following week "resolutions of respect " inspired by the sad event ? Beginning with, "Whereas, the Supreme Exalted Trustful Knight of the Universe has in His omnipotent wisdom seen fit to call Knight Jones from his earthly labors to the Great Lodge above; and, whereas, Hiram Chapter has lost a noble brother and the community a useful citizen,"and so on, to "Resolved, that these resolutions be spread on the records of the lodge and a copy be given to the afflicted family," they make a public testimonial of worth not to be despised. Naturally, in the card of thanks, along with "the kind friends and neighbors who assisted us in our late bereavement," are mentioned directly and specifically the " brothers of Hiram Chapter " as worthy of recognition by the grateful widow and children.

There be those who profess to see something ridiculous in the wearing of robes and plumes. They sneer at the sight of lodge parade, each participant adorned in a conventionalized mediaeval armament, or sporting semi-military gorgeousness. They say it is silly for grown men to refer to each other in grandiose terms, and to assume dignities that are neither of state nor church. And sometimes this side of it does appeal even to the most hardened joiner. The average man grows weary of too much gold lace and fancy dress, hence there is a tendency to-day toward simpler uniforms and less ostentatious display. The stronger the order, the less is it likely to seek undue adornment.

After all, it is not the ritual nor the robes that make a lodge strong; it is the teaching that is behind it. In even the avowedly beneficiary orders is taught something higher than paying monthly assessments. The underlying principles of charity, hope, and brotherhood are linked with protection in a way that cannot fail to make an impression upon the candidate for lodge honors. Here and there is a touch of fun; some of the degrees have trials that test men's good nature to the utmost, but they are usually taken "on the side," or as separate functions from the regular initiation, and have nothing to do with the real work of the lodge. The horse-play of the college fraternity finds little encouragement in the modern idea of good lodge management. It is realized that an order to be successful must appeal to men's reason and intelligence rather than to their love of amusement.

The past seven years have been a time of remarkable growth in lodge membership. Prosperity influences this as other things. To many the price of a lodge membership is a luxury; in hard times the assessments often become a burden. Not to mention the various brotherhoods of workers, which are properly labor unions rather than secret societies, the increase in strength has been notable. More frequent than ever before has been the call to "work" in initiation of petitioner (sic) for degrees. With an abundance of funds, the citizen is a much more willing subject for the solicitor of the lodge, and he finds more time to enjoy whatever benefits may be derived. Wealth pours into the coffers of the organizations. Costly temples, owned by the orders and equipped with every appliance for the conduct of the sessions as well as for the comfort of the members, have been erected in the larger cities.

To the far Western farms, where the dwellers were a few years ago working out their material destiny through trial and tribulation, the lodge has reached, and thousands of prosperous husbandmen drive into the nearest town once a week, or every fortnight, to mingle with the village residents in a society's halls. Efforts to conduct permanently lodges exclusively for farmers have not been generally successful, though in parts of the country such orders have met with considerable prosperity.

From the president of the nation down to the humblest citizen the fascination of grip and password enthralls. It is not that the lodge is a secret organization, although that is a part; it is not that its membership is chosen with caution, although such exclusiveness undoubtedly makes it more eagerly sought; it is not that it gives direct benefits or that it offers protection to the family when the bread earner has departed, — not these things alone make the lodge popular. Greater than they is the desire for social companionship, the love of fellowship, the power of community of interest. Not a substitute for club or church, yet filling a place in men's lives that neither occupies, the lodge has developed the old-time guild idea and fitted it to modern conditions, and is an institution that exerts a tremendous power in business, in politics, and in society. So rapidly does it increase in popularity that it shows little indication of ever wielding less power over men's destinies than it does to-day.

Hugh Weir's "The Romance of the Secret Society" provides an overview of the status of fraternal organizations at the end of the first decade of the twentieth century. In doing so, he provides thumbnail histories of the Freemasons, the Odd Fellows, and the Red Men. Although Weir distinguishes between the legendary and factual histories of the Masons, he is not as careful in his treatment of the Red Men. Historians may find Weir's economic analysis of fraternalism particularly useful.

THE ROMANCE OF THE SECRET SOCIETY
Hugh C. Weir
1911
The World Today 21 (1911), 866-71.

1. Nine Million Oath-Bound Men

NINE MILLION men, drawn from the four compass points, compose the most unique army in the world's history. It is the army of the secret fraternities of the United States. It reaches to all sections, all classes and all creeds. Its power is the most absolute known to mankind. Its members are bound by oaths of life and death. Its secrets are so well guarded that in spite of the millions among whom they are shared, they have never reached the outside world. If its members acted in unison at the polls they would possess three million more votes than elected William H. Taft President of the United States. Their roster would equal the combined population of Alabama, Arizona, Arkansas, California, Colorado, Connecticut, Delaware, the District of Columbia, and Florida.

And yet the average man who is not a lodge member, and for that matter the average man who is one, has no conception of the tremendous development of the secret fraternities of this country. It is a development which, in spite of its gigantic scope, has materialized with a quietness attracting so little attention as to be almost startling. And the swiftness of its growth is no less remarkable. Fully seventy-five per cent of the nine-million membership of American secret fraternities has been attained in a period of twenty-five years. Fifty years ago half of the organizations with an enrollment to-day ranging from one hundred thousand to five hundred thousand, had no existence. These brotherhoods of strange oaths and secret pledges and hidden rituals, embracing in their membership one man in every four in this country, have sprung up almost in a generation.

What are we to read from this amazing record! What is the dynamic power behind the secret fraternity — this power that governs as many persons as are numbered in the combined membership of Baptist, Presbyterian, United Brethren, Episcopalian, Unitarian and Congregational churches? Whether you belong in a secret society or not, whether you believe in the principle of the secret society or not, you must admit that it has grown to one of the greatest factors of modern society.

Viewed from a fair, impartial angle is this factor for good or harm? There are those sociological investigators who tell us that the goal of human brotherhood is impractical, that it is a magnificent dream, but only a dream. Is the curious development of the secret fraternity an argument to prove these pessimistic reasoners in the wrong, an argument to convince those of us who doubt, that the world is, indeed creeping toward the era of brotherhood. Or is the secret fraternity properly to be regarded as a brotherhood? Its named as such, true; its advertised purpose is such, but behind its initiations and rituals and numbers does it represent the real brotherhood of man? In the literature of the lodge, this is called the Golden Era of Fraternity. Is it? What is the interpretation which an unbiased tribunal would place on this sweeping statement of the fraternal society?

In the United States there are now 125,000 distinct and individual lodges of American secret societies. Many of them own towering buildings of their own devoting one or two floors to their own use and deriving a handsome income from the rent of the remainder. Others are housed in unpretentious backrooms of obscure villages. The scale ranges from the dingy, third-story hall of a Kansas county seat, to the imposing Masonic Temple, of Chicago. Totaling the annual expenses required in the maintenance of the secret fraternity lodge rooms — rent, fixtures, light, heat — and allowing the conservative average of $50 for each lodge, although in some cases it would be nearly $50,000, we find that the enormous sum of $6,250,000 is required each year for the bare expenses of meeting places for our fraternal societies. Some experienced lodge men would double this estimate, even when the incomes from office and store rent of the fraternal buildings of the great cities are deducted.

To this amount we must add also the expenses of uniforms and lodge regalia, for the modern secret society often carries through its services with Oriental splendor, and conservative business men who would scorn any other garments but quietest suits in their everyday life, appear in the lodge room with flowing vestments that would put their wives' wardrobes to shame. The item of plumed hats in a single lodge of pretension may amount to $10,000. And when we consider the cost of the gorgeously designed robes, sheep-skin aprons, belts, swords and various lodge-room fittings necessary to carry through the elaborate rituals, it is not difficult to understand that the costumes and furnishings of American fraternities cost anywhere from $12,000,000 to $20,000,000! Of course, there must be rich men's lodges and poor men's lodges in such an estimate. A man of ordinary income could not afford to belong to a fraternity spending $75,000 or $100,000 on its costumes and appointments, but when we find that even the humble lodges maintain elaborately uniformed "degree teams" the national bill for lodge-room splendor is staggering. Certainly it reveals a love of mysticism and pomp and gorgeous extravagance in the supposedly prosaic American man, calculated to upset many national traditions!

But we have not yet reached the end of the expense account of our fraternities. We must consider the hundreds of lodge banquets given every year - many of them the most sumptuous feasts designed in this country - convention costs, the traveling expenses of officials and delegations, the thousands of testimonials and gifts to retiring officers. Eighteen years ago one fraternal writer estimated these items to amount to $250,000,000 in a year's time, and our lodge membership has almost doubled since that date!

As an adjunct to many of the fraternal societies, there are military companies, drilled in the manual of arms with all of the thoroughness of the army. The extent of these companies is shown by the astonishing fact that their membership is four times the enrollment of the United States regular army. The cost of their equipment, instruction and maintenance must be considered apart from other lodge expenses, and it is apparent that it must reach an enormous sum, running into the millions at the most conservative per capita estimate.

So much for one side of the ponderous ledger before us. There is another and even more significant side, that of lodge philanthropy, a subject with almost as many varied angles as there are different societies. We hear a great deal about the charity of the secret fraternity, and there is, doubtless, much that we do not hear anything about. To the layman not familiar with the scope of modern fraternities, philanthropy seems the be-all and the end-all of the lodge room. The sum distributed by American lodges during the past twenty years in so-termed "benefits," as a matter of fact is staggering. Even eliminating the Masons, the Odd Fellows, and the Pythians, it is estimated that during this period at least $600,000,000 was expended; From the three former organizations, a modest reckoning adds $400,000,000 more, and this, despite the fact that the Masons is not primarily a charitable organization and that no official record is kept of its philanthropic work. Many fraternal experts will tell you that unrecorded lodge philanthropies will amount to half as much as official benefits. In any event, it is conservative to say that considerably over $1,000,000,000 was expended in the past decade by American secret societies in the relief of human want and suffering.

Statistics are dry reading. To the average man, there is little difference between millions and billions. But the financial feature of the secret fraternities of this country is important as one of the emphasized details showing the extent and use of the nation-wide power which they have attained. The enormous sums spent by the modern fraternity in decorations, costumes, amusements, may seem nothing more than a huge waste. The glamour and splendor made possible by these millions may appeal (sic) to the man who is not a lodge member as absurd. They are details, however, which must be reckoned in their true proportion, if we would find and measure the position which the secret fraternity holds in American society. Equally true is the feature of philanthropy and benefits. The billion dollars spent in relief work may seem dwarfed by comparison with the enormous sums which have been expended in the creation and development of the lodges behind it, but it is at least an evidence of resources that appear the more startling when we consider the millions of members who have contributed them. Philanthropies of a billion dollars make a gigantic credit-mark, and if the lodges, from which they have come, spend five times as much for plumes and uniforms and swords and the other paraphernalia of secret pomp and display, the two facts at least give us a curious viewpoint from which to digest the practical worth of the fraternal society.

Let us turn our attention from the lodge, considered collectively, to the lodge member considered individually. What walks of life are represented in the nine million membership of American secret societies? The answer is surprising, not because of one especial rank but because of the many ranks. Our fraternal lodges are peculiarly and significantly democratic. One might think in view of the magnificence of their display that they are the rich man's playthings. The rich man as a class, however, plays a minor part in the activities of the lodge room. It is one of the fundamental truths of the modern fraternity that its membership does not emphasize either extreme of society. Neither the very rich man nor the very poor man is prominent in its roster. What may seem like a contradictory statement is simple of explanation.

The man of great wealth or social position resents the democracy which the lodge by its very name makes it impossible to eliminate. Even raising the barriers of excessive entrance fees and prohibitive dues, a man with a sufficient bank-roll and conventional morality can obtain admittance regardless of his position in society, or lack of it. Recognition by the "Smart Set" is not and could not be one of the requisites of the fraternal society however conservative and however wealthy. In addition, the rich man has his club life, and the lodge room is unnecessary to his scheme of existence. A censorship can be established over members of the club, which is impossible over the members of the lodge. At the other extreme of society, the very poor man as a rule has neither the money for dues, however slight, nor the training or ambition to appreciate the pomp of the ritual. The philanthropies of the lodge are bestowed because of adversity. The poverty which it relieves is an incident rather than a condition, excepting, perhaps the fraternal homes of the country.

The great bulk of the members of modern secret society is drawn from what is popularly and rather vaguely termed, the middle classes. While occasionally there may be a very wealthy man rising to lodge prominence, the fact remains that, if we except a few scattered lodges without in any way excepting the particular fraternities of which they are part, nine-tenths of the strength of the secret society comes from the prosaic every-day walks of life, the bread-winners whether their income be $2 a day or $2 an hour. The men who cast seventy-five per cent of the ballots at the polls, who represent the sinews of modern business and professional life, if not always leaders, contribute the membership of fraternal orders.

Again, the secret society is essentially American. With only an occasional exception, its history is confined to this country, its development has been recorded in this country, and ninety-nine per cent its members are American citizens. In no other nation of the world and in no other decade of history has the secret fraternity attained the strength which it now wields in America. As we study its power and its use and abuse of that power we must bear always in mind that it is an American institution, even though it has transplanted the barbaric pomp of ancient Egypt to modern American soil.

The most pronounced exception to the list of fraternities with a distinctly American origin and development is the Masons, the oldest, and in point of numerological strength, the second largest secret fraternity in the world. Masonic tradition is among the most ancient and picturesque in all history. While a distinct line must be maintained between fact and legend in a study of the Masons, the traditions of the order, even if not to be accepted as proved history, at least serve as an illuminating angle from which to view the scope and characteristics of the society.

Tradition defines the origin of the Masonic order in the reign of King Solomon, and gives no less a personage than that storied ruler as its organizer. As the legend goes, Solomon was assisted in the formation of the brotherhood by King Hiram, of Tyre, and Hiram Abif, the son of a widow of Naphthali, who became the master architect of Solomon's Temple. Continuing the interesting details of Masonic legend, the brotherhood, after its formation, at least one thousand years before Christ, continued through the turbulent period following the destruction of Solomon's Temple by Nebuchadnezzar, with a power so secret and well organized, that it was through the instrumentality of the fraternity that the five books of Moses were preserved from destruction and handed down to posterity. The discovery of Masonic emblems in the Egyptian obelisk at Alexandria, known as Cleopatra's Needle, is accepted by many students as additional verification that the order flourished in the days of antiquity.

Whether or not these legends of Masonry are accepted at par value, it is certain that a startling resemblance exists between the present insignia of the order and the emblems of the various secret cults which existed before Christ such as the Eleusinians, Pythagoreans and Rosicrucians. Particularly is this true in the use of the Masonic aprons and the peculiar applications of the forty-seventh problem of Euclid in the ritualistic work of the fraternity.

The most generally accepted theory in regard to the origin of Masonry, however, fixes its origin in the Middle Ages as the successor of the building associations of Europe like the Steimmetzen or Stone Masons of Germany. These early societies dated from the Benedictine monasteries of the eleventh and twelfth centuries, the erection of the more pretentious buildings of a growing civilization requiring the association of skilled craftsmen for lengthy periods, who found the advantages of a close affiliation of interests. These organizations increased so rapidly that by the latter part of the thirteenth century, a combination was effected in Germany under the name of the *Bauhutten,* governed by one code of laws, recognizing one set of secret signs and passwords, and operating under one central authority, the *Haupthutte* of Strassburg. Until the seventeenth century, admission was granted only to craftsmen, but at this time the scope of the order was broadened and gentlemen were received into membership.

The first modern organization to bear the name of Masons, however, was that termed the Masonic Grand Lodge, formed in London in 1717. Within forty years the society had spread into Ireland, Scotland, France, Holland, Russia, Spain, Italy and America. Operative skill in the building arts, the original requirement of membership, was eliminated, and instead of a knowledge of architecture, a Masonic ritual was gradually formed, embodying a statement of moral principles and aims, which candidates were obliged to master and subscribe to. Symbolic Masonry was introduced into this country by the British during colonial days, and the first lodges in the United States were operated under English authority. Following the Declaration of Independence of the United States, in 1776, came a similar declaration from the American Masons, who, in 1777, elected the first grand master on this side of the Atlantic. Among the early Masons in this country appear the names of George Washington and Benjamin Franklin. The membership of American Masonic lodges to-day exceeds 1,500,000.

One of the most curious chapters in the history of Masonry centers around the branch of Knights Templar. Addison, a leading

American Masonic authority, dates the origin of the Templars back to 1113, when nine knights joined themselves together in a brotherhood of arms for the purpose of guiding and protecting pilgrims on their way to Jerusalem. They were so poor that they were forced to ride two on a horse, and yet so strong was the spirit of their religious fervor, that by the close of the twelfth century, their order numbered thirty thousand members.

As it grew in members it also grew in wealth until King Philip, of France, planned to secure their treasures for himself. In 1307, the grand master, James de Molay, and sixty knights on their way to Paris to formulate plans for another crusade, were seized by order of the king and accused of worshiping idols. As a result, they were put to torture, and fifty-nine of the band were burned at the stake by Dominican friars. De Molay was imprisoned for a number of years and finally forced to suffer the same fate as his devoted followers. Modern research, however, while admitting the truth of the tragic events summarized above, is skeptical of the lineal connection between the ancient order and its modern revival. Even though the historic proof be lacking, as in the legends of the Masons, there is no doubt that the spirit of the first Templars has been reflected as nearly as possible in the rituals of their modern brethren. To America belongs the creation of the first Masonic order of Templars, the investiture being recorded in Boston under the date of 1769 although where the ritual came from or by whose authority it was used is one of the many mysteries of Masonry that has never been solved.

The largest fraternal order in existence in point of membership is the Odd Fellows. Although founded in England, its American history is entirely distinct from its British record. The first authenticated date in Odd Fellowship is that of 1748 when the Aristarchus Lodge was organized at the old Globe Tavern in London. During the latter part of the eighteenth century, a tide of sentiment against secret societies swept England, as a result of which Parliament instituted such drastic laws that for years the progress of the order was practically suspended.

The first lodge of Odd Fellows in this country was formed in 1819 in Baltimore. The circumstances of its founding are significant as emphasizing the slight beginnings from which many of the powerful fraternities of today have developed. In the year 1818

Thomas Wildey, an English Odd Fellow, settled in Maryland. Odd Fellowship was strange to American soil. Indeed, fraternal organizations of any character, with the exception of the Masons, were practically unknown. Whether Wildey craved companionship in his new surroundings or whether he was animated by a broader desire to found a fraternal lodge, he had been in this country less than a year when, in company with a brother lodge-member from England, he invited the men of the neighborhood to meet at his home. At that first gathering there were but five present, but plans were set on foot for a series of regular gatherings, which gradually developed from merely social features to an emphasis of higher elements of fraternity, until, in the following year, Washington Lodge No 1 of Odd Fellows was formed and a charter from England applied for.

British jurisdiction, however, did not commend itself to the spirit of Yankee independence, and the English charter was surrendered. The ambitious plan was conceived of establishing a great American brotherhood with a system of government modeled after that of the United States. In each state, grand lodges were formed with jurisdiction over the local branch of the society, and in turn contributing representatives to the national governing body of the order. The membership of the Odd Fellows to-day is rapidly approaching the two million mark—the development of a century.

The oldest fraternity with a purely American history is that of the Red Men, an outgrowth from the historic Sons of Liberty of pre-Revolutionary fame. The Sons of Liberty was established in 1764 as a result of the Stamp Act, and operated for years as a secret society of minutemen, prepared to assemble at a moment's notice in the cause of independence. In 1774 the order was instrumental in calling a session of the Continental Congress. Branches sprang up in different sections of the country. An organization was formed in Georgia, termed the Liberty Boys, which drove out the British governors. For the first half of the nineteenth century little was heard of the society but in the Civil War period it was revived in a measure by the Knights of Golden Circle. The Red Men, as a distinct order, was organized in 1834, incorporating the principles of the Sons of Liberty, and describing its various details of organization with Indian names. Its present enrollment is five-hundred-thousand.

It is one of the curious facts of American fraternities that the majority are a development of the past forty years, and that, twenty years ago, organizations with an enrollment today of 200,000, had not yet been formed. For instance, the Modern Woodmen of America, the third largest fraternal order in this country, with a membership of more than 1,000,000 was not created until 1883. The Knights of Pythias, the fourth in point of members, with an enrollment of 850,000, organized in 1864. The Woodmen of the World, with a membership of nearly 600,000 was not formed until 1890. The Royal Arcanum, with an enrollment of 300,000 started in Boston in 1877 with only nine members. The Independent Order of Foresters, with a membership of 250,000 was formed in 1874. The Macabees with 300,000 members today, was not established until 1883.

No other country of the world has such a remarkable record. What is the reason for it? What is the force that brings nine-million men together at weekly or monthly intervals for the transaction of "lodge business"? What is the magnet that has developed fraternities of a third of a million membership in twenty years? The element of secrecy? The oath of silence? The fascination of elaborately costumed "degree" work, with its suggestion of long-forgotten ages? Or is it the spirit of American comradeship and union which makes possible a bond that would be smothered under the formality and suspicion of older, more conservative nations?

Does the lodge act as a substitute for the club and the tavern and respond to the demands of masculine gossip? Or, striking to a higher angle, is it the consciousness of protection in time of need which appeals to the lodge member? Is it the shrewd, canny provision against the proverbial rainy day? Or can we accept the conclusion of the idealist, and view the spread of the modern fraternity as the dawn of a new era of brotherhood?

The secret society has been reviled and ridiculed. It has been denounced from pulpit, press and legislature. Laws have been made against it. Sociologists have seen in it the root of much of our domestic unrest. It has been buffeted and eulogized as has no other institution of modern society. And it is flourishing to-day more than ever before. The reason, after all, is so simple that it can be expressed in one sentence. Behind the theories of the sociologist, behind the attacks of pulpit and government, behind the censure and ridicule of its enemies and the praise of its patrons, the American secret fraternity exists to-day because, above and beyond all else, it is essentially democratic.

Written in the irreverent, entertaining journalistic style characteristic of the 1920s that reached its fullest expression in Sinclair Lewis's Babbitt, *Charles Merz's "Halt! Who Comes There?" simultaneously celebrates and mocks fraternalism's conventions while allowing readers in the twenty-first century to glimpse the mundane reality of the activities which transpired within America's lodge rooms. Through mentions of automobiles, radio, moving pictures, and urbanization, Merz indicates that, while American life was being reshaped by technology, fraternalism assisted Americans in fending off social alienation and linked city-dwellers to residents of the nation's small towns.*

HALT! WHO COMES THERE?
Charles Merz
1923
The New Republic 25 (August 15, 1923), 327-28.

IT is lodge night for the Olympian, and a dusty row of rubber-tired chariots lines the curb near Centre Hall.

Lodge night for the Olympians plays no favorites; it belongs to both the cities and the towns. Some things you will find alone on Broadway: Spearmint twins who shoulder arms in twenty foot electric lights – swift flashes of an "L" train as it charges across town – pillowed elbows seven flights above the street, braced against a window-sill to watch the crowds below.

Other things belong to Main Street, sights that Broadway seldom sees: hitching posts and plow stores – church picnics, Old Home Weeks, summer wagons with a red umbrella on a pole.

East is East and West is West. But the roads cross once at Centre Hall. It is a far cry from Harlem River to a canteen in the plains. But Centre Hall has bridged them both, as typical of one as the other.

From the street you climb a flight of stairs to the gateway of Valhalla. There is an average door of varnished oak, concealing on its farthest side the Lord High Seneschal: none other, in this case, than Bruno Shafer – clerk by day in the Sheffield Grocery, guardian by night of all that lies beyond the pale. You knock three times; pause for a heart-beat; knock three times again. Panel enough to disclose a lawn tie and two waistcoat buttons opens. "Halt, Stranger! Who comes there?"

"Brother seeking light and council."

"Advance brother. Give the countersign."

Abracadabra. . . Eucalyptus. . . Cornucopia. . . Four syllables, at any rate. The oak door swings slowly on its hinges. There is a hasty and embarrassed fumbling in the dark ante-room for a fraternal handshake. The inner door swings wide upon the shrine of shrines.

It is a great hall that roofs the roller-skating rink downstairs. An organ in one corner vis-à-vis a phosphorescent stove. Chandeliers festooned with paper bunting curled crisp at the edges from the heat of bright electric bulbs. Row on row of folding-chairs, wax yellow, blisteringly bright: upholstered only with vague memories of funerals and Commencement Day. A dais at the room's end, serving as the throne of Charlemagne one night, another as the grotto of Elijah.

For Centre Hall is common ground, the trysting-place of many clans. Olympians have it once a week on Tuesdays. Wednesdays come the Redmen. Thursdays, the Daughters of Rebecca. Fridays, the Ladies of the Khedive's Palace. Saturday is Odd Fellows night. Sunday night the floor is scrubbed. Mondays come the Knights and Ladies of Granada.

It is a problem, nightly, how to shift the bare accoutrements of Centre Hall to give its empty stretches color for the evening scene. Lodge rituals revolve around the telling of a twice-told tale. King Arthur and his knightly court; Solomon and his temple, the good news brought to Ghent; Archimedes and the fulcrum, Jonah and the whale. For the Olympians, lodge night is a barbecue of the immortals – high on the slope above a vale of Tempe no one here has ever seen.

Jove sits on the dais: Jove in the person of Robert Grasty, vice-president and general manager of Barge & Tuttle Trucking. Befitting his high office, Jove alone of all the lodge may wear a hat in temple: a tall and slightly concave boulder, chipped from the mould of 1883. Around his shoulders is a purple toga, lightning playing in and out the hem. His comrades salute him with the cry, "Hail, Jupiter!" when they remember not to call him Bob.

Left and right of Jove himself, on smaller thrones less perilously perched, sit those two brothers who drew lots with him to parcel out the universe: Neptune, with a sea-green scarf around his throat and a firm grip on his trident; Pluto, wrapped in robes of night, dawn breaking gently through the elbows. In a lodge less picturesque than the Olympians they might bear humdrum titles. First and second deacon, possibly. Or first and second warden. They constitute, upon the sometimes faltering attention of the lodge, a first and second mortgage.

Jove raps his chair-arm with a bolt of wood thunder.

"Brother Mercury!"

A red robe rises near the door.

"Hail, Jupiter!"

"Your office, Brother Mercury?"

"To see that the approaches to the temple are defended."

"To your duty, boldly."

Mercury advances to the door, red robe following behind him. Two raps. From the ante-room, a muffled echo."

"The approaches to the temple are defended, Jupiter."

"Who stands guard?"

"The Seneschal."

"His station?"

"Outside the inner door, with a drawn sword in his hand."

"So be it."

Another bolt of thunder.

"Brothers, it is my order that Grover Cleveland Temple, No. 867, Commandery 55, District 37, A. A. of O. O., be now declared in session. Brethren will take due notice thereof and govern themselves accordingly."

Fred Corey, near the corner window on the left, whacks two brethren in the row before him. "That means you! Cut out the noise."

"Who's making any noise? Let go my collar."

A sudden low reverberating roar, as Brother Orpheus pulls out the bass stops on the organ. Jove removes his hat. The lodge rises to the opening verse of "Come, Olympians, Now the Happy Hour Strikes." There is a decided tenor from the corner where the professional choristers are grouped: a quick leaping to the trigger for the first words and the Hallelujahs; a rhythmic um-tum-tum to fit forgotten snatches in between.

Jove restores his opera hat. The lodge proceeds to unfinished business.

There is no unfinished business.

"Reports of committees?"

No reports.

"New business?"

No new business.

"We shall proceed to the consecration of new members," Jove announces. "Brother Mercury, see that the mortals in the ante-room are prepared for their ascent to the imperialistic heights."

Mercury departs; to return shortly with three candidates – arms trussed behind them, eyes blinded with a fold. For an hour, now, they have been sitting in the darkness – unaware of one another's presence; nothing to see; nothing to hear except the dim echoes of "Come, Olympians," sung within, and the faint distant rattle of a dumb-waiter ascending with the evening's stock of coffee and ice cream. There is a myth that they should wait half-paralyzed with fear. But A. has been memorizing for an impromptu speech for after-dinner. B. has been wishing he could see his watch. C. has been wondering if this is going to be worth the $15 he has paid for it.

"Three mortals from the outer night," announces Mercury, "three mortals who have spent their days in darkness, now seek inner light."

A trifle ill at ease, none too certain there is not a trap-door yawning for a headlong flight, shuffling their feet as if they moved on iron rails, the neophytes are led around the chamber. Lost waifs tailing the Elysian fields: from a dozen unexpected quarters they are halted, challenged, searched, made to kneel, and made to rise; pledged, plighted, covenanted, sworn by all that's holy; wrapped in sheets of canvas, lowered into mattressed graves, mourned as lost, brought back to life miraculously.

"Even as the pilgrim toils through the darkness of the night to dawn," intones the hoarse voice of weary Jove, "even as the shepherd mounts the wooded hill to scan the heavens for the first shafts of a welcome dawn, so, Brothers, do you climb our thrice-blessed mountain."

Jove pauses for a glass of water.

"I Say to you" –

"Let there be light!"

Comes light in all its glory! Off with broad cloth blindfolds! Unleash the sixty watts of every frosted bulb on Mt. Olympus! Three new brothers blink into the purple robe of Jove.

Through the kitchen doorway sails an appetizing sniff of coffee.

. . . .

Lodges multiply by thousands, new ones every day. Redmen, Woodmen, Klansmen, Icemen, Elks, Moose, Eagles, Beagles, Bears.

Insurance benefits, in case of illness; perhaps new customers, embraced as brothers. Yes. And an appeal to instincts usually suppressed. Desire to "belong." Desire to peer inside of anything closed outside: to lift the veil before the shrine. Desire to wear regalia – helmets, togas, sandals, police hats, buttons, bearskins – anything that deifies the human form.

All that counts. But there is more.

Once we had a neighborhood. People lived next door to friends. There was no talk of "community spirit." Communities had it, without trying.

That is less true, nowadays. Friends in cities live a mile apart. Even in villages, factory, radio, motor car and moving picture are pushing sections of the old communities apart, sandwiching new interests in between.

What are lodges, anyway – for all their Joves and Neptunes, their rituals and their myths of gay dogs who have left their wives at home – but homesick tribesmen hunting their lost clans?

Look at the curb next time you walk past Centre Hall. The dusty row of rubber-tired chariots reaches to the corner.

In "Sweet Land of Secrecy," Charles Merz expands his earlier short article to provide a light-hearted but detailed overview of fraternalism in the 1920s, claiming it as characteristically American while seeking an explanation for its overwhelming popularity. Salesmanship and economic benefits, he claims, cannot fully explain Americans' love for their lodges. Ultimately, Merz argues that the dramatic rituals and romantic overtones of secret orders allowed Americans to escape the prosaic and drab daily existence offered by an industrializing nation.

SWEET LAND OF SECRECY: THE STRANGE SPECTACLE OF AMERICAN FRATERNALISM
Charles Merz
1927
The Harper's Magazine 154 (1927), 329-334

CENTER hall is a blaze of lights. The curb is parked with motors. Any American in search of something really characteristic of his father-land, weighing the merits of the Woolworth Building and the county fair; the roller-coaster and the nineteenth hole, the non-stop elevator and the family Ford, must reckon with the claims of lodge night. The growth of lodges in this country is stupendous. There were, at the last census, some sixty million adult people in the United States. There are, on the basis of trustworthy figures, some eight hundred different secret orders with some thirty million members. In 1926 half of us have a watch-charm and a countersign. We are the world's great joiners.

We join everything. We join the Gideons and the Rotarians and the Kiwanians and the Democrats and the Republicans and the Single Taxers and the Epworth Leaguers and the Friends of Self-Determination for Rhodesia, to say nothing of almost innumerable country clubs and luncheon clubs and motor clubs and discussion clubs and societies for the prevention of this and the prevention of that and the achievement of the other. All this is above and beyond the thirty million. The thirty million includes only members of those bona fide secret orders with a ritual which are real luxuries in life and real playgrounds for a national ego. It includes members of vast organizations like the Woodmen and the Knights of Pythias and the Odd Fellows and the Daughters of Rebekah, each of which carries on its own roster more than half a million members. It includes the Maccabees who meet in "Hives," the Red Men who meet in "Tribes," the Prophets who meet in "Grottos," the Watchmen who meet in "Forts,'" the Stags who meet in "Droves," the Owls who meet in "Nests," and the Eagles who meet in "Aeries." It includes these new and rapidly growing secret orders, the Beavers, Lions, Serpents, Roosters, Orioles, Deer, Geese, Goats, and Bears. It includes organizations like the Elks and the Foresters and the Modern Order of White Mahatmas and the Concatenated Order of the Hoo-Hoo, the Christian Knights and Heroines of Ethiopia of the Eastern and Western Hemispheres, the Sheiks of the Mosque and the Iridescent Order of Iris and the Benevolent Order of Monkeys and the Hooded Ladies of the Mystic Den.

Who really knows his country without at least one password?

II

A few of the many brightly named and highly varied orders which thrive in these modern times are venerable and of long standing. Freemasonry on this side of the Atlantic dates back to Colonial times; it was brought into New Jersey as early as 1729, and had established itself in all of the original Colonies before the Revolution. In its first patchwork form Odd-Fellowship came from England early in the 1800's. There are other cases of this sort, but not many. The great bulk the eight hundred or so secret orders which now function on the American scene are neither foreign in origin venerable in age; they are one hundred per cent native and distinctly modern. Few of them go back to the days of the Civil War, or even to the days of the Spanish War; some of the most successful have been thought up and created entirely within the last two decades. Of the big ten, the Owls, the Eagles and the Deer each with more than half a million members, date entirely within the 1900s. The Moose, organized in 1888, were practically non-existent till the magic hand of James J. Davis took hold of them and made a stodgy organization something imposing enough to put James J. Davis in the Cabinet.

The life-curve of these more numerous societies of native origin follow a more or less consistent line.

They begin either as the nationally planned projects of experienced organizers who believe that the national market is not surfeited or local societies organized for a local purpose but capable of swift expansion. Under the former head might be cited a great variety of orders including most of those which borrow their titles from four-footed friends. Of the latter a good example is the Elks. "Elkology" has been defined in these more recent years as "by far more comprehensive than theology since it not only contains the theory of a God but the new application of his existence"; but in humbler days "Elkology" was only the good-fellowship of a somewhat jolly benevolent society founded in New York in 1866 as a protest against the excise laws, and deriving its name from a moose head in Barnum's old museum, mistaken by the founders for an elk.

Necessarily, the start is modest. Sometimes it is haphazard, sometimes elaborately planned. In either case there follows for each new order a period of intensive competition. This is the second state of the life-curve and it brings elimination. Some societies catch on, and so survive. Some go under. The history of fraternalism has its casualties: the Knights of the Golden Circle and the Knights of Agar and the Chevaliers of Pythias and a good many hundred others. Some die because they hit upon hard times. Some die because the insurance projects upon which they were built turn out to have been miscalculated. This fate overtook the Order of Solon, the Order of Vesta, the Order of the Royal Ark and others. Still others die because they have been hitched unhappily to a political situation and the political situation sinks beneath them. Thus the Patriots of America went under with free silver in the campaign of '96.

The failures lie in unhallowed ground, but at least lie at rest. For the survivors competition never ends. Sometimes quiet competition, with no public boosting. Sometimes the publicity expert is called in, given a drum, and told to beat it. "Drive" follows "drive." The Ladies of the Mystic Circle challenge the Knights of the Mystic Circle to a contest for new members. Rival organizations push their claims in the advertising pages of a country-wide fraternal press. "Our ritual," says the Fraternal Order of Beavers, "stacks up with any order in existence — brief snappy opening ceremony, including beautiful patriotic flag exercises. . . Special dramatic degree exemplifying the Beavers in the Valley of the Turquemenau and their conflict with the Iroquois." Perhaps your fancy turns to other lines. "Our ritual," asserts the Ancient and Illustrious Order of the Knights of Malta, "is the sole repository of the rites and ceremonies practiced during the Middle Ages, preserved in their entirety but presented in more exquisite style by the aid of modern invention." To the Holy Land with Burton Holmes. The choice is varied. It is the boast of Melter, one of the orders of the Supreme Tribe of Ben Hur that here is the "funniest side degree known to fraternalism." It is the pledge of the Loyal Sons of America that "our goal is five million." It is the claim of the Eastern Order of Magian Masters that its charter comes from "chosen messengers of the Holy Ghost."

And does this drive go over? Sometimes not. There are scores of orders which have flared toward greatness, then died back. There are scores of others whose memberships have never gone above ten thousand but whose constitutions are still hearty. There are others which have begun booming suddenly and never stopped. Why? Simply because of well-planned plugging? Possibly. More likely because of something inherently attractive in the set-up of the new order which actually catches on. Who really knows what goes into the making of a best seller?

Once this latter stage is reached — the stage of real eminence in numbers — there remain two hazards. The first is imitation: an immediate stampede into the field of a host of new societies all patterned on the model of the latest winner. The second is the familiar hazard which has beset every successful institution in the history of human effort, whether the institution was a secret order, a church, a political party, or a school of poets: namely, schism. Jealousies arise, factions appear, it is alleged that the majority is not abiding by tradition, that the clique in control of the Woodmen or the Orioles is not interpreting Woodmanism or Oriolology in the spirit of its founders. Friction grows. A quarrel follows. One wing of the Ancient Order of Foresters breaks away (1874) and forms the Independent Order of Foresters. Another wing of the Ancient Order of Foresters breaks away (1889) and forms the Foresters of America. One wing of the Order of Owls quarrels with the other (1912), and from the controversy springs full-fledged the Order of Ancient Oaks. This is secession. In the case of the Owls, it has happened twenty times since 1906. It is happening constantly in one organization or another. Sometimes it results in the destruction of the parent order. Sometimes the parent order snuffs life from its upstart rival. But note this:

Never has the net effect been to destroy fraternalism itself, or to check its growth, or to reduce its numbers. Schisms may come and schisms may go, but the gate still swings to the double knock and the whispered password. Into a nation overrun with secret fraternal orders come each year new secret fraternal orders which somehow live and prosper. Mere fear of crowding does not faze them. The Elks are followed by the Moose, the Moose are followed by the Stags, the Stags are followed by the Buffaloes, the Buffaloes are followed by the Deer, the Deer are followed by the Reindeer; it is almost demonstrably true, and not a mere conceit of the imagination that within a decade we shall have the Caribou and then the Musk-Ox. Each year the procession lengthens. The apparent fact that this America of ours is already super-organized with bucks and birds and knights and seers is only an incentive. Super-organized? Come, brothers, super-organize some more. On they come: new orders stumbling over themselves into a world in which there is ostensibly not the slightest room for them, yet finding room and settling down and waxing great and adding millions to their rosters. We have reached a stage, in point of numbers, when half the adult population of America now owns a fez, scimitar, a secret code, two feet of plume, a cutlass, or a pair of Anatolian breeches.

There is nothing like it elsewhere in all Christendom.

What explains it?

III

A modern economist might have a ready explanation.

All of this, he might say, is simply a somewhat colorful demonstration of the fact that men organize willingly for economic motives. In this case, whatever they may think of the swords they swing and the plumes they wear and the horns they blow, they are really organizing chiefly for two purposes: (a) to participate in the advantages of the group insurance plans which are characteristic of most lodges, and (b) to make friends and bring in business.

No doubt there is truth in this. Insurance benefits are an integral part of most secret orders, and not infrequently the point they chiefly stress. Especially is this true in the orders which have still to make a name. Thus the Loyal Order of Buffaloes, "a great big, broad-minded, non-sectarian fraternal, sociable, and charitable society," points out that it provides death benefits, accident benefits, sickness benefits, disability benefits, insurance bureaus, and the free services of physician—"all for $6 charter fee and 75 cents a month."

Nor is there, any doubt, so far as the other major economic factor is concerned, that a large part of the joining done in this country is done for the purpose of acquiring brothers who will not only take the everlasting oath, but also open cash accounts. In one of the last public addresses of President Harding - himself an Elk, a Moose, a Mason, a Shriner, and a Tall Cedar of Lebanon – there occurs a story of two gentlemen who came to Marion, Ohio, and joined the two fraternities "with the largest memberships" solely for purposes of commerce. Probably there are few localities which lack instances of this careful choosing.

But when this much is said, and when it is admitted that fraternal orders have their business side, it is apparent that there is still a good deal of ground which this explanation of their popularity does not cover. For it does not explain why men who wish to enjoy insurance benefits do not organize economically for that purpose without going to the bother and expense of dressing themselves as Algerian zouaves each time they meet. It does not explain why men who wish to attract customers to the stores they run should find pleasure in memorizing long passages of archaic ritual and challenging their neighbors with a halberd. After all, there are almost countless social clubs and insurance societies where men and women can make business contacts and protect themselves against the losses of ill health. American fraternalism is something more than this. The economic interpretation is all right as far as it goes, but it leaves unsaid what is important.

That if something like half the adult population of America now belongs to secret orders it is because American fraternalism is something more than a chance to make money or to save it, and the real gateway to a never-never land.

Here is John Jones, a plain bank teller of 211 E. Fourth Street, almost anywhere. But here also is John Jones, on Tuesday evenings from seven-thirty to eleven, a Sir Knight Errant of the Mystic Order of Granada. It is characteristic of secret orders that the names they bear are high spirited and resounding, on a plane above the routine affairs of daily living. The Shriners are not simply Shriners; they are members of the Ancient Arabic Order of Nobles of the Mystic Shrine. The Grottos are not simply Grottos; they are members of the Mystic Order of Veiled Prophets of the Enchanted Realm. There are many other "Mystic"orders. There are many "Illustrious" orders, many "Imperial" orders, many "'Exalted" orders. Frequently there are orders which are several of these at once. On the heels of the Illustrious and Exalted Order of Crusaders may come the Imperial and Illustrious Order of the Mystic and Exalted Cross. These are good adjectives, and possibly by this time some five million Americans have identified themselves with at least one of them. Possibly five million more Americans have identified themselves with two other adjectives which prefix the names of at least fifty thriving orders. These two are "Royal" and Ancient"; and the popularity of each is understandable in a nation which has neither royalty nor antiquity, but a vicarious enthusiasm for them both.

To live in a modern world and be an ancient; to live in a humdrum world and be a knight; to live in a gabby world and have a secret — all this is possible. It is the essence of fraternalism that it does its best to make it possible. An illustrious name is only a beginning. When the password is given and the inner door swings back, it is upon a world as different from the world outside as ingenuity can make it. No mere Presiding Officer sits on the dais; we, live in a democracy, but if there is one secret order which has chosen to pattern itself on the Republic, and call its presiding officer a President, the name of that society is not on record. On the dais sits a Monarch or a Master, a supreme Seignior, an Illustrious Potentate, a Grand Illuminator, or a Maharajah. No secretary is a secretary in this world of dreams come true; he is a Thrice Illustrious Scribe. No treasurer is a treasurer; he is an August keeper of the Strong-Box. No citizen is a citizen; he is a knight, a monk, a priest, a dervish, or an ogre. Never mind if the light is bad and the toga needs a safety-pin. . . . Whose hands have never trembled as he tied a mask behind his ears or combed the fine gold fringe of a glossy pair of epaulettes or stuck in his hat the splendid plume that made of him a Don Quixote? Lodge night for the Red Men brings out the tomahawks. Lodge night for the Shriners brings out the fezzes. Lodge night for the Odd Fellows, when the Third Encampment meets, brings out the purple gowns, the yellow belts, the miters, and the breast-plates. All over America six nights a week, from one to five million men and women are dressing themselves as brahmins, Pharaohs, cannibals, vikings, princes, furies, hermits, druids, Galahads, sorcerers, Maltese, and Tibetans.

For what purpose?

If I tell, swears the Woodman, "may I be dashed to pieces as I now dash this fragile vessel into fragments!"

If I tell, swears the Maccabee, "may my left arm be cut off above the elbow!"

If I tell, swears the Shriner, "may my eyeballs be pierced to the center with a three-edged blade, my feet be flayed, and I be forced to walk the hot sands upon the sterile shores of the Red Sea until the flaming sun shall strike me with living plague, and may Allah, the god of Arab, Moslem, and Mohammedan, the god of my fathers, support me to the entire fulfillment of the same, Amen, Amen, Amen."

What secrets possibly demand protection with these mighty oaths? Never mind the secrets. When the enthusiastic nephew of the neighbor across the street has been digging with two comrades in the lot behind the Baptist Church and comes home hungry, with something in a basket, do not ask what he has found. It is the key to the seventh treasure chest of Captain Kidd.

IV

"Raise the right hand on a level with the face, the last two fingers closed, the two forefingers extended, slightly apart, the thumb Nesting on the third finger, back of the hand to the front, signifying 'Who are you? — Answer: The same sign with the left hand, meaning 'A Friend'"

Thus do the good ladies of the Degree of Pocahontas greet one another "in distress." And no one contemplating the thought of a lodge full of ladies raising right and left hands alternately to signal "Who are you?" and receive the answer "Friend" can doubt that into the routine business of grocery errands, carpet-sweepers, pillow-slips, literary clubs, and laundry lists American fraternalism has brought something agreeably and generically different.

This is notoriously a new world, and in it many things are done prosaically, and not a great deal is done glamorously. Possibly there never was a time when many things really were done glamorously.

But at least we picture such a time, and embellish it with open roads and heroes who were pioneers and knights of the green forest making merry in a world that had no time-clocks. In some such world is cast much of our folklore and most of our early fiction. We may be forgiven if we look back to it occasionally from this other world in which we live: a very modern American world of mass production, uptown locals, carbon copies, 5:16's, yours received and contents noted, references, cross-references, and headlines.

Do not smile if the Foresters of America, a quarter of a million strong, meet once a week to reaffirm their faith, and in the secrecy of an oath-bound lodge enact a ritual "which touches upon the adventures of Robin Hood and brings in Biblical events relative to the Garden of Eden." A wind whistles through Sherwood Forest, which has been baked dry in steam-heated offices with dictaphones and restless fly-screens.

Do not smile if once a month the Red Men gather at the stake and (Ritual, p. 30) the Junior Sagamore cries, "Warriors prepare for the execution! Make ready and pile high the fagots!" Man does not live by bread alone, nor by oil-burning furnaces, superheterodynes, and electrical pianos.

Regularly once a week, from one end of a broad country to the other, the Knights of Pythias meet to re-enact the fable of Damon and his faithful friend, the Yeomen to play Ivanhoe, the Odd Fellows to offer some new Isaac in expiation for his brothers' sins. Tell draws his bow once more; Caesar spurns his crown; in a new world Lancelot and Miles Standish, Charlemagne and Barbara Frietchie, Hector and Pocahontas live again.

Lodge night in a thousand towns and cities: Center Hall a blaze of lights, its chandeliers festooned with paper bunting. Guards at the gates – a blowsy veil at the mystic shrine – crossed flags above the booming organ – row on row of folding chairs, wax-yellow, cushionless, but upholstered with rich memories.

From the street outside you climb a flight of well-worn stairs to the second landing. There is a door of varnished oak, behind which stands the Lord High Seneschal. It is just an average door; but beyond lies mystery, drama, opportunity to share great names and take a hand in deeds well done, the satisfaction of "belonging."

You knock three times, pause for a heart beat, knock three times again. . . . Panel slides back enough to disclose a lawn tie and two waistcoat buttons. . . Advance, stranger, and give the countersign!"

A whispered word. . . . The door swings slowly on its hinges.

It will continue to swing as long as life is drab enough for grown men to play Indian.

Milton Lehman's elegiac portrait of fraternalism in the years immediately following the Second World War originally appeared in the official magazine of the US Chamber of Commerce. Lehman depicts many of the older organizations which were driven by secret rituals and insurance benefits as moribund, while working-class clubs providing clubrooms to serve as male sanctuaries reach ascendancy. The feeling of American exceptionalism that characterized the Cold War years is expressed in a quotation from Earl Warren, who had previously been the Grand Master of Masons for the State of California and later served as the Chief Justice of the United States Supreme Court.

IT TAKES THREE TO MAKE A LODGE
Milton Lehman
1949
Nation's Business (37)(September 1949), 40-42, 58-61.

W. N. SWINDELL, one of the last of the vanishing Red Men, sometimes thinks back to a night at the turn of the century. He was standing in front of a drugstore in Anacostia, D.C., with some of the boys. They were watching pretty girls go past, when Swindell heard someone hollering for help in a building across the street.

"What's that hollering?" he demanded.

"Why that's the Improved Order of Red Men," said one of the boys," "They're holding a secret initiation."

Young Swindell, now 72, went to investigate and was invited in. "They made me a brother," he says today. "They gave me feathers to wear and told me the secrets. I held every station in the Mineola tribe from Guard of the Wigwam to Keeper of the Wampum, but I never did find out what the hollering was about."

Still, there was considerable hollering in those days. Preachers stormed that the secret orders were leading men away from church and family in the arms of perdition. Politicians debated the merits of secret fraternities and Charles Francis Adams, the somber first citizen of Boston, declaimed, "A more perfect agent for devising and executing conspiracies against church and state could hardly have been conceived."

There were dozens of secret orders then, active in every city and township in the country. The man of distinction wore his lodge pin proudly. He kept his bright uniforms in better repair than his business suits and preserved his ceremonial plumage in a hatbox filled with black pepper, believed a sure proof against predatory insects. He could detect a brother on his travels through the whispered password and the secret grip, accomplished by much twisting of thumbs, forefingers and knuckles. "Give me the grip, brother!" was a national challenge to the confines of the lodge.

The lodge itself was sacred, part of an old tradition that man deserved a place away from the house. The tradition went back at least to the head-hunters of Borneo, who set aside one shack in their village for men only. The latter-day lodge was also a stronghold for the embattled male. Into the lodge the members came on meeting night. In plumed hat or feathers, a man would rule for an evening as Sovereign Commander or Sir Knight, Grand Potentate or Great Incohonee. But now the old order has changed. Slowly at first, then with the relentlessness of a moving iceberg, the lodge has turned and twisted in its course. The shadow cast by the ladies' auxiliary has darkened: some ladies have even managed to enter the sanctum of the meeting hall! The pride in secrecy has subsided; many of the top-secret brotherhoods are fading, replaced by more outgoing societies like the Eagles, Elks and Moose, by service clubs like Rotary, Lions and Kiwanis, and by veterans organizations of two world wars. Of the old orders, only a few, like the Masons, are attracting younger Americans and really thriving. Others are breathing heavily, while their aging brethren look wistfully back to the days when they were young and powerful. "Something," as Swindell puts it, "has gone out of America."

Recently, I visited Alexandria, Va., and Chambersburg, Pa., both active lodge towns, to see what was missing. The Red Men, I found, were gone from both places and so were the Royal Arcanum, the Knights of the Golden Eagle and the Knights of Friendship. In Chambersburg, the Junior Order of the United American Mechanics still turns out for the Community Softball League, but there are few junior members. In Alexandria, a lonely veteran of the Knights of the Maccabees, explained:

"In the old days, folks entertained themselves. The women turned out for the sewing circle and the men went all out for the lodge. But now, folks want to be entertained. First came the automobiles, then movies and now television. It's the same all over the country. Unless you turn the lodge into a card room and beer parlor, you won't draw the brothers."

In both towns I visited, the Elks, Eagles, and Moose are doing well, stressing the virtues of public charity and a private clubroom, rather than secret rites. While the new-style orders, like the old, attract members through health benefits, there is less concern for fraternal security. One reason, perhaps, is that the newer orders have fought for security as a national program. When Franklin D. Roosevelt signed the Social Security Act of 1935, he gave the pen he used and the flag that flew over the Capitol that day to the Fraternal Order of Eagles. The Eagles, he said, had pointed the way.

Most of the old-time joiners grow nostalgic as they consider the fading fraternalism. But a few are bitter about the failure of several defunct societies to pay off promised benefits. After hard times and dwindling memberships, some of the orders expired before their members.

In the heyday of secret orders, many citizens, like Swindell, joined out of pure curiosity. "I just wanted to find out the secrets," he observed. "And I wouldn't tell you what they are even now. But everybody knows the origin of the Red Men and it won't hurt to tell that. It began with the Boston Tea Party, when the Sons of Tammany disguised themselves as Indians and threw the tea into the Boston Harbor. They were standing up for their rights – that's what the Red Men believe in."

Using Indian symbols, the Red Men called their lodge a wigwam and their leader the Great Incohonee. When the wives finally pressured the men for a ladies' auxiliary, they named it the Order of Pocahontas. A few years ago, national headquarters launched a campaign for new members, awarding an engraved tomahawk to the most successful recruiters.

The love of ritual itself was an attraction to young Americans, although it startled many a visitor from the older, blasé countries of Europe. It was a visiting Frenchman who first observed: "*Mon Dieu, it takes only three Americans to make a lodge!*" But many Americans, from the President down to the humblest citizen, saw secret orders as a necessity of life. "It's an inborn instinct to belong to a secret society," the Masons used to say.

Whether instinctive or not, the secret societies are less active than they used to be. Harry W. Mong, job printer of Chambersburg, still looks back fondly to the days when he went on initiating junkets to Harrisburg and Pittsburgh for the Knights of Pythias. "Everybody wanted us to officiate," he said, "because we had a crack degree team – the best in Pennsylvania."

In those days, a man would join a lodge to get out of the house at night, as well as to share fraternal spirit. One aging joiner, out of earshot of his little woman, confessed: "Oh, it was a busy life. On Monday nights, the Knights of Friendship met. On Tuesday, there was the Patriotic Order of the Sons of America. On Wednesday, the wife didn't mind because I had to go to choir rehearsal at the church, and she could come along. On Thursday, the Junior Order of United American Mechanics got together and on Friday, somebody always called a committee meeting."

Today, the joiners are much less occupied. Even the Independent Order of Odd Fellows, with 2,000,000, has trouble getting a quorum at meetings. Although the IOOF is still active in Chambersburg and Alexandria, fraternal energy has lapsed. In Alexandria, Elmer Mudd, postmaster, and Cliff Cunningham, undertaker, still say "you can spend a lifetime in Odd Fellowship." And at Christmas, Wilmer Scott, rotund proprietor of the Palace Cleaners, officiates as Santa Claus at a party for the children. But Alexandria sees less of the Odd Fellows than it once did.

"We started out with plain folks," said the fraternal undertaker, "and we kept our dues and initiation fee down so they could afford to come in. I used to march in parades all over the country, but I'm too old now. Besides, there aren't so many parades."

Sixty-one-year-old George Showalter, garage mechanic, has been an Odd Fellow in Chambersburg for more than 30 years. He was rushed to membership by a rural postman and a friendly tombstone cutter named John Bennett. "Old John told me that in the Odd Fellows, everything was fair and square," he said, "and that's the reason I joined. It didn't matter whether you were rich or poor, important or just trying to make a living."

The Odd Fellows initiation is less colorful now than it used to be, Showalter believes. "In the old days," he recalled, "we had a lot fancier uniform and we didn't mind people noticing us. But now even the ritual is more make-believe, especially here in the East."

Two of the secret orders are now holding members primarily through insurance policies, with a bond somewhat more fraternal than Prudential or Metropolitan Life. The Knights of the Maccabees were founded in 1878 in London, Ontario, honoring the Biblical exploits of Judas Maccabaeus. Establishing "tents" for the men, "hives" for the women and "courts" for the children, the Maccabees admitted brethren regardless of age, sex, or physical fitness. For a while, the order was in danger of collapse until some hardheaded business men from Michigan put it on a sound insurance basis.

The Modern Woodmen of America is also a fraternal insurance order. Its "distinguishing feature," according to Past Sovereign Banker Morris Sheppard, is to "combine the abstract principle of fraternity with the mathematical principle of insurance." Of these two, insurance has prevailed. While the order recently distributed American flags to civic organizations and wrist compasses to scoutmasters of the Boy Scouts, headquarters is more concerned about insurance payments. Last year, they paid out $10,411,198.78 in benefits to members.

The Knights of Columbus also provides its members with insurance policies, but has held them primarily through church and welfare activities. Founded in 1882, by Father Michael J. McGivney in New Haven, Conn., the K of C is an organization of 700,000 Catholic brethren. Nationally, the Knights have supported parochial schools, Americanism and worked in relief of the major disasters in America.

In Chambersburg, Past Grand Knight Edward Geary, clerk at the Montgomery House, told me how the local council helped Italian prisoners assigned to the nearby Letterkenny Ordnance Depot after Italy's wartime surrender. "We held block parties to get them acquainted with folks in town," said Geary, "and we built them a chapel at the Depot." The council also sponsors a local Boy Scout troop and at Christmas supplies the children in parochial schools with oranges and candy. "People," said Geary, "have respect for a man who belongs to an organization."

Among the secret orders, the Freemasons are unique. They have withstood the rivalry of insurance societies and the competition of free-wheeling clubhouse fraternities. At one time the most violently attacked, they have held on to their secrets and steadily increased their memberships. Today there are more than 4,000,000 Masons in America and 1,000,000 more throughout the world.

In Alexandria, site of the Mason's National Memorial, there are three lodges, all booming. Gray-haired C. Philip Heishley, custodian of the Memorial, observes: "We are so busy initiating Masons we can hardly keep up with it. We have to meet several times a month to get them all in." In Chambersburg, the George Washington Lodge No. 143 has doubled its membership since the war. But most of the Masons I spoke with told me they haven't attended any meetings in months. "I joined because the most successful men in town are Masons, and it's really an honor to be accepted," said a Chambersburg realtor.

Masonry in America dates back to Colonial days, when frontiersmen met in the woods to conduct their rites. One of the oldest secret fraternities, Freemasonry began in London, England, in 1717 and soon spread around the world. But its roots grew fastest in America.

Troubled feelings between Masons and the clergy started in the 1820's after the so-called "Morgan Incident," when a Methodist preacher declared "The three most wicked places in the community are right around us – Sam Brandt's tavern across the street, a den of iniquity on the opposite corner, and the Masonic Temple next door."

The "Morgan Incident" began in Batavia, N.Y., when Capt. William Morgan, veteran of the War of 1812, threatened to expose the secrets of Masonry in print. Suddenly arrested for petty larceny, Morgan was a few days later removed from jail by men in closed carriages. All trace of him was lost. After several years, the decomposed body of a man was found on the shores of Lake Ontario. The body was claimed by both Captain Morgan's wife, and by the family of a Canadian fisherman who had drowned at sea.

Thereupon, Masonry and all secret orders were loudly attacked by the press, politicians and preachers. Many orders disbanded. In Rhode Island and Vermont, laws were passed prohibiting the administration of secret oaths.

Sobered by these attacks, the secret orders eventually recovered, but their pride in secrecy had suffered. The newer orders that developed – among them Elks, Moose and Eagles – believed more in good works and clambakes. Earl Warren, recent Republican candidate for vice president, was addressing the Eagles when he declared: "These great fraternities that we have in this country are distinctly an American institution. They have done a great deal to form our national character. We do care for the poor and the helpless and all those who are struggling for their rightful place in the sun as individuals. We do this not as cold charity, but as a matter of social responsibility."

The Fraternal Order of Eagles was founded in 1898 by a Seattle lumberman named Jon Considine. Calling themselves the "Great Order of the Common Man," some Eagles still protest the restriction to "men of the white race." Although the initiations are private, there's not much concern over secrecy. The ritual is brief and there are few secret words. On national and local levels, the Eagles have campaigned successfully for old-age pension laws, the GI Bill of Rights, the Social Security Act and Mother's Day. In addition to benefits and mutual aid, the Eagles sponsor youth guidance programs and boys' clubs in many cities.

The Eagles arrived in Alexandria in 1902, and today there are 2,400 members in the town. Alexandria is a big freight center and many of the Eagles work on the railroad, coming to the red-brick clubhouse in off-duty hours. The rathskellar, a large basement room with aging chandeliers and a chipped mirror, has card tables and a bar that serves beer and sandwiches.

"The telephone's ringing all the time," said Ed Young, secretary of the Aerie, who stays on duty day and night to collect dues and answer the phone. In 16 years with the Eagles, Young has become apprehensive about women, a state of mind the old-time lodgeman would have found incomprehensible. "Around dinner time," he said, "the wives start calling. I make the men take the calls, even if I have to go downstairs to fetch them. Sometimes an Eagle will say, 'Tell her I'm not here,' but I won't do it. And when a man tells his wife he's going to the Eagles and he's not here when she calls, I say so. I don't want to get in dutch with the ladies."

While the Eagles report almost 1,500,000 members, the Benevolent and Protective Order of Elks is nearing the 1,000,000 mark. Older than the Eagles, the BPOE was founded in 1868 in New York on "four cardinal virtues – Charity, Justice, Brotherly Love and Fidelity." In 70 years, the Elks have established a $1,000,000 home for aged members and spent up to $3,000,000 a year in charitable and welfare work. Their total assets are more than $100,000,000.

The Elks' Lodge in Alexandria, according to Dr. Robert S. Barrett, Past Grand Exalted Ruler, has increased since the war. There are now 750 members. Somewhat plushier than the Eagles', the Elks'

Lodge is complete with rathskellar, television set, ballroom and open-air beer garden.

An Elk for 48 years, Dr. Barrett joined "because this was a group of men who had a good time. If you're an Elk, you're welcome wherever there's a lodge." Dr. Barrett figures that he's visited 300 Elk lodges throughout the country. Along the way, he helped establish Elk hospitals for crippled children.

In Chambersburg as well as Alexandria, the Elks have been active in charity. In G. M. Berger's tailor shop, Chambersburg's Past Exalted Ruler talked of good works. Last year, he told me, the Elks gave $3,600 to the local Boy Scouts and Girl Scouts and $2,500 in food baskets to the poor at Christmas. They gave bed clothes, food and lodging to two families whose houses burned down; they comforted the families of departed brethren and conducted graveside services.

With little concern for secrecy, the Elks believe in simple rituals. Their fraternal anthem is "Auld Lang Syne" and their symbol, the Elk, was chosen because "it is distinctly American. It lives in herds. It is quick and keen of perception and while it is usually gentle and even timorous, it is strong and valiant in defense of its own." The Elks' comforting prospectus to the new recruit would seem pallid to the old-style joiner. "The initiation is wholly devoid of any feature which will embarrass or annoy the candidate or subject him to ridicule or to any discomfort."

The Loyal Order of Moose considers its symbol even more American than the Elk. "The Moose," they say, "is a challenger. It wages war on the enemies of the herd, battling stubbornly to protect its own. It takes only what it needs and doesn't rob its fellows. It loves freedom and ascending with mighty strides it seeks the heights. Leaving the low hills to the earth dwellers below it takes its place among the clouds."

With its head in the clouds, the Moose is firmly planted on solid ground. With an organization of 750,000 and gross assets of $70,000,000, the Moose has distributed $51,000,000 in sick and death benefits to its members since its founding. Moosehaven, its home for the aged at Orange Park, Fla., is a thriving community where elderly Moose may spend the winter of their lives. And Mooseheart, its proudest accomplishment, is a $32,000,000 model community for children of deceased members.

Mooseheart also generates new lodges for the Loyal Order. Last year, Thomas J. Bowen, salesman for Proctor and Gamble in Chambersburg, wrote a letter to Moose headquarters. He had grown up in Mooseheart, he said, and he couldn't see why there wasn't a lodge in his new home town.

The Chambersburg Moose Lodge is now nine months old, but in that time it has initiated 582 members. While the Elks' initiation fee is $75, you can join the Moose for only $10. "We're an average workingman's fraternity," said Paul Martin, insurance agent and secretary of the new lodge. "Some day we'll have a big clubhouse, but already Chambersburg knows we're around." Today the clubhouse is the converted White Rose Diner with the vital moosehead mounted on one wall. A handsome large-nostrilled specimen, the moosehead was borrowed from the lodge at Hanover, Pa. "Hanover had a couple of spares," Martin declared.

On Mother's Day, the lodge held open house for the ladies and showed motion pictures of Mooseheart. Last Christmas, it held a free movie party in the Rosedale Theater for the children and at Easter it bought 180 dozen eggs, colored them and hid them in the shrubs of Municipal Park. The kids who found the most eggs won live rabbits.

For the mourners of the secret society, however, this vigor of the new order seems unimpressive. "They don't have the old-time spirit and they don't keep secrets," one elderly joiner complained. "Why, I can remember that when every building went up, we were called on to dedicate it. When there was a holiday, we'd be fighting to get on the platform. When there was a burying, every lodge turned out, arguing to see who would lead the funeral."

Perhaps, as the aging gentleman observed, the spirit is missing. Possibly the heyday of the secret order is past, although you can start a hot argument on that score with many a Mason. But meanwhile, the Elks and the Moose are stomping through the woods, seeking the heights, and the Eagles are screaming overhead.

In this wide-ranging essay, Schlesinger discusses the role of voluntary associations in American life from the seventeenth to the twentieth centuries. In so-doing he places fraternal, oath-bound organizations into the greater context of religious, professional, and political groups. Written during a period of history in which Americans were preoccupied with the role of totalitarian governments, this essay posits that America's voluntary societies are manifestations of the limited role of government within the national life. Schlesinger, a historian of social and cultural movements, argues that associative bodies serve as "irregular or unofficial governments" which meet the needs of America's citizens.

BIOGRAPHY OF A NATION OF JOINERS
Arthur M. Schlesinger
1944
American Historical Review, 50 (October 1944) 1-25.[1]

AT first thought it seems paradoxical that a country famed for being individualistic should provide the world's greatest example of joiners. How this came about is the object of this sketch, but the illusion of paradox may be dispelled at once. To Americans individualism has meant, not the individual's independence of other individuals, but his and their freedom from governmental restraint. Traditionally, the people have tended to minimize collective organization as represented by the state while exercising the largest possible liberty in forming their own voluntary organizations. This conception of a political authority too weak to interfere with men's ordinary pursuits actually created the necessity for self-constituted associations to do things beyond the capacity of a single person, and by reverse effect the success of such endeavors proved a continuing argument against the growth of stronger government. The tendency was reinforced by the absence of fixed social classes. As Alexis de Tocqueville pointed out in the 1830's, men in aristocratic countries do not have the same reason "to combine in order to act," for "Every wealthy and powerful citizen constitutes the head of a permanent and compulsory association, composed of all those who are dependent upon him, or whom he makes subservient to the execution of his designs." The "independent and feeble" citizens of a democratic nation, lacking these advantages, must "learn voluntarily to help one another."[2]

The trend toward collective action began slowly in American history, but it gathered impetus as the years passed, new opportunities beckoned, and people perceived the benefits to be gained. Each fresh application of the associative principle opened the way for further ventures and at the same time helped to provide the needed experience. In the end, no department of human existence remained unaffected. Because the subject in its entirety is too vast for more than a bird's-eye view here, this discussion centers upon voluntary bodies of sizable membership, reasonably long duration, and fairly large territorial extent, and it proceeds by means of sampling rather than complete coverage. Even as so limited, the theme is inconveniently large, for it includes incorporated as well as unincorporated groups, secret societies as well as open ones, organizations for religious, economic, and political purposes as well as those seeking humanitarian, cultural, and recreational ends. By a canon of humor the term "joiner" is generally restricted to a member of fraternal orders, but the fact is that this particular proclivity, far from being a unique development, was merely a somewhat belated manifestation of a spirit which had come to penetrate nearly every aspect of American life.

I

During the first century or more of the colonial period the people displayed little aptitude for large co-operative undertakings. They had had scant experience in doing things collectively in Europe. Moreover, the population was small, towns were few, and communication was difficult. Nevertheless, in one important phase of life, that of religion, the principle of association struck quick an effective root. In a majority of the colonies the settlers found they had not escaped the restrictions of an established church by removing to America, for in New England the dominant Puritans devised their own counterpart of the Old World system and in the Southern provinces the Anglicans transplanted the system existing at home. This union of church and state went hard with nonconformists, for these early Americans took their religion more seriously than has any later generation. Fortunately, the field was open equally to all beliefs in the intermediate region -- Pennsylvania, Delaware, New Jersey, Rhode Island, and most of New York -- and there the various groups operated on a basis of free association and self-support. Even in the colonies with official churches, the dissenters insisted upon setting up their own places of worship alongside those that were public-supported, though this subjected them to a species of double taxation. The plan of voluntarism (or voluntaryism) as it was worked out in the different provinces amazed most onlookers from Europe, who could not understand why anyone should pay for the maintenance of religion when he was not obliged to. The colonists in organizing their own devotional societies instituted a system which would eventually prevail in all American denominations.

In other than spiritual concerns, however, men preferred to go their individual ways. It was not until toward the middle of the eighteenth century, when towns had grown larger and more numerous, that people ventured somewhat timidly to extend the principle of voluntary group action to other interests. Associations for local civic purposes, though not unknown earlier, now assumed far greater prominence, as the career of Philadelphia's leading citizen bears witness. Benjamin Franklin, who in so many other ways fore-shadowed the modern American, qualifies further as an organizer and joiner. Besides forming the Junto, a secret club of artisans and tradesmen, he started a subscription library, an academy for the education of youth, and a volunteer company of fire fighters, and he also took part in founding a hospital and a fire insurance company. In addition to these community organizations, he founded the American Philosophical Society, our oldest learned body, served for a time as provincial grand master of the Masons, and helped to promote a Western land company.

For various reasons the larger-scale undertakings proved far less successful than the local ones. Distances between the principal towns were still great and communications slow; most persons viewed oath-bound lodges with distrust, if not alarm; and the British government was dubious as to the wisdom of encouraging Western colonization schemes. The American Philosophical Society, which aspired to an inter-provincial membership, languished for some years after its formation in 1743; and the Masonic order, introduced into the leading cities from England in the 1730's, excited public antagonism as being aristocratic in tendency and subversive of good morals. On one occasion the New York members were "complimented with Snow Balls and Dirt" while marching through the streets.[3] In Philadelphia popular anger over an apprentice's death in a bogus initiation caused Masonic activities to cease from 1738 to 1749.[4] The land company in which Franklin was active encountered inter-colonial jealousies as well as ministerial objections and delays. Nevertheless this Vandalia project, as a profit-making scheme, bespoke a more natural interest of the times, as is shown by the fact that Franklin's group was only one of many that were formed. Such undertakings had become possible as surplus capital increased in the colonial towns. Since the best coastal lands were now largely in private hands, men with money to invest looked to the untenanted tracts beyond the mountains, and a rising speculative fever caused them to league together in order to obtain governmental concessions. Beginning about the middle of the eighteenth century, various groups of provincials, some with English associates, organized such enterprises as the Ohio Company, the Mississippi Company, the Illinois Company, the Wabash Land Company, and the Transylvania Company.[5] Though none of these actually succeeded, the widespread interest they represented foreshadowed the future extension of the associative device to a wide diversity of capitalistic purposes.

Considerably more effective were the colonists' strivings for united political action. For this the home government was unwittingly responsible, for until the British authorities in the 1760's and 1770's adopted a policy of closer imperial control, political parties had been unknown on a continental scale and tended to be temporary even in the separate provinces. Now, alarmed by common fears of parliamentary taxation and threats to their trade, the people not only formed local groups of protest but also acted in concert with similar bodies in other colonies. These interprovincial alliances constituted the first national parties in American history.

The Stamp Act emergency of 1764-66 produced a multifarious network of such agencies up and down the seaboard: merchants' committees, active in stirring legislatures to opposition; secret mechanics' organizations, which under the name of Sons of Liberty sometimes resorted to terroristic methods and other bands of citizens who joined together to boycott British manufactures. The Stamp Act Congress brought many of the leaders together for the first time face to face. As crisis piled upon crisis, these organs were supplemented by still others, notably the so-called committees of correspondence which in New England were appointed by town meetings but elsewhere emanated usually from unofficial gatherings. When parliament embarked upon drastic coercive proceedings after the Boston Tea Party, the patriots formed provincial congresses and conventions, and proceeded to assemble the First Continental Congress, which, though not avowedly or constitutionally a government, functioned like one, extending and reinvigorating the committee system and adopting measures of economic opposition which all persons must obey on pain of being publicly blacklisted. Through the associative process the insurgent elements thus reared a structure which, as a Tory feelingly remarked, "takes the Government out of the hands of the Governour, Council, and General Assembly; and the execution of the laws out of the hands of the Civil Magistrates and Juries."[6] Organized now from center to circumference, the patriot party presently unsheathed the sword against the British and eventually declared America's independence. Under conditions of extreme provocation the people thus demonstrated their capacity for common action for political ends.

II

In this hesitant and halting way the colonial era saw the emergence of what was to become a dominant American trait. Prompted originally by a passion for liberty of worship, and for a long time going no further, the associative impulse began to invade more mundane undertakings as the break with England approached. Though it achieved decisive results only in the realm of public affairs, the foundations were laid for future progress in other respects as well. National independence hastened these tendencies. The philosophy of natural rights underlying the Revolution exalted the individual's capacity to act for himself; the military struggle taught men from different sections valuable lessons in practical co-operation; the mounting sense of national consciousness suggested new vistas of achievement; and Britain was powerless to interpose a restraining hand. A little later, after a decade of political instability, the adoption of the Constitution stimulated still further applications of the collective principle.

In the domain of spiritual concerns the complete divorce of church and state was now effected, first in the South and later in New England. Voluntarism thus became the practice of all devotional associations. Jefferson's famous Virginia statute of religious liberty affirmed that "the rights hereby asserted are of the natural rights of mankind."[7] Such denominations as had maintained Old World connections proceeded to sever them in order to reorganize upon a separate American basis. Moreover, many of the states enacted general laws specifically granting church groups equal opportunities of incorporation— a foretaste of the system that the next generation would apply to business groups.[8] A further innovation was the formation of benevolent societies, religious in inspiration but nonsectarian in personnel and direction. Profiting by British example, these creations, usually the out-growth of local bodies, labored to awaken an interest in Christianity beyond church circles and even beyond the United States.[9] The principal agencies were the American Board of Commissioners for Foreign Missions (1810), the American Bible Society (1816), the American Sunday School Union (1824), the American Tract Society (1825), and the American Home Missionary Society (1826). While each of these organizations discharged a particular function, all stood for a Biblical rather than a doctrinal approach to religion, and they preserved their independence of denominational interference by maintaining financial self-sufficiency. This concern of the devout for the spiritually neglected was a halfway house to the humanitarian reform societies of the Jacksonian period.

Meanwhile, in the economic sphere, the associative spirit flowered in a profusion of local capitalistic enterprises, notably for building toll roads and establishing banks. The first agricultural improvement societies also made their appearance, some of them statewide in extent. Distances continued to emphasize restricted projects; yet, as in the case of religious benevolence, larger ones were also undertaken. With British oversight removed, aggressive men, sometimes employing unscrupulous methods, joined forces to secure from Congress or the state legislatures extensive land grants in the Mississippi Valley. Such men as Manasseh Cutler of Massachusetts, Rufus Putnam of Connecticut, Robert Morris of Pennsylvania, and Patrick Henry of Virginia participated in some of the earlier schemes. On its own motion the Federal government, utilizing powers derived from the newly ratified Constitution, incorporated a bank of the United States under private control, with branches in the leading seaboard cities; and in 1816, five years after the charter expired, Congress set up a Second United States Bank for a twenty-year period with a much larger capitalization. As yet, however, economic undertakings of interstate or national scope were the exception rather than the rule.

The adoption of the Constitution unintentionally provided also a firmer basis for voluntary political associations. The Founding Fathers had thought of parties as transitory combinations of legislators, coalescing and dissolving as new measures were considered, but the device of checks and balances would have rendered such a system difficult, if not unworkable. The requirement of electing the President, Senate, and House in three different ways entailed the danger that these organs of government would each go its separate way unless some voluntary agency unknown to the Constitution geared them together. To supply this unifying element the Federalist and Republican parties quickly took shape, the one looking to Hamilton and the other to Jefferson for inspiration. Thus were instituted those permanent groupings of voters which, as the suffrage was broadened, later generations would mold into even more powerful instruments of political action.

The various extensions of collective enterprise during this first half-century of national independence did not go unchallenged by persons and groups who feared the effects upon either their own or the public welfare. Certain of the churches resented the encroaching activities of the benevolent societies "subject to no ecclesiastical responsibility, and adopting no formula of faith by which their religious tenets may be ascertained."[10] These adjunct bodies were also charged with drying up sources of funds which might otherwise have replenished denominational coffers. The growing rift in the Presbyterian fold over the question of voluntary associations led directly to the great schism of 1837 between the Old School and New School contingents.

Capitalistic associations aroused hostility because of the special legal advantages they enjoyed at the expense of possible competitors. Few colonial economic enterprises had been incorporated, not even the land companies. But now, enticed by new and more exciting prospects of profit, commercial groups turned increasingly to the legislatures for charters conferring such privileges as rights of way, limited liability for debts, and permanence of organization. To many persons the government's action in bestowing exclusive favors seemed to ally it with the "large monied interests" and to violate the "natural and legal rights of mankind."[11]   They saw no more reason for a union of business and state than of church and state. A Philadelphia pamphleteer in 1792, maintaining that wealth already wielded undue influence, continued: "Laws, it is said, cannot equalize men, —no— but ought they, for that reason, to aggravate the inequality which they cannot cure? ... It is not the distinction of titles which constitutes an aristocracy; it is the principle of partial association."[12]   Though some critics objected to any incorporation at all, most wished to replace the practice of granting particular charters with a system of general incorporation open to all able to meet the specified conditions. In the national arena the dispute over corporate privileges centered in the struggle over chartering the First United States Bank. Behind the constitutional controversy lay deep-seated democratic objections to the establishment of a financial monopoly. The Supreme Court in the Dartmouth College case (1819), while not passing upon the issue of equality of privilege, gave great impetus to the associative trend for a time by promulgating the doctrine of the freedom of charters from later alteration by sole action of the lawmaking authority.

Political associations also encountered opposition, with President Washington particularly vocal on the subject. The Democratic Societies, which sprang up in most of the states during his second administration to agitate for popular rights and carry on pro-French propaganda, kindled his fears for the maintenance of orderly government. In denouncing to Congress the "self-created societies" that had instigated the Whiskey Insurrection in western Pennsylvania his words were intended to apply equally to the Democratic clubs.[13] Returning to the theme in his Farewell Address, he specifically condemned "all combinations and associations, under whatever plausible character, with the real design to direct, control, counteract, or awe the regular deliberation and action of the constituted authorities." Lest he be understood as not including political parties, he added, "In governments of a monarchical cast patriotism may look with indulgence, if not with favor, upon the spirit of party. But in those of the popular character, in governments purely elective, it is a spirit not to be encouraged."[14]

Local social and literary clubs, on the other hand, excited little criticism, and even the Masonic fraternity seemed to have lived down its earlier unpopularity, though portents of future trouble appeared in the increasing strictures on its unorthodox religious ideals by church groups.[15] By contrast, a new national secret order, the Society of the Cincinnati, raised a whirlwind of wrath which the country did not soon forget. Formed in 1783 by Revolutionary officers on the basis of hereditary membership, the organization struck many as a potential military threat to the people's freedom as well as the scheme of an exclusive class to perpetuate a species of un-American nobility. The press volleyed against it, Rhode Island considered disfranchising persons who joined it, and the Massachusetts legislature proclaimed it "dangerous to the peace, liberty, and safety of the Union."[16] Such fears were doubtless hysterical, but the Cincinnati suffered a blight from which it did not recover until after the Civil War. Nor were the veterans of any of the intervening wars able to establish effective societies.

III

Notwithstanding the occasional dikes of resistance the associative current steadily gathered momentum during the first half century of national independence. In the next generation it seemed to many to reach flood proportions.

"In truth," wrote William Ellery Channing as early as 1829,

> one of the most remarkable circumstances or features of our age is the energy with which the principle of combination, or of action by joint forces, by associated numbers, is manifesting itself. . . . Those who have one great object find one another out through a vast extent of country, join their forces, settle their mode of operation, and act together with the uniformity of a disciplined army."[17]

Without a knowledge of these organizations, he said, one would fail to perceive the "most powerful springs" of social action. Alexis de Tocqueville, the Frenchman who visited the United States in 1831-32, quickly sensed their importance. "The power of association," he noted in his diary, "has reached its uttermost development in America," and as the luminous discussion in his published work shows, he marveled at "the extreme skill with which the inhabitants ... succeed in proposing a common object to the exertions of a great many men, and in getting them voluntarily to pursue it."[18] To posterity, of course, the accomplishments appear less impressive than to people at the time, who compared the situation with earlier America or with what they knew of Europe.

What caused this passion for joining? Channing attributed it to the "immense facility given to intercourse by modern improvements, by increased commerce and traveling, by the post-office, by the steam-boat, and especially by the press, - by newspapers, periodicals, tracts, and other publications." And to these agencies, of course, were presently added the canal, the railroad, and the telegraph. Though physical distances grew constantly longer, new means of communication made them shorter. As Channing remarked, "The grand manoeuvre to which Napoleon owed his victories - we mean the concentration of great numbers on a single point - is now placed within the reach of all parties and sects."[19] But the will to make use of these instrumentalities needs also to be accounted for, and here the explanation lies in certain other changes in American life. The rising importance of the plain people, symbolized in politics by Jackson's election as President, dramatized social and economic injustices hitherto unrecognized, and inspired the humane, and sometimes the victims themselves, to unite for correcting them. European example, especially that of England, also played a part, for in the Old World, too, a new tenderness was being shown for the underprivileged. Moreover, as cities increased both in number and size, voluntary effort could be more easily mobilized. People of kindred interests could be quickly assembled, agitation organized, mass meetings held, committees put to work. And besides being centers of surplus enthusiasm, cities were centers of surplus capital, supplying the principal financial sinews for joint under-takings whether to reinforce or modify the existing order.

Nowhere were the results more striking than in the field of humanitarian reform. The earlier concern for bruised and neglected souls now widened to take in bruised and neglected minds and bodies. Christian altruism combined with democratic idealism to produce what seemed to the ill-disposed an interferiority complex. Typical of the new creations were the American Temperance Society (1826), the American Peace Society (1828), the General Union for Promoting the Christian Observance of the Sabbath (1828), the American Lyceum Association (1830), the American Anti-Slavery Society (1833) and the American and Foreign Sabbath Union (1842). If to these national bodies be added countless smaller ones devoted to such aims as improving penal methods, advancing the cause of public education, and redeeming "Females who have Deviated from the Paths of Virtue," one can understand Orestes A. Brownson's sour comment: "Matters have come to such a pass, that a peaceable man can hardly venture to eat or drink, or to go to bed or to get up, to correct his children or to kiss his wife, without obtaining the permission and direction of some moral . . . society."[20]

Since every reform association bespoke a minority opinion, it had to devise means to persuade or frighten the majority into adopting the desired course of action. For this purpose the crusading groups borrowed and improved upon the methods already developed by the nonsectarian benevolent societies. The procedure quickly became standardized. As described by a contemporary, the first step was to choose an "imposing" designation for the organization; next "a list of respectable names must be obtained, as members and patrons"; then "a secretary and an adequate corps of assistants must be appointed and provided for from the first fruits of collections; a band of popular lecturers must be commissioned, and sent forth as agents on the wide public; the press with its many-winged messengers, is put in operation"; finally, "subsidiary societies are multiplied over the length and breadth of the land."[21] In structure the reform movements resembled the Federal political system, with local units loosely linked together in state branches and these in turn sending representatives to a national body. By 1835 the 1,200,000 members of the American Temperance Society were distributed in 8,000 local affiliates with an over-all organization in every state but one.[22] Two years later the American Anti-Slavery Society, whose constituency was in fact strictly Northern, had grown to more than a thousand local groups and seven state associations. In addition, both of these bodies (and the American Peace Society as well) maintained youth auxiliaries and separate branches for women.

To carry on their work effectively the humanitarian societies required funds as well as moral zeal. For example, the American Anti-Slavery Society between 1836 and 1840 reported an annual revenue of from $26,000 to $50,000, not counting the receipts of affiliates. As in the case of kindred organizations, this financial support came partly from membership dues and from collections at public gatherings, partly from large and small gifts and bequests, and partly from the sale of publications. Publication activities, however, were designed less to raise money than to supplement oral propaganda. Every reform group fathered weekly or monthly periodicals, distributed reports of its annual conventions, and issued great quantities of leaflets and pamphlets, including fiction, songbooks, almanacs, and cartoons or "pictorial representations." In the single year 1840-41 the American Temperance Union circulated 433,000 pieces of printed matter and in the three preceding years the American Anti-Slavery Society sent out 796,000. Another practice was to pelt the government with memorials. The abolitionists' persistence in petitioning the House of Representatives led that body to adopt a "gag rule" whose repeal ex-President John Quincy Adams finally accomplished in 1844 after a historic eight-year battle.

With varying effect the reformers also enlisted the support of church, school, and stage. At one juncture more than a thousand ministers agreed to preach annual peace sermons; efforts were made to insert favorable matter in textbooks; and such plays as *Uncle Tom's Cabin* and *Ten Nights in a Bar-room* swayed countless thousands. Use was also made of symbols and ceremonials. Olive Leaf Circles attracted female foes of war, Cold Water Armies recruited children fighters against the "Demon Rum," and for nearly everybody bazaars, parades, banners, and badges mixed fun with serious purpose. So successfully did these pioneer reformers develop the techniques of propaganda that later generations have been able to contribute little beyond taking advantage of new technological devices such as the movies and the radio. The South for the most part remained immune to the agitation, fearing lest the institution of slavery perish in an assault on other social abuses.

Some reformers, impatient of gaining their ends through the slow process of persuasion, ventured to try out their ideas in experimental communities away from the haunts of men. Others, equally ardent but more practical-minded, endeavored to dragoon the unconvinced into conformity through legislative coercion. This helps to explain the interest in petitions and also the greater attention to lobbying. One wing of the abolitionists, discarding halfway measures, launched the Liberty party. The increasing resort to political methods was a natural consequence of the swift spread of manhood suffrage in the generation before the Civil War. Parties themselves were transformed by the admission to the polls of the hitherto unenfranchised. Political chieftains learned to regiment the vastly enlarged electorate and to please and influence the mass mind. As means to this end, these years marked the extension of the spoils system to the Federal government, the growth of party machines, and the introduction of national nominating conventions and of political platforms. Campaign appeals were increasingly directed at people's emotions rather than at their reason. The voter was now attracted by such partisan symbols as the log cabin (in which William Henry Harrison was alleged to reside), by torchlight processions, and by slogans like "Fifty-four-forty or fight!" It is evident that political associations learned much from the example of the humanitarian associations.

The increased democratic emphasis in politics also facilitated the adoption of the principle of impartiality in granting incorporation rights to capitalistic associations. In the national arena President Jackson waged victorious battle against renewing the exclusive privileges of the Second United States Bank, while in the states, his followers and sympathizers warred unceasingly to abolish "any and all monopolies by legislation."[23] Others supported the proposal in order to assure their equality with competitors in taking advantage of the vastly expanding opportunities in transportation, manufacturing, and finance. As a result, legislature after legislature provided for establishing corporations by general law instead of by special act, a third of the states anchoring the requirement in their constitutions.[24] Though many businesses continued to operate as unchartered associations, the legal machinery now existed for that vast growth of corporate enterprise which was eventually to dominate the American scene. The practice of obtaining a charter in a lax state in order to do business in stricter ones belongs to that later time.

With far less approval from the commercial classes, indeed against their active resistance, the rapid growth of industry begot a new type of organization, the trade union, which had long been struggling for birth. Wage earners, confronted with conditions of employment that prevented decency of living, resorted to united action in self-defense. Combining here and there in local crafts, they soon established nation-wide unions in some trades, and from 1834 to 1837 they succeeded in maintaining a national labor federation.

At the peak of success, in 1836, the total membership in the five principal cities approximated three hundred thousand distributed in one hundred and sixty local unions.[25] Though the movement suffered severe setbacks and gained only a wavering tolerance of the courts, it nevertheless exemplified the special techniques that later set it apart from all other kinds of collective undertakings: the strike, the boycott, the sympathetic strike, picketing, the closed shop, and the trade agreement. As yet, however, labor's future in the family of voluntary associations seemed far from clear.

The zeal for joining also affected professional and intellectual workers. Here the motive was less economic - though the regulation of fees was sometimes one of the objects - than to improve common standards, foster research, and disseminate knowledge through meetings and publications. These associations differed from the older American Philosophical Society in not limiting the number of members and in pursuing more highly specialized interests. Some were the outgrowth of earlier local or state societies and "academies." After the American Statistical Association set the example in 1839, such kindred bodies appeared as the American Ethnological Society (1842), the American Medical Association (1847), the American Society of Engineers and Architects (1852), the National Education Association (1852), and the American Entomological Society (1859). In 1848 the American Association for the Advancement of Science was formed to unite investigators in all scientific fields. Only research workers in the humanities and social sciences failed to heed the call to national action, but these departments of learning were as yet only feebly staffed.

With one section of the population after another yielding to the associative contagion it is not surprising that the long-standing aversion to secret societies should collapse. But the collapse came after an unprecedented outburst of hostility against the principal oath-bound brotherhood.[26] The Antimasonic movement was rooted in the antagonism of country to town, where most of the lodges were to be found; in objections of the orthodox to the order's diluted Christianity; in lower-class resentment against the well-to-do, who usually composed the membership; and in fear of the boastful claims of Masons to a controlling influence in political and economic life. The spark that set off the explosion was the abduction and alleged murder in 1826 of William Morgan of Batavia, New York, who, having become dissatisfied with the fraternity, had written a book to expose its secrets. Though Morgan's disappearance was plainly the work of overzealous individuals, popular prejudice refused to make any distinction. The smoldering anger blazed up through the rural parts of the East and edged into the South and the Mississippi Valley. Lodges in wholesale numbers perished in the flames, New York state alone losing over four hundred. Churches expelled Masonic clergymen and members; legislatures instituted investigations; Vermont and at least two other states prohibited secret-society oaths; and Rhode Island required all lodges to publish their proceedings in annual reports. Astute men such as Thurlow Weed in upstate New York and Thaddeus Stevens in Pennsylvania saw an opportunity to use the movement as a rallying point for the forces opposed to Jackson. So far did these political opportunists carry the Antimasons from their original purpose that in 1832 William Wirt, the party's first and only presidential nominee, actually avoided denouncing the order. The Antimasons won only Vermont's seven electoral votes.

Though the political antagonism toward Masonry (or oath-bound societies) lived on for several years in a few states, and though as late as 1882 a National Christian Association Opposed to Secret Societies erected a monument to William Morgan at Batavia with the inscription "Murdered by the Masons," the election of 1832 marked a decisive turning point in the American attitude toward oath-bound associations. Even if the Antimasonic party had not been betrayed by its professed friends, it could have displayed little strength, for it had not correctly diagnosed the malady. What had really offended democratic sensitiveness was not the secrecy but the exclusiveness. Just as people wished to multiply economic corporations through a general system of chartering, so they desired to have enough fraternal organizations for all who cared to join.[27] The plain citizen sometimes wearied of his plainness and, wanting rites as well as rights, hankered for the ceremonials, grandiloquent titles, and exotic costumes of a mystic brotherhood. Moreover, the impersonality of city life put a premium on the comradeship thus afforded. Lodge membership might also help one's business or political ambitions. Add to these motives the financial advantages usually accruing from sickness and death benefits, and the proliferation of fraternal associations following the decline of the

Antimasonic crusade is not hard to understand. Henceforth secrecy and degrees and regalia became an asset instead of a liability.

Within two years of Wirt's defeat the Order of Druids was introduced from England, and the United States had created the first adult secret society of its own: the Red Men, to whose ranks only palefaces were admitted.[28] In 1843 the Odd Fellows, who had been in America for nearly twenty-five years, cast off their dependence on the English parent body and swiftly boosted their membership from 30,000 at the time of withdrawal to 200,000 in 1860. "The American," grumbled Thoreau mindful of his Walden solitude, "has dwindled into an Odd Fellow, -one who may be known by the development of his organ of gregariousness, and a manifest lack of intellect and cheerful self-reliance."[29] Meanwhile the Masons accomplished a slow recovery which before the Civil War wiped out their earlier losses, and in the colleges national Greek-letter fraternities, most of them recently founded, played an increasingly important role. The great foreign influx of these years added to the variety with the Ancient Order of Hibernians, brought over by Irish Catholics in 1836, and with the B'nai B'rith (1843) and similar bodies formed by German Jews after arriving.[30] The foes of immigration returned the compliment by churning up nativist and anti-Catholic sentiment through such secret societies as the Order of United Americans (1844), the United American Mechanics (1845), the Order of the Star-Spangled Banner (1849), and the Brotherhood of the Union (1850). Even the total-abstinence forces now resorted to oath-bound orders, setting afoot the Sons of Temperance (1842), the Templars of Honor (1845), and the Good Templars (1851). Within eight years the Sons numbered 6,000 lodges and 245,000 members, a larger total than that of either the Odd Fellows or the Masons.[31] Secret associations, though late in gaining respectability, were in America to stay.

IV

The progress in associationalism before the Civil War was a prelude to far greater advances in the years to come. All the earlier favoring conditions now operated with magnified force. Cities were bigger, more numerous, and more generally distributed throughout the land. They were also bound together by swifter communications:

the improved telegraph, the expanding web of railways, the invention of the telephone, and, somewhat later, the coming of the motorcar and the radio. Newspapers not only grew in number and circulation but, themselves obeying the associative impulse, developed chains, syndicated features, and co-operative news-gathering methods, thereby further increasing the tendency to common thought and action. Moreover, a heightened sense of nationality followed the Civil War. That struggle decided that the Americans were to be one people, not two. The effect was to redouble Northern endeavors to plan far-flung undertakings, while the Southerners, no longer hampered by their "peculiar institution," soon fell into line. So thoroughly did the "habit of forming associations"-- James Bryce's phrase— interpenetrate American life that it becomes possible to understand practically all the important economic and social developments merely by examining the activities of voluntary organizations.[32]

Capitalistic associations, battening on fast-growing markets and access to cheap and abundant raw materials, assumed dinosaur proportions. Within eight years after the peace a House investigating committee reported, "This country is fast becoming filled with gigantic corporations wielding and controlling immense aggregations of money and thereby commanding great influence and power."[33] In the years ahead they strove for monopolistic dominion. By means of pools, rate agreements, interlocking directorates, trusts, mergers, holding companies, and other devices, legal or illegal, they reduced large sections of the population to a species of economic vassalage. The United States Steel Corporation, formed in 1901, combined under one ownership 228 companies scattered in 127 cities and 18 states, and possessed a capitalization nearly thirty times as great as that of the Second United States Bank. Three years later 318 consolidations (not including transportation lines and other public utilities) represented the fusing of nearly 5300 separate companies.[34]

The wage earners responded by extending and strengthening their own associations. They established many new national unions, they experimented for a time with the one-big-union idea as members of the Knights of Labor, and in 1881 they joined in founding the more successful American Federation of Labor, a body which by 1900 represented 82 national unions, 16 state federations, 118 city central unions, and 550,000 individual members.[35] These gains were made in the teeth of determined opposition from employers' associations, legislatures, and courts. The farmers, who likewise blamed Big Business for their ills, also resorted to organization against the foe, first in the Patrons of Husbandry or Grangers, and then in the more aggressive Northern and Southern Farmers' Alliances. The latter groups established the People's party to accomplish their political demands and, by polling twenty-two electoral votes and a million popular votes in 1892, frightened the Democrats into making free silver their battle cry in the next election. Most important of all, these agrarian bodies accustomed the agricultural population to pressure-group tactics and thereby paved the way for such associations as the National Farmers' Union, the Farmers' Nonpartisan League, and the American Farm Bureau Federation in the next century. Aided by modern means of communication, the once isolated husbandman thus also became a joiner.

Meanwhile, in the crowded urban centers, humanitarians intensified their earlier efforts and discovered many new outlets for reform zeal. Representative of these multifarious interests were the American Prison Association, the National Conference of Social Work, the Women's Christian Temperance Union, and the Society for the Prevention of Cruelty to Children, all formed in the 1870's, and the American Red Cross Society, the National Divorce Reform League, the National Arbitration League, and the Indian Rights Association, which came along in the 1880's. In many of these bodies women were the leading spirits, but they also established special groups for their own advancement. The two nation-wide suffrage associations, founded in 1869, signified one type of activity. Less militant members of the sex congregated in local clubs for self-culture, which became so plentiful by 1889 as to warrant the creation of the General Federation of Women's Clubs.

With even greater energy associations were multiplied for the promotion of professional and research interests.[36] Industry's competitive demand for technological improvement as well as the ambition of universities to enlarge the sum total of human knowledge caused specialization increasingly to dominate the individual worker and the societies he established. Sometimes the organizations arose out of a process of peeling away from an older trunk. Thus the American Society of Civil Engineers, which had grown out of the Society of Engineers and Architects (1852), bore a numerous offspring after the Civil War in the American Institute of Mining and Metallurgical Engineers, the American Society of Mechanical Engineers, the National Association of Power Engineers, the American Institute of Electrical Engineers, the American Order of Steam Engineers, the American Society of Naval Engineers, and the American Railway Engineering Association, with more to follow in the twentieth century. In some scientific branches a brand-new start was necessary, as in the case of the American Chemical Society (1876) and the American Association of Anatomists (1888). Scholars and practitioners in nonscientific fields followed suit. Soon librarians, archaeologists, modern-language specialists, historians, economists, mural painters, and musicians, not to mention other groups, were paying dues, electing national officers, and flocking to conventions with their kind.

But perhaps the most striking upsurge of voluntary associations was in the domain of leisure. Confronted with an increasing amount of idle time because of shorter hours of work and other favoring conditions, most people met the situation by banding together with others and having their use of leisure more or less arranged for them. Oath-bound brotherhoods now issued forth into what a contemporary called the "Golden Age of fraternity."[37] Between 1865 and 1880 seventy-eight beneficiary fraternal orders were founded; between 1880 and 1890 a hundred and twenty-four; and between 1890 and 1901 three hundred and sixty-six more.[38] Though many of them soon died, well over 5,000,000 names of men and women were inscribed on the rosters of 70,000 local lodges as the century closed, not including the 150,000 college youth distributed among 900 chapters of fraternities and sororities."[39]

These secret orders did not monopolize the field, for even apart from women's clubs three other sorts of leisure-time groups made their appearance. For one thing, the Civil War stimulated both sides to establish commemorative associations of the survivors, with parallel women's societies and, in the course of time, special organizations for the veterans' sons and daughters. The largest of this numerous brood, the Grand Army of the Republic, had 350,000 members in 1887.[40] The centennial celebrations of Revolutionary events, starting with Concord and Lexington in 1875, were responsible for a second flock of associations. If many persons wished merely to live off the unearned increment of ancestral reputations, others felt a need to assert the old American spirit against the engulfing tide of immigration from southern and eastern Europe. Among the more noteworthy of these pedigreed clans were the Sons of the American Revolution, the Daughters of the American Revolution, the Colonial Dames, the Society of Colonial Wars, and the Society of Mayflower Descendants, all dating from the late eighties and early nineties. Less exclusive in appeal was the third group of organizations, those mirroring the increasing popularity of sports. Foreshadowed by the National Association of Base Ball Players (1858), the contagion now spread to nearly all other games and forms of exercise -- archery, cycling, canoeing, college football, lawn tennis, croquet, polo, golf. Generally the object was either to standardize rules of play for amateurs or to put the contests on a professional and commercial basis. By these various means the American people, after a long period of hesitation and soul-searching, extended the associative principle to their hours of relaxation and rest.

V

To the vast and intricate mosaic of organizations evolved during the nineteenth century the twentieth has as yet added little new or significant. Popular alarm at the overweening power of capitalistic combinations has, however caused both the state and national governments to place increasing curbs on their freedom of action, while labor's right to organize and to pursue trade-union methods has at last been accorded full legal sanction. Secret fraternal orders reached their peak membership of over ten million in the mid-1920's, after which they began to decline, partly perhaps as a result of such competing attractions as the cheap motor car, the talking movies, and the radio.[41]   A contributing factor was the rapid growth of International Rotary and similar businessmen's luncheon clubs, founded in the second decade of the century. For the younger generation a new type of association appeared in the Boy Scouts (1910). The irrepressible spirit of gregariousness sometimes broke out also in unexpected forms. Thus the period since the first World War has seen the rise of the National Horseshoe Pitchers' Association, the Guild of Former Pipe Organ Pumpers, the Circus Fans' Association of America, the American Sunbathing Association, and the Association of Department Store Santa Clauses.

Related to the associative movement is the revamping of the calendar through the device of special "weeks."According to one enumeration, the United States year consists of a hundred and thirty-five weeks instead of the traditional fifty-two-an increase that involves, of course, considerable duplication.[42] Both benevolence and self-interest explain this new dimension of time. Among the designated occasions which all good citizens are expected to observe are Better Speech Week, Courtesy Week, Fire Prevention Week, Honesty Week, Thrift Week, and Walk-and-Be-Healthy Week, while the voice of the advertiser rings through Apple Week, Book Week, Canned Foods Week, Linoleum Week, and Pharmacy Week. Thus was devised a mechanism for reaching into the family circle and getting people to think and act in the same way when the ties of mutual interest would not support a dues-paying organization and the holding of national conventions. The more influential "weeks" were publicized with badges, seals, stickers, and posters. It seemed as if social inventiveness had reached its limit.

VI

"At the name of a society," wrote Ralph Waldo Emerson, "all my repulsions play, all my quills rise and sharpen." As he saw it, men clubbed together on the principle: "I have failed, and you have failed, but perhaps together we shall not fail."[43] The historical record shows, however, that his uncompromising stand against the herd instinct neither persuaded his countrymen or fairly delineated their motives and accomplishments. Out of the loins of religious voluntarism in colonial times had issued a numerous progeny, each new generation outstripping the old in the number and variety of its creations. These instrumentalities grew out of deep-felt human desires as a highly dynamic society continually disclosed fresh needs and opportunities. "From a handful of individuals we have become a nation of institutions," Henry Watterson once summarized his country's history.[44] It usually denoted strength rather than weakness when one man multiplied himself by uniting with others. Restating Emerson's thought with keener insight, William Ellery Channing declared, "Men, it is justly said, can do jointly what they cannot do singly."[45] It is true, of course, that the associative impulse tended to feed upon itself, sometimes leading to an infatuation that provoked the mirth of onlookers, but such excesses should not be permitted to hide the deeper significance of this powerful force in American life.

As a result of its workings, every community large or small has assumed a cellular structure, with these subdivisions of humanity intricately interlaced and overlapping. In the course of years there has evolved what Channing more than a century ago called "a sort of irregular government created within our constitutional government."[46] Day in and day out, this irregular government, by enlisting the constant participation of its members, stirs more interest and often possesses greater reality than the constitutional authority. Nor is comparison with the political state a mere figure of speech, for voluntary bodies actually exhibit many of the attributes of government. Despite the diversity among associations as to function and scope, the fact of membership usually generates a pride of belonging and a sense of devotion that endow their purposes and decisions with an obligatory character. It is as though the emotional fervor, even the bigotry, once centering in religious fellowship, has pervaded the labor union, the National Association of Manufacturers, the political party, and the Daughters of the American Revolution. Moreover, such organizations generally operate on the basis of a constitution or charter, possess both elected and appointed officials, prescribe standards of conduct, compel obedience to rules and regulations by means of fines, suspensions, and expulsions, and impose a species of taxation in the guise of dues and assessments. Their fiscal operations frequently eclipse those of governmental units. Though this fact is most familiar in the case of business corporations, the financial aspect of religious, political, and other associations may also be considerable. An authority writing on fraternal benefit societies in 1919 cited their aggregate annual income at $165,000,000 and placed the total amount of insurance carried on members' lives at $9,500,000,000.[47]

These irregular or unofficial governments have external as well as internal relations. It might seem that voluntary bodies could be divided between those which mind their own business and those which mind other people's business, but the distinction is unreal since all in some degree impinge upon the life about them. Recreational, no less than professional and learned, groups seek to maintain codes of ethics and levels of technical competence that indirectly affect the public at large. Capitalistic and labor organizations influence general conditions of employment and, when locked in battle, may disrupt the normal existence of a community. Moreover, nearly all associations resort at times to pressure tactics in relation to government. Though designed primarily for other purposes, the Methodist Church fronted the movement for prohibition, the League of American Wheelmen in its day induced many states to provide good roads for bicycle riders, and the G. A. R. labored successfully for higher Federal pensions. In recent times such activities have assumed increasing importance. In 1942 a total of 628, organizations maintained offices in Washington to supply arguments and witnesses for or against various types of legislation. Ten spoke for financial groups, eleven for foreign-language memberships, thirteen for lawyers' bodies, fourteen for youth or young people's interests, fifteen for minority elements, twenty-four for different phases of education, forty-two for labor, forty-two for one or another kind of political or economic creed, forty-three for veterans' or military organizations, and one hundred and eighty-two for business and manufacturing.[48] And this enumeration omits political parties, which operate the machinery that alone can gratify the desires of the pressure groups. It hardly needs to be said that these lobbying activities sometimes injure the public welfare. Only as long as all communities of interest are able to express themselves freely and adequately can the democratic process be regarded as working effectively. The problem is one of balance, just as bodily health depends upon a due equilibrium of physiological factors.

Emerson's objections to group undertakings rested largely on the view that the many cramp and diminish the single individual, stealing away his self-reliance as the price of acting in concert with others.[49] But, as Burke once observed, "All government, indeed every human benefit and enjoyment, every virtue, and every prudent act, is founded on compromise and barter."[50] Moreover, nothing has been more characteristic of voluntary bodies than the proneness of dissidents to exercise what the president of the American Society of Newspaper Editors recently termed "the God-given right of every American to resign, tell why, and raise hell."[51] A process of splitting and splintering, or what sociologists like to call "schismatic differentiation," has marked the course of practically every sort of association.[52] The history of religious denominations teems with instances, but hardly more so than that of humanitarian movements, labor organizations, political parties, and patriotic societies.

Sometimes the cause is an attitude of dogma-eat-dogma, sometimes the rivalry of ambitious leaders, sometimes a wrangle over such questions as eligibility rules for membership or the methods of implementing accepted objectives. Oath-bound orders have been torn by similar ructions. For example, the Royal Order of Foresters was the English progenitor of at least ten American brotherhoods containing the words "Foresters" or "Forestry" in their titles.[53] If internal strife has wasted a good deal of associational energy, it also indicates the existence of a vigorous spirit of nonconformity.

Probably a graver criticism of voluntary bodies than Emerson's is the extent to which men do things as members of an organization that they would be ashamed or afraid to do as individuals. The outstanding example is afforded by capitalistic groups, where a sense of fractional responsibility often leads a stockholder or official to sanction acts contrary to his usual standard of ethics. But business and financial corporations are impersonal institutions to a degree that most associations are not, and in recent years, as we have seen, the power of government has been increasingly invoked to keep them within their legitimate bounds. The same element of fractional responsibility enters into ephemeral organizations that are avowedly law-defying. Nearly every great national crisis has produced one or more of them: the Knights of the Golden Circle and other Copperhead societies during the Civil War; the Ku Klux Klan, the Knights of the White Camelia, and similar Southern bodies in the period of Reconstruction; the modernized Ku Klux Klan that skyrocketed into prominence after the first war with Germany; and the jumble of Silver Shirts, Black Shirts, White Shirts, United States Fascists, Christian Fronters, and German-American Bundists who skulked in the shadows cast by the Great Depression and the ideological conflict over totalitarianism. All these were secret oath-bound companies carrying on treasonable or terroristic activities and usually having military features and aims. In every case the members profited by the public's habituation to the principle of freedom of association, but sooner or later their lawless exploits brought down upon their heads the destroying sword of constituted authority.

The career of these few, short-lived organizations stands in marked contrast to the great and continuing role in society played by the numerous secret fraternal orders. These with rare exceptions have acted as bulwarks of conservatism, their constant endeavor being to emphasize conventional moral and ethical standards, transmit existing social values, and avoid entangling alliances with political movements. Furthermore, as a writer in the *Century Magazine* once pointed out, their very existence has constituted a "great American safety-valve for these ambitions for precedence which our national life generates, fosters, and stimulates, without adequate provision for their gratification."[54] The burden of championing minority rights and unpopular causes has been borne by other types of association, notably humanitarian, labor, and reform bodies. These have helped to educate the public to the need for continuing change and improvement and in their aspect as pressure groups have done much to keep legislatures and political parties in step with the times.

Considering the central importance of the voluntary organization in American history there is no doubt it has provided the people with their greatest school of self-government. Rubbing minds as well as elbows, they have been trained from youth to take common counsel, choose leaders, harmonize differences, and obey the expressed will of the majority. In mastering the associative way they have mastered the democratic way.[55] Moreover, through what Professor Julius Goebel has called "the creative magic of mere association," they have learned to conduct most of the major concerns of life, spiritual, economic, political, social, cultural, and recreational.[56] To this fact James Bryce attributed the high level of executive competence he found everywhere in America - talents which he likened to those possessed by "administrative rulers, generals, diplomatists."[57] By comparison, the much vaunted role of the New England town meeting as a seedbed of popular government seems almost negligible. The habits so engendered have armed the people to take swift and effective steps in moments of emergency. On the advancing frontier the pioneers joined together for house-raisings, for protecting squatters' rights against lawful claimants, for safeguarding the community against desperadoes, and for allied purposes.[58] In times of war impromptu organizations arise as if by spontaneous generation to invigorate the national will and to supplement the government's military measures in a thousand ways. This instinctive resort to collective action is one of the strongest taproots of the nation's well-being.

It was with calculated foresight that the Axis dictators insured their rise to power by repressing or abolishing political, religious, labor, and other voluntary groups. They dared not tolerate these guardians of the people's liberties and, at the very least, regarded them, in Hobbes's phrase, as "worms within the entrails of a natural man," detracting from the absolute allegiance which they believed citizens to owe to the state. Hence joiners were among the earliest casualties of the totalitarian system. But under a reign of freedom self-constituted bodies have seldom been a divisive factor and never for long. Reaching out with interlocking membership to all parts of the country, embracing all ages, classes, creeds, and ethnic groups, they have constantly demonstrated the underlying unity that warrants diversity. They have served as a great cementing force for national integration.

ENDNOTES

1. The author, a former president of the American Historical Association, is Francis Lee Higginson professor in Harvard University.

2. Alexis de Tocquevile, *Democracy in America* (Henry Reeve, trans., New York, 1900), II, 115.

3. Carl Bridenbaugh, *Cities in the Wilderness* (New York, 1938), p.436.

4. Melvin M. Johnson, *The Beginning of Freemasonry in America* (New York, 1924), pp. 191-92, 205.

5. See Shaw Livermore, *Early American Land Companies* (New York, 1939), *passim.*

6. *New-York Gazetteer*, Feb. 16, 1775.

7. William W. Hening, comp., *Statutes at Large of Virginia*, XII, 86.

8. Joseph S. Davis, *Essays in the Earlier History of American Corporations* (Cambridge, 1917), II, I6-17.

9. [James Walker], "Associations for Benevolent Purposes," *Christian Examiner*, II (1825), 241-52. See also Oliver W. Elsbree, *The Rise of the Missionary Spirit in America, 1790-1815* (Williamsport, 1928), and James O. Oliphant, "The American Missionary Spirit, 1828-1835," *Church History*, VII (1938), 125-37.

10. William W. Sweet, ed., *The Presbyterians, 1783-1840* (New York, 1936), p. 829. See his *The Story of Religions in America* (New York, 1930), pp. 368-72, for the attitude of Western Baptists.

11. Davis, *Essays*, II, 304, 305, quoting contemporary critics.

12. *Ibid.*, I, 440, quoting from *Five Letters to the Yeomanry of the United States*, probably by George Logan.

13. See his *Writings*, ed. Worthington C. Ford (New York, I889), XII, 454-55, 465-66.

14. James D. Richardson, comp., *Messages and Papers of the Presidents*

(Washington, 1896-99), I, 163, 217, 2I9. The fullest account of the political clubs is Eugene P. Link, *Democratic- Republican Societies* (New York, 1942).

15. Charles McCarthy, "The Antimasonic Party," American Historical Association, *Report for 1902*, 1, 542-43; David M. Ludlum, *Social Ferment in Vermont* (New York, 1939), pp. 90-93.

16. John B. McMaster, *A History of the People of the United States* (New York, 1883-1913), 1, 167-76.

17. "Remarks on Associations" in W. E. Channing, *Works* (Boston, 1875), p. 139, an article which first appeared unsigned in the *Christian Examiner*, VII (1829), 105-40. Among others, Daniel Webster likewise held that the great characteristic of the age was that "public improvements are brought about by a voluntary association and combination." Quoted in U. S. Commissioner of Agriculture, *Report for 1866*, p. 525. Harriet Martineatu in *Society in America* (New York, 1837), I1, 299, praised the organizations for "mechanical objects" and for indoctrinating public opinion, but saw little good in those for moral self-improvement.

18. George W. Pierson, *Tocqueville and Beaumont in America* (New York, 1938), p. 479; Tocqueville, I, 19I, II, 114-15, 117-18, 127.

19. Channing, p. 139.

20. Quoted in Arthur M. Schlesinger, Jr., *Orestes A. Brownson* (Boston, 1939), p. 8o. The best general account of these early reform organizations is Alice F. Tyler, *Freedom's Ferment* (Minneapolis, 1944).

21. Calvin Colton, *Protestant Jesuitism* (New York, 1836), pp. 53-54.

22. The statistics regarding reform societies are derived from the appropriate annual reports.

23. The phrase is quoted from a "Declaration of Principles" in Fitzwilliam Byrdsall, *The History of the Loco-foco or Equal Rights Party* (New York, 1842), p. 39. See also Carl Russell Fish, *The Rise of the Common Man* (New York, 1927), pp. 50-61.

24. Theodore G. Gronert, *The Corporation in the State Constitutional Conventions of 1835- 1860* (Fayetteville, 1924). "The North is indebted for its great wealth and prosperity to the readiness with which it forms associations for all industrial and commercial purposes," wrote George Fitzhugh in *Sociology for the South* (Richmond, 1854), p. 27.

25. John R. Commons and others, *History of Labour in the United States* (New York, 1918), I, 424.

26. This account is based largely on McCarthy, "Antimasonic Party"; Ludlum, pp. 88-89, 101-111; Dixon Ryan Fox, *The Decline of Aristocracy in the Politics of New York* (New York, 1918), pp. 337-43; Emerson Davis, *The Half Century* (Boston, 1851), pp. 163-68; and J. M. Foster, "Secret Societies and the State," *Arena*, XIX (1898), 233-34. *Ed's note: The Foster article is reprinted in this volume.*

27. Thus, Massachusetts *Senate Document*, no. 87 (1836), 42, speaks of the

"obvious and intimate relation between the exclusive selfishness of secret, oath bound societies and the monopolies and exclusive privileges of special legislation."

28. For these and the other oath-bound societies, see Albert C. Stevens, comp., *The Cyclopaedia of Fraternities* (New York, 1899). *Ed's note: An article by Stevens is reprinted in this volume.*

29. Henry D. Thoreau, *Cape Cod and Miscellanies*, in *Complete Works* (Boston, 1929), pp. 364-65. Apparently contemporaries used the term "Odd Fellow" as synonymous with lodge member. See also Fitzhugh, pp. 44, 68.

30. The role of ethnic associations in America has never been carefully studied, though some suggestive references appear in Robert E. Park and Herbert A. Miller, *Old World Traits Transrplanted* (New York, 1921), pp. 11 9-44, 287-96. Most immigrant societies seem to have been nonsecret.

31. John A. Krout, *The Origins of Prohibition* (New York, I925), p. 211.

32. Bryce, echoing Tocqueville, remarked, "Associations are created, extended- and worked in the United States more quickly and effectively than in any other country.' *The American Commonwealth* (2-vol. ed., London, 1888), II, 239.

33. Quoted in James F. Rhodes, *History of the United States* (New York, 1892-1919), VII, 19.

34. John Moody, *The Truth about the Trusts* (New York, 1904), p. 486.

35. Lewis L. Lorwin, *The American Federation of Labor* (Washington, 1933), pp. 484, 488.

36. For a comparative study of the methods and social role of professional and business organizations, with some attention to labor associations and farm co-operatives, see Carl F. Taeusch, *Professional and Business Ethics* (New York, 1926).

37. W. S. Harwood, "Secret Societies in the United States," *North American Review*, CLXIV (I897), 622-23. *Ed's note: reprinted in this volume.*

38. Balthasar H. Meyer, "Fraternal Beneficiary Societies in the United States," *American Journal of Sociology*, VI (I901), 655-56; Walter Basye, *History and Operation of Fraternal Insurance* (Rochester, 1919), pp. 209, 211. *Ed's note: The Meyer article is reprinted in this volume.*

39. Stevens, p. xv; Arthur M. Schlesinger, *The Rise of the City* (New York, 1933), pp. 209, 211.

40. Noel P. Gist, *Secret Societies, a Cultural Study of Fraternalism* (Columbia, Mo., 1940), p. 38. *Ed's note: Two articles by Gist are reprinted in this volume.*

41. Ibid., pp. 41-43.

42. Boston *Herald*, Oct. 14, 1927.

43. Robert M. Gay, *Emerson* (Garden City, N. Y., 1928), p. 142; Ralph W. Emerson, *Works* (Boston, 1883-87), III, 252.

44. Quoted in John P. Davis, *Corporations* (New York, 1905), 1, 4n.

45. Channing, 139.

46. Ibid., 149. For recent observations on this aspect of associations, see

Guy Stanton Ford, *On and Off the Campus* (Minneapolis, 1938), 149-151; Beardsley Ruml, *Government, Business and Values* (New York, 1943), pp. 5-29; and Charles E. Merriam, *Public and Private Government* (New Haven, 1944), pp. 3-19.

47. Basye, p. 16.

48. *United States News* (Washington), July 24, 1942, p. 19. According to E. Pendleton Herring, *Group Representation before Congress* (Washington,1929), p. 19, the total was at least 530 in 1929.

49. Emerson, I, 264-65, III, 253, and elsewhere.

50. Edmund Burke, *Speeches and Letters on American Affairs* (London, 1908), 130-31.

51. Boston *Globe*, July 9, 1943.

52. Merle Curti cites examples of reform associations in "The Changing Pattern of Certain Humanitarian Organizations," American Academy of Political and Social Science, *Annals*, CLXXIX (1935), 59-61.

53. Stevens, pp. 127, 223; Gist,p. 47.

54. Walter B. Hill, "The Great American Safety-Valve," *Century*, XLIV (1892), 383. *Ed's note: Reprinted in this volume.*

55. For an early statement of this view, see a quotation from Charles J. Ingersoll's *A Discourse Concerning the Influence of America on the Mind* (Philadelphia, 1823) in the *North American Review*, XLII (1824), 168-69.

56. The quoted phrase is from the introduction to Livermore, p. xv.

57. Bryce, II, 40, 44, 239-40, 407-408, 516.

58. See Frederick J. Turner's discussion in *The Frontier in American History* (New York, 1920), pp. 343-44.

David Brion Davis situates the Anti-Masonic movement of the 1820s and 1830s within the religious, economic, and political contexts of Jacksonian America. He argues that the radical transformations of an expanding and increasingly diverse nation caused many Americans to perceive caustic conspiracies which sought to subvert American ideals. These individuals, whom Davis terms "nativists," sought to convince the antebellum public that Freemasonry, Catholicism, and Mormonism constituted conspiracies which compelled adherents to degrade the national identity and thus endanger the country's glorious destiny. Davis's compelling analysis of American reactions to social transformation identifies modes of thought which are recognizable within the political discourse of our own time.

SOME THEMES OF COUNTER-SUBVERSION.
An Analysis of Anti-Masonic, Anti-Catholic, and Anti-Mormon Literature
David Brion Davis
1960
The Mississippi Valley Historical Review 47(2) (Sep., 1960), 205-224.

Reprint permission granted by author

DURING the second quarter of the nineteenth century, when danger of foreign invasion appeared increasingly remote, Americans were told by various respected leaders that Freemasons had infiltrated the government and had seized control of the courts, that Mormons were undermining political and economic freedom in the West, and that Roman Catholic priests, receiving instructions from Rome, had made frightening progress in a plot to subject the nation to popish despotism. This fear of internal subversion was channeled into a number of powerful counter movements which attracted wide public support. The literature produced by these movements evoked images of a great American enemy that closely resembled traditional European stereotypes of conspiracy and subversion. In Europe, however, the idea of subversion implied a threat to the established order - to the king, the church, or the ruling aristocracy - rather than to ideals or a way of life. If free Americans borrowed their images of subversion from frightened kings and uneasy aristocrats, these images had to be shaped and blended to fit American conditions. The movements would have to come from the people, and the themes of counter-subversion would be likely to reflect their fears, prejudices, hopes, and perhaps even unconscious desires.

There are obvious dangers in treating such reactions against imagined subversion as part of a single tendency or spirit of an age.[1] Anti-Catholicism was nourished by ethnic conflict and uneasiness over immigration in the expanding cities of the Northeast; anti-Mormonism arose largely from a contest for economic and political power between western settlers and a group that voluntarily withdrew from society and claimed the undivided allegiance of its members.[2] Anti-Masonry, on the other hand, was directed against a group thoroughly integrated in American society and did not reflect a clear division of economic, religious, or political interests.[3] Moreover, anti-Masonry gained power in the late 1820's and soon spent its energies as it became absorbed in national politics; anti-Catholicism reached its maximum force in national politics a full generation later;[4] anti-Mormonism, though increasing in intensity in the 1850's, became an important national issue only after the Civil War.[5] These movements seem even more widely separated when we note that Freemasonry was traditionally associated with anti-Catholicism and that Mormonism itself absorbed considerable anti-Masonic and anti-Catholic sentiment.[6]

Despite such obvious differences, there were certain similarities in these campaigns against subversion. All three gained widespread support in the northeastern states within the space of a generation; anti-Masonry and anti-Catholicism resulted in the sudden emergence of separate political parties; and in 1856 the new Republican party explicitly condemned the Mormons' most controversial institution. The movements of counter-subversion differed markedly in historical origin, but as the image of an un-American conspiracy took form in the nativist press, in sensational exposes, in the countless fantasies of treason and mysterious criminality, the lines separating Mason, Catholic, and Mormon became almost indistinguishable.

The similar pattern of Masonic, Catholic, and Mormon subversion was frequently noticed by alarmist writers. The *Anti-Masonic Review* informed its readers in 1829 that whether one looked at Jesuitism or   Freemasonry, "the organization, the power, and the secret operation, are the same; except that Freemasonry is much the more secret and complicated of the two."[7] William Hogan, an ex-priest and vitriolic anti-Catholic, compared the menace of Catholicism with that of Mormonism.[8] And many later anti-Mormon writers agreed with Josiah Strong that Brigham Young "out-popes the Roman" and described the Mormon hierarchy as being similar to the Catholic. It was probably not accidental that Samuel F. B. Morse analyzed the Catholic conspiracy in essentially the same terms his father had used in exposing the Society of the Illuminati, supposedly a radical branch of Freemasonry,[9] or that writers of sensational fiction in the 1840's and 1850's depicted an atheistic and unprincipled Catholic Church obviously modeled on Charles Brockden Brown's earlier fictional version of the Illuminati.[10]

If Masons, Catholics, and Mormons bore little resemblance to one another in actuality, as imagined enemies they merged into a nearly common stereotype. Behind specious professions of philanthropy or religious sentiment, nativists[11] discerned a group of unscrupulous leaders plotting to subvert the American social order. Though rank-and-file members were not individually evil, they were blinded and corrupted by a persuasive ideology that justified treason and gross immorality in the interest of the subversive group. Trapped in the meshes of a machine-like organization, deluded by a false sense of loyalty and moral obligation, these dupes followed orders like professional soldiers and labored unknowingly to abolish free society, to enslave their fellow men, and to overthrow divine principles of law and justice. Should an occasional member free himself from bondage to superstition and fraudulent authority, he could still be disciplined by the threat of death or dreadful tortures. There were no limits to the ambitious designs of leaders equipped with such organizations. According to nativist prophets, they chose to subvert American society because control of America meant control of the world's destiny.

Some of these beliefs were common in earlier and later European interpretations of conspiracy. American images of Masonic, Catholic, and Mormon subversion were no doubt a compound of traditional myths concerning Jacobite agents, scheming Jesuits, and fanatical heretics, and of dark legends involving the Holy Vehm and Rosicrucians. What distinguished the stereotypes of Mason, Catholic, and Mormon was the way in which they were seen to embody those traits that were precise antitheses of American ideals. The subversive group was essentially an inverted image of Jacksonian democracy and the cult of the common man; as such it not only challenged the dominant values but stimulated those suppressed needs and yearnings that are unfulfilled in a mobile, rootless, and individualistic society. It was therefore both frightening and fascinating.

It is well known that expansion and material progress in the Jacksonian era evoked a fervid optimism and that nationalists became intoxicated with visions of America's millennial glory. The simultaneous growth of prosperity and social democracy seemed to prove that Providence would bless a nation that allowed her citizens maximum liberty. When each individual was left free to pursue happiness in his own way, unhampered by the tyranny of custom or special privilege, justice and well-being would inevitably emerge. But if a doctrine of laissez-faire individualism seemed to promise material expansion and prosperity, it also raised disturbing problems. As one early anti-Mormon writer expressed it: What was to prevent liberty and popular sovereignty from sweeping away "the old landmarks of Christendom, and the glorious old common law of our fathers"? How was the individual to preserve a sense of continuity with the past, or identify himself with a given cause or tradition? What, indeed, was to insure a common loyalty and a fundamental unity among the people?

Such questions acquired a special urgency as economic growth intensified mobility, destroyed old ways of life, and transformed traditional symbols of status and prestige. Though most Americans took pride in their material progress, they also expressed a yearning for reassurance and security, for unity in some cause transcending individual self-interest. This need for meaningful group activity was filled in part by religious revivals, reform movements, and a proliferation of fraternal orders and associations. In politics Americans tended to assume the posture of what Marvin Meyers has termed "venturesome conservative," mitigating their acquisitive impulses by an appeal for unity against extraneous forces that allegedly threatened a noble heritage of republican ideals. Without abandoning a belief in progress through laissez-faire individualism, the Jacksonians achieved a sense of unity and righteousness by styling themselves as restorers of tradition.[12] Perhaps no theme is so evident in the Jacksonian era as the strained attempt to provide America with a glorious heritage and a noble destiny. With only a loose and often ephemeral attachment to places and institutions, many Americans felt a compelling need to articulate their loyalties, to prove their faith, and to demonstrate their allegiance to certain ideals and institutions. By so doing they acquired a sense of self-identity and personal direction in an otherwise rootless and shiftless environment.

But was abstract nationalism sufficient to reassure a nation strained by sectional conflict, divided by an increasing number of sects and associations, and perplexed by the unexpected consequences of rapid growth? One might desire to protect the Republic against her enemies, to preserve the glorious traditions of the Founders, and to help insure continued expansion and prosperity, but first it was necessary to discover an enemy by distinguishing subversion from simple diversity. If Freemasons seemed to predominate in the economic and political life of a given area, was one's joining them shrewd business judgment or a betrayal of republican tradition?[13] Should Maryland citizens heed the warnings of anti-Masonic itinerants, or conclude that anti-Masonry was itself a conspiracy hatched by scheming Yankees?[14] Were Roman Catholics plotting to destroy public schools and a free press, the twin guardians of American democracy, or were they exercising democratic rights of self-expression and self-protection?[15] Did equality of opportunity and equality before the law mean that Americans should accept the land claims of Mormons or tolerate as jurors men who "swear that they have wrought miracles and supernatural cures"? Or should one agree with the Reverend Finis Ewing that "the 'Mormons' are the common enemies of mankind and ought to be destroyed"?[16]

Few men questioned traditional beliefs in freedom of conscience and the right of association. Yet what was to prevent "all the errors and worn out theories of the Old World, of schisms in the early Church, the monkish age and the rationalistic period," from flourishing in such salubrious air?[17] Nativists often praised the work of benevolent societies, but they were disturbed by the thought that monstrous conspiracies might also "show kindness and patriotism, when it is necessary for their better concealment; and oftentimes do much good for the sole purpose of getting a better opportunity to do evil."[18] When confronted by so many sects and associations, how was the patriot to distinguish the loyal from the disloyal? It was clear that mere disagreement over theology or economic policy was invalid as a test, since honest men disputed over the significance of baptism or the wisdom of protective tariffs. But neither could one rely on expressions of allegiance to common democratic principles, since subversives would cunningly profess to believe in freedom and toleration of dissent as long as they remained a powerless minority.

As nativists studied this troubling question, they discovered that most groups and denominations claimed only a partial loyalty from their members, freely subordinating themselves to the higher and more abstract demands of the Constitution, Christianity, and American public opinion. Moreover, they openly exposed their objects and activities to public scrutiny and exercised little discrimination in enlisting members. Some groups, however, dominated a larger portion of their members' lives, demanded unlimited allegiance as a condition of membership, and excluded certain activities from the gaze of a curious public.

Of all governments, said Richard Rush, ours was the one with most to fear from secret societies, since popular sovereignty by its very nature required perfect freedom of public inquiry and judgment.[19] In a virtuous republic why should anyone fear publicity or desire to conceal activities, unless those activities were somehow contrary to the public interest? When no one could be quite sure what the public interest was, and when no one could take for granted a secure and well-defined place in the social order, it was most difficult to acknowledge legitimate spheres of privacy. Most Americans of the Jacksonian era appeared willing to tolerate diversity and even eccentricity, but when they saw themselves excluded and even barred from witnessing certain proceedings, they imagined a "mystic power" conspiring to enslave them.

Readers might be amused by the first exposures of Masonic ritual, since they learned that pompous and dignified citizens, who had once impressed non-Masons with allusions to high degrees and elaborate ceremonies, had in actuality been forced to stand blindfolded and clad in ridiculous garb, with a long rope noosed around their necks. But genuine anti-Masons were not content with simple ridicule. Since intelligent and distinguished men had been members of the fraternity, "it must have in its interior something more than the usual revelatons *(sic)* of its mysteries declare."[20] Surely leading citizens would not meet at night and undergo degrading and humiliating initiations just for the sake of novelty. The alleged murder of William Morgan raised an astonishing public furor because it supposedly revealed the inner secret of Freemasonry. Perverted by a false ideology, Masons had renounced all obligations to the general public, to the laws of the land, and even to the command of God. Hence they threatened not a particular party's program or a denomination's creed, but stood opposed to all justice, democracy, and religion.[21]

The distinguishing mark of Masonic, Catholic, and Mormon conspiracies was a secrecy that cloaked the members' unconditional loyalty to an autonomous body. Since the organizations had corrupted the private moral judgment of their members, Americans could not rely on the ordinary forces of progress to spread truth and enlightenment among their ranks. Yet the affairs of such organizations were not outside the jurisdiction of democratic government, for no body politic could be asked to tolerate a power that was designed to destroy it.[22] Once the true nature of subversive groups was thoroughly understood, the alternatives were as clear as life and death. How could democracy and Catholicism coexist when, as Edward Beecher warned, "The systems are diametrically opposed: one must and will exterminate the other"?[23] Because Freemasons had so deeply penetrated state and national governments, only drastic remedies could restore the nation to its democratic purity.[24] And later, Americans faced an "irrepressible conflict" with Mormonism, for it was said that either free institutions or Mormon despotism must ultimately annihilate the other.[25]

We may well ask why nativists magnified the division between unpopular minorities and the American public, so that Masons, Catholics, and Mormons seemed so menacing that they could not be accorded the usual rights and privileges of a free society. Obviously the literature of counter-subversion reflected concrete rivalries and conflicts of interest between competing groups, but it is important to note that the subversive bore no racial or ethnic stigma and was not even accused of inherent depravity.[26] Since group membership was a matter of intellectual and emotional loyalty, no *physical* barrier prevented a Mason, Catholic, or Mormon from apostatizing and joining the dominant in-group, providing always that he escaped assassination from his previous masters. This suggests that counter-subversion was more than a rationale for group rivalry and was related to the general problem of ideological unity and diversity in a free society. When a "system of delusion" insulated members of a group from the unifying and disciplining force of public opinion, there was no authority to command an allegiance to common principles. This was why oaths of loyalty assumed great importance for nativists. Though the ex-Catholic William Hogan stated repeatedly that Jesuit spies respected no oaths except those to the Church, he inconsistently told Masons and Odd Fellows that they could prevent infiltration by requiring new members to swear they were not Catholics.[27] It was precisely the absence of distinguishing outward traits that made the enemy so dangerous, and true loyalty so difficult to prove.

When the images of different enemies conform to a similar pattern, it is highly probable that this pattern reflects important tensions within a given culture. The themes of nativist literature suggest that its authors simplified problems of personal insecurity and adjustment to bewildering social change by trying to unite Americans of diverse political, religious, and economic interests against a common enemy. Just as revivalists sought to stimulate Christian fellowship by awakening men to the horrors of sin, so nativists used apocalyptic images to ignite human passions, destroy selfish indifference, and join patriots in a cohesive brotherhood. Such themes were only faintly secularized. When God saw his "lov'd Columbia" imperiled by the hideous monster of Freemasonry, He realized that only a martyr's blood could rouse the hearts of the people and save them from bondage to the Prince of Darkness. By having God will Morgan's death, this anti-Mason showed he was more concerned with national virtue and unity than with Freemasonry, which was only a providential instrument for testing republican strength.[28]

Similarly, for the anti-Catholic "this brilliant new world" was once "young and beautiful; it abounded in all the luxuries of nature; it promised all that was desirable to man." But the Roman Church, seeing "these irresistible temptations, thirsting with avarice and yearning for the reestablishment of her falling greatness, soon commenced pouring in among its unsuspecting people hoardes *(sic)* of Jesuits and other friars." If Americans were to continue their narrow pursuit of self-interest, oblivious to the "Popish colleges, and nunneries, and monastic institutions," indifferent to manifold signs of corruption and decay, how could the nation expect "that the moral breezes of heaven should breathe upon her, and restore to her again that strong and healthy constitution, which her ancestors have left to her sons"?[29] The theme of an Adamic fall from paradise was horrifying, but it was used to inspire determined action and thus unity. If Methodists were "criminally indifferent" to the Mormon question, and if "avaricious merchants, soulless corporations, and a subsidized press" ignored Mormon iniquities, there was all the more reason that the *"will of the people* must prevail."[30]

Without explicitly rejecting the philosophy of laissez-faire individualism, with its toleration of dissent and innovation, nativist literature conveyed a sense of common dedication to a noble cause and sacred tradition. Though the nation had begun with the blessings of God and with the noblest institutions known to man, the people had somehow become selfish and complacent, divided by petty disputes, and insensitive to signs of danger. In his sermons attacking such self-interest, such indifference to public concerns, and such a lack of devotion to common ideals and sentiments, the nativist revealed the true source of his anguish. Indeed, he seemed at times to recognize an almost beneficent side to subversive organizations, since they joined the nation in a glorious crusade and thus kept it from moral and social disintegration.

The exposure of subversion was a means of promoting unity, but it also served to clarify national values and provide the individual ego with a sense of high moral sanction and imputed righteousness. Nativists identified themselves repeatedly with a strangely incoherent tradition in which images of Pilgrims, Minute Men, Founding Fathers, and true Christians appeared in a confusing montage. Opposed to this heritage of stability and perfect integrity, to this society founded on the highest principles of divine and natural law, were organizations formed by the grossest frauds and impostures, and based on the wickedest impulses of human nature. Bitterly refuting Masonic claims to ancient tradition and Christian sanction, anti-Masons charged that the Order was of recent origin, that it was shaped by Jews, Jesuits, and French atheists as an engine for spreading infidelity, and that it was employed by kings and aristocrats to undermine republican institutions.[31] If the illustrious Franklin and Washington had been duped by Masonry, this only proved how treacherous was its appeal and how subtly persuasive were its pretensions.[32] Though the Catholic Church had an undeniable claim to tradition, nativists argued that it had originated in stupendous frauds and forgeries "in comparison with which the forgeries of Mormonism are completely thrown into the shade."[33] Yet anti-Mormons saw an even more sinister conspiracy based on the "shrewd cunning" of Joseph Smith, who convinced gullible souls that he conversed with angels and received direct revelations from the Lord.[34]

By emphasizing the fraudulent character of their opponents' claims, nativists sought to establish the legitimacy and just authority of American institutions. Masonic rituals, Roman Catholic sacraments, and Mormon revelations were preposterous hoaxes used to delude naive or superstitious minds; but public schools, a free press, and jury trials were eternally valid prerequisites for a free and virtuous society.

Moreover, the finest values of an enlightened nation stood out in bold relief when contrasted with the corrupting tendencies of subversive groups. Perversion of the sexual instinct seemed inevitably to accompany religious error.[35] Deprived of the tender affections of normal married love, shut off from the elevating sentiments of fatherhood, Catholic priests looked on women only as insensitive objects for the gratification of their frustrated desires.[36] In similar fashion polygamy struck at the heart of a morality based on the inspiring influence of woman's affections: "It renders man coarse, tyrannical, brutal, and heartless. It deals death to all sentiments of true manhood. It enslaves and ruins woman. It crucifies every God-given feeling of her nature."[37] Some anti-Mormons concluded that plural marriage could only have been established among foreigners who had never learned to respect women. But the more common explanation was that the false ideology of Mormonism had deadened the moral sense and liberated man's wild sexual impulse from the normal restraints of civilization. Such degradation of women and corruption of man served to highlight the importance of democratic marriage, a respect for women, and careful cultivation of the finer sensibilities.[38]

But if nativist literature was a medium for articulating common values and exhorting individuals to transcend self-interest and join in a dedicated union against evil, it also performed a more subtle function. Why, we may ask, did nativist literature dwell so persistently on themes of brutal sadism and sexual immorality'? Why did its authors describe sin in such minute details, endowing even the worst offenses of their enemies with a certain fascinating appeal?

Freemasons, it was said, could commit any crime and indulge any passion when "upon the square," and Catholics and Mormons were even less inhibited by internal moral restraints. Nativists expressed horror over this freedom from conscience and conventional morality, but they could not conceal a throbbing note of envy. What was it like to be a member of a cohesive brotherhood that casually abrogated the laws of God and man, enforcing unity and obedience with dark and mysterious powers? As nativists speculated on this question, they projected their own fears and desires into a fantasy of licentious orgies and fearful punishments.

Such a projection of forbidden desires can be seen in the exaggeration of the stereotyped enemy's powers, which made him appear at times as a virtual superman. Catholic and Mormon leaders, never hindered by conscience or respect for traditional morality, were curiously superior to ordinary Americans in cunning, in exercising power over others, and especially in captivating gullible women.[39] It was an ancient theme of anti-Catholic literature that friars and priests were somehow more potent and sexually attractive than married laymen, and were thus astonishingly successful at seducing supposedly virtuous wives.[40] Americans were cautioned repeatedly that no priest recognized Protestant marriages as valid, and might consider any wife legitimate prey.[41] Furthermore, priests had access to the pornographic teachings of Dens and Liguori, sinister names that aroused the curiosity of anti-Catholics, and hence learned subtle techniques of seduction perfected over the centuries. Speaking with the authority of an ex-priest, William Hogan described the shocking result: "I have seen husbands unsuspiciously and hospitably entertaining the very priest who seduced their wives in the confessional, and was the parent of some of the children who sat at the same table with them, each of the wives unconscious of the other's guilt, and the husbands of both, not even suspecting them."[42] Such blatant immorality was horrifying, but everyone was apparently happy in this domestic scene, and we may suspect that the image was not entirely repugnant to husbands who, despite their respect for the Lord's Commandments, occasionally coveted their neighbors' wives.

The literature of counter-subversion could also embody the somewhat different projective fantasies of women. Ann Eliza Young dramatized her seduction by the Prophet Brigham, whose almost superhuman powers enchanted her and paralyzed her will. Though she submitted finally only because her parents were in danger of being ruined by the Church, she clearly indicated that it was an exciting privilege to be pursued by a Great Man.[43] When Anti-Mormons claimed that Joseph Smith and other prominent Saints knew the mysteries of Animal Magnetism, or were endowed with the highest degree of "amativeness" in their phrenological makeup, this did not detract from their covert appeal.[44] In a ridiculous fantasy written by Maria Ward, such alluring qualities were extended even to Mormon women. Many bold-hearted girls could doubtless identify themselves with Anna Bradish, a fearless Amazon of a creature, who rode like a man; killed without compunction, and had no pity for weak women who failed to look out for themselves. Tall, elegant, and "intellectual," Anna was attractive enough to arouse the insatiable desires of Brigham Young, though she ultimately rejected him and renounced Mormonism.[45]

While nativists affirmed their faith in Protestant monogamy, they obviously took pleasure in imagining the variety of sexual experience supposedly available to their enemies. By picturing themselves exposed to similar temptations, they assumed they could know how priests and Mormons actually sinned.[46] Imagine, said innumerable anti-Catholic writers, a beautiful young woman kneeling before an ardent young priest in a deserted room. As she confesses, he leans over, looking into her eyes, until their heads are nearly touching. Day after day she reveals to him her innermost secrets, secrets she would not think of unveiling to her parents, her dearest friends, or even her suitor. By skillful questioning the priest fills her mind with immodest and even sensual ideas, "until this wretch has worked up her passions to a tension almost snapping, and then becomes his easy prey." How could any man resist such provocative temptations, and how could any girl's virtue withstand such a test?[47]

We should recall that this literature was written in a period of increasing anxiety and uncertainty over sexual values and the proper role of woman. As ministers and journalists pointed with alarm at the spread of prostitution, the incidence of divorce, and the lax and hypocritical morality of the growing cities, a discussion of licentious subversives offered a convenient means for the projection of guilt as well as desire. The sins of individuals, or of the nation as a whole, could be pushed off upon the shoulders of the enemy and there punished in righteous anger.[48]

Specific instances of such projection are not difficult to find. John C. Bennett, whom the Mormons expelled from the Church as a result of his flagrant sexual immorality, invented the fantasy of "The Mormon Seraglio" which persisted in later anti-Mormon writings. According to Bennett, the Mormons maintained secret orders of beautiful prostitutes who were mostly reserved for various officials of the Church. He claimed, moreover, that any wife refusing to accept polygamy might be forced to join the lowest order and thus become available to any Mormon who desired her.[49]

Another example of projection can be seen in the letters of a young lieutenant who stopped in Utah in 1854 on his way to California. Convinced that Mormon women could be easily seduced, the lieutenant wrote frankly of his amorous adventures with a married woman. "Everybody has got one," he wrote with obvious pride, "except the Colonel and Major. The Doctor has got three – mother and two daughters. The mother cooks for him and the daughters sleep with him." But though he described Utah as "a great country," the lieutenant waxed indignant over polygamy, which he condemned as self-righteously as any anti-Mormon minister: "To see one man openly parading half a dozen or more women to church . . . is the devil according to my ideas of morality virtue and decency."[50]

If the consciences of many Americans were troubled by the growth of red light districts in major cities, they could divert their attention to the "legalized brothels" called nunneries, for which no one was responsible but lecherous Catholic priests. If others were disturbed by the moral implications of divorce, they could point in horror at the Mormon elder who took his quota of wives all at once. The literature of counter-subversion could thus serve the double purpose of vicariously fulfilling repressed desires, and of releasing the tension and guilt arising from rapid social change and conflicting values.

Though the enemy's sexual freedom might at first seem enticing, it was always made repugnant in the end by associations with perversion or brutal cruelty. Both Catholics and Mormons were accused of practicing nearly every form of incest.[51] The persistent emphasis on this theme might indicate deep-rooted feelings of fear and guilt, but it also helped demonstrate, on a more objective level, the loathsome consequences of unrestrained lust. Sheer brutality and a delight in human suffering were supposed to be the even more horrible results of sexual depravity. Masons disemboweled or slit the throats of their victims; Catholics cut unborn infants from their mothers' wombs and threw them to the dogs before their parents' eyes; Mormons raped and lashed recalcitrant women, or seared their mouths with red-hot irons.[52] This obsession with details of sadism, which reached pathological proportions in much of the literature, showed a furious determination to purge the enemy of every admirable quality. The imagined enemy might serve at first as an outlet for forbidden desires, but nativist authors escaped from guilt by finally making him an agent of unmitigated aggression. In such a role the subversive seemed to deserve both righteous anger and the most terrible punishments.

The nativist escape from guilt was more clearly revealed in the themes of confession and conversion. For most American Protestants the crucial step in anyone's life was a profession of true faith resulting from a genuine religious experience. Only when a man became conscious of his inner guilt, when he struggled against the temptations of Satan, could he prepare his soul for the infusion of the regenerative spirit. Those most deeply involved in sin often made the most dramatic conversions. It is not surprising that conversion to nativism followed the same pattern, since nativists sought unity and moral certainty in the regenerative spirit of nationalism. Men who had been associated in some way with un-American conspiracies were not only capable of spectacular confessions of guilt, but were best equipped to expose the insidious work of supposedly harmless organizations. Even those who lacked such an exciting history of corruption usually made some confession of guilt, though it might involve only a previous indifference to subversive groups. Like ardent Christians, nativists searched in their own experiences for the meanings of sin, delusion, awakening to truth, and liberation from spiritual bondage. These personal confessions proved that one had recognized and conquered evil, and also served as ritual cleansings preparatory to full acceptance in a group of dedicated patriots.

Anti-Masons were perhaps the ones most given to confessions of guilt and most alert to subtle distinctions of loyalty arid disloyalty. Many leaders of this movement, expressing guilt over their own "shameful experience and knowledge" of Masonry, felt a compelling obligation to exhort their former associates to "come out, and be separate from masonic abominations."[53] Even when an anti-Mason could say with John Quincy Adams that "I am not, never was, and never shall be a Freemason," he would often admit that he had once admired the Order, or had even considered applying for admission.[54]

Since a willingness to sacrifice oneself was an unmistakable sign of loyalty and virtue, ex-Masons gloried in exaggerating the dangers they faced and the harm that their revelations supposedly inflicted on the enemy. In contrast to hardened Freemasons, who refused to answer questions in court concerning their fraternal associations, the seceders claimed to reveal the inmost secrets of the Order, and by so doing to risk property, reputation, and life.[55] Once the ex-Mason had dared to speak the truth, his character would surely be maligned, his motives impugned, and his life threatened. But, he declared, even if he shared the fate of the illustrious Morgan, he would die knowing that he had done his duty.

Such self-dramatization reached extravagant heights in the ranting confessions of many apostate Catholics and Mormons. Maria Monk and her various imitators told of shocking encounters with sin in its most sensational forms, of bondage to vice and superstition, and of melodramatic escapes from popish despotism. A host of "ex-Mormon wives" described their gradual recognition of Mormon frauds and iniquities, the anguish and misery of plural marriage, and their breath-taking flights over deserts or mountains. The female apostate was especially vulnerable to vengeful retaliation, since she could easily be kidnapped by crafty priests and nuns, or dreadfully punished by Brigham Young's Destroying Angels.[56] At the very least, her reputation could be smirched by foul lies and insinuations. But her willingness to risk honor and life for the sake of her country and for the dignity of all womankind was eloquent proof of her redemption. What man could be assured of so noble a role?

The apostate's pose sometimes assumed paranoid dimensions.

William Hogan warned that only the former priest could properly gauge the Catholic threat to American liberties and saw himself as providentially appointed to save his Protestant countrymen. "For twenty years," he wrote, "I have warned them of approaching danger, but their politicians were deaf, and their Protestant theologians remained religiously coiled up in fancied security, overrating their own powers and undervaluing that of Papists." Pursued by vengeful Jesuits, denounced and calumniated for alleged crimes, Hogan pictured himself single-handedly defending American freedom: "No one, before me, dared to encounter their scurrilous abuse. I resolved to silence them; and I have done so. The very mention of my name is a terror to them now." After surviving the worst of Catholic persecution, Hogan claimed to have at last aroused his countrymen and to have reduced the hierarchy to abject terror.[57]

As the nativist searched for participation in a noble cause, for unity in a group sanctioned by tradition and authority, he professed a belief in democracy and equal rights. Yet in his very zeal for freedom he curiously assumed many of the characteristics of the imagined enemy. By condemning the subversive's fanatical allegiance to an ideology, he affirmed a similarly uncritical acceptance of a different ideology; by attacking the subversive's intolerance of dissent, he worked to eliminate dissent and diversity of opinion; by censuring the subversive for alleged licentiousness, he engaged in sensual fantasies; by criticizing the subversive's loyalty to an organization, he sought to prove his unconditional loyalty to the established order. The nativist moved even farther in the direction of his enemies when he formed tightly-knit societies and parties which were often secret and which subordinated the individual to the single purpose of the group. Though the nativists generally agreed that the worst evil of subversives was their subordination of means to ends, they themselves recommended the most radical means to purge the nation of troublesome groups and to enforce unquestioned loyalty to the state.

In his image of an evil group conspiring against the nation's welfare, and in his vision of a glorious millennium that was to dawn after the enemy's defeat, the nativist found satisfaction for many desires. His own interests became legitimate and dignified by fusion with the national interest, and various opponents became loosely associated with the un-American conspiracy. Thus Freemasonry in

New York State was linked in the nativist mind with economic and political interests that were thought to discriminate against certain groups and regions; southerners imagined a union of abolitionists and Catholics to promote unrest and rebellion among slaves; gentile businessmen in Utah merged anti-Mormonism with plans for exploiting mines and lands.

Then too the nativist could style himself as a restorer of the past, as a defender of a stable order against disturbing changes, and at the same time proclaim his faith in future progress. By focusing his attention on the imaginary threat of a secret conspiracy, he found an outlet for many irrational impulses, yet professed his loyalty to the ideals of equal rights and government by law. He paid lip service to the doctrine of laissez-faire individualism, but preached selfless dedication to a transcendent cause. The imposing threat of subversion justified a group loyalty and subordination of the individual that would otherwise have been unacceptable. In a rootless environment shaken by bewildering social change the nativist found unity and meaning by conspiring against imaginary conspiracies.

ENDNOTES

1. For an alternative to the method followed in this article, see John Higham's perceptive essay, "Another Look at Nativism," *Catholic Historical Review* (Washington), XLIV (July, 1958), 147-58. Higham rejects the ideological approach to nativism and stresses the importance of concrete ethnic tensions, "status rivalries," and face-to-face conflicts in explaining prejudice. Though much can be said for this sociological emphasis, as opposed to a search for irrational myths and stereotypes, the method suggested by Higham can easily lead to a simple "stimulus-response" view of prejudice. Awareness of actual conflicts in status and self-interest should not obscure the social and psychological functions of nativism, nor ·distract attention from themes that may reflect fundamental tensions within a culture.

2. For a brilliant analysis of Mormon-Gentile conflict, see Thomas F. O'Dea, *The Mormons* (Chicago, 1958).

3. Freemasons were blamed for various unrelated economic and political grievances, but anti-Masonry showed no uniform division according to class, occupation, or political affiliation. See Charles McCarthy, "The Anti-Masonic Party," American Historical Association, *Annual Report for the Year 1902*, Vol. I (Washington, 1903) ,370-73, 406-408. I am also indebted to Lorman A. Ratner, whose "Antimasonry in New York State: A Study in Pre ·Civil War Reform" (M.A thesis, Cornell University, 1958) substantiates this conclusion.

4. For a detailed analysis of the issues and development of anti-

Catholicism, see Ray A. Billington, *The Protestant Crusade, 1800-1860* (New York, 1938).

5. It should be noted, however, that national attention was attracted by the Mountain Meadows Massacre and by Albert Sidney Johnston's punitive expedition to Utah.

6. For anti-Catholic references in *The Book of Mormon,* see I Nephi 13 :4-9; II Nephi 6 :12, 28 :18. Parallels between Masons and the "Gadianton robbers" have been frequently discussed.

7. *Anti -Masonic Review and Magazine* (New York), II (October, 1829) , 225 ·34. It was even claimed that Jesuits had been protected by Frederick the Great because they were mostly Freemasons and shared the same diabolical designs. See *Free Masonry: A Poem, In Three Cantos, Accompanied with Notes, Illustrative of the History, Policy, Principles, Bc. of the Masonic Institution. Shewing the Coincidence of Its Spirit and Designwith Ancient Jesuitism ... By a Citizen of Massachusetts* (Leicester, Mass., 1830), 134.

8. William Hogan, *Popery! As It Was and as It Is: Also, Auricular Confession: and Popish Nunneries,* two books in one edition (Hartford, 1855), 32-33.

9. Jedidiah Morse, *A Sermon Preached at Charleston, November* 29, 1798, on *the Anniversary Thanksgiving in Massachusetts* (Boston, 1799); Vernon Stauffer, *The New England Clergy and the Bavarian Illuminati* (New York, 1918), 98-99, 233, 246-48.

10. In Ned Buntline's *The G'hals of New York* (New York, 1850) the Jesuits seem to be connected with all secret conspiracies, and their American leader, Father Kerwin, is probably modeled on Brown's Carwin. George Lippard admired Brown, dedicated a novel to him, and was also fascinated by secret societies and diabolical plots to enslave America. In *New York: Its Upper Ten and Lower Million* (New York, 1853), the Catholic leaders are Illuminati-like atheists who plan revolutions, manipulate public opinion, and stop at no crime in their lust for wealth and power. These amoral supermen were clearly inspired by such characters as Brown's Ormond, as well as by the anti-Catholic writings of Eugène Sue and others.

11. Though the term "nativist" is usually limited to opponents of immigration, it is used here to include anti-Masons and anti-Mormons. This seems justified in view of the fact that these alarmists saw themselves as defenders of native traditions and identified Masonry and Mormonism with forces alien to American life.

12. For a lucid and provocative discussion of this "restoration theme," see Marvin Meyers, *The Jacksonian Persuasion* (Stanford, 1957), 162-64.

13. Hiram B. Hopkins, *Renunciation of Free Masonry* (Boston, 1830), 4-7.

14. Jacob Lefever of Hagerstown appealed to regional loyalty and urged citizens of Maryland to forget their differences and unite against "foreign influence" from an area notorious for its "tricks and frauds," *Free-Masonry Unmasked: or Minutes of the Trial of a Suit in the Court of Common Pleas of Adams*

County, Wheren Thaddeus Stevens, Esq. Was Plaintiff, and Jacob Lefever, Defendant (Gettysburg, 1835), pp. xiii-xiv.

15. *The Cloven Foot: or Popery Aiming at Political Supremacy in the United States, By the Rector of Oldenwold* (New York, 1855), 170-79.

16. William Mulder and A. Russell Mortensen (eds.), *Among the Mormons: Historic Accounts by Contemporary Observers* (New York, 1958), 76·79. The quotation is from the minutes of an anti-Mormon meeting in Jackson County, Missouri, July 20, 1833.

17. John H. Beadle, *Life in Utah: or, the Mysteries and Crimes of Mormonism* (Philadelphia, [1872]), 5.

18. *Anti-Masonic Review,* I (December, 1828), 3-4.

19. Letter of May 4, 1831, printed in *The Anti-Masonic Almanac, for the Year 1832,* ed. by Edward Giddins (Utica, 1831), 29-30.

20. *Anti-Masonic Review,* I (December, 1828), 6·7; Lebbeus Armstrong, *Masonry Proved to Be a Work of Darkness, Repugnant to the Christian Religion; and Inimical to a Republican Government* (New York, 1830), 16.

21. *The Anti-Masonic Almanack, for the Year 1828: Calculated for the Horizon of Rochester, N.Y. by Edward Giddins* (Rochester, 1827), entry for November and December, 1828; Armstrong, *Masonry, 14.*

22. Hogan, *Popery, 32-33.*

23. Edward Beecher, *The Papal Conspiracy Exposed, and Protestantism Defended, in the Light of Reason, History, and Scripture* (Boston, 1855), 29.

24. *Anti-Masonic Review,* I (February, 1829), 71.

25. Mulder and Mortensen (eds.), *Among the Mormons, 407;* Jennie Anderson Froiseth (ed.), *The Women of Mormonism: or, the Story of Polygamy as Told by the Victims Themselves* (Detroit, 1881-1882), 367-68.

26. It is true that anti-Catholics sometimes stressed the inferiority of lower-class immigrants and that anti-Mormons occasionally claimed that Mormon converts were made among the most degraded and ignorant classes of Europe. This theme increased in importance toward the end of the century, but it seldom implied that Catholics and Mormons were physically incapable of being liberated and joined to the dominant group. Racism was not an original or an essential part of the counter-subversive's ideology. Even when Mormons were attacked for coarseness, credulity, and vulgarity, these traits were usually thought to be the product of their beliefs and institutions. See Mrs. B. G. Ferris, "Life among the Mormons," *Putnam's Monthly Magazine* (New York), VI (August, October, 1855), 144, 376-77.

27. Hogan, *Popery, 35.*

28. *Free Masonry: A Poem, 55-58.*

29. Hogan, *Popery,* 7-8; *Auricular Confession, 264-65.*

30. Froiseth (ed.), *Women of Mormonism,* 285-87, 291-92.

31. *Free Masonry: A Poem,* 29·37; *Anti-Masonic Review,* I (June, 1829), 203-207. The charge was often repeated that higher degrees of Freemasonry, were

created by the "school of Voltaire" and introduced to America by Jewish immigrants. Masonry was also seen as an "auxiliary to British foreign policy."

32. This question was most troubling to anti-Masons. Though some tried to side-step the issue by quoting Washington against "self-created societies," as if he had been referring to the Masons, others flatly declared that Washington had been hoodwinked, just as distinguished jurists had once been deluded by a belief in witchcraft. Of course Washington had been unaware of Masonic iniquities, but he had lent his name to the cause and had thus served as a decoy for the ensnarement of others. See *Free Masonry: A Poem*, 38; *Anti-Masonic Review*, I (January, 1829), 49, 54; *The Anti-Masonic Almanac, for the Year of the Christian Era 1830* (Rochester, 1829),32.

33. Beecher, *Papal Conspiracy Exposed, 39 1.*

34. Beadle, *Life in Utah*, 30-34.

35. *Ibid.,* 332-33. According to Beadle, religious error and sexual perversion were related "because the same constitution of mind and temperament which gives rise to one, powerfully predisposes toward the other."

36. *Cloven Foot*, 294-5.

37. Froiseth (ed.), *Women of Mormonism*, 113.

38. Though Horace Greeley was moderate in his judgment of Mormonism, he wrote: "I joyfully trust that the genius of the Nineteenth Century tends to a solution of the problem of Woman's sphere and destiny radically different from this," Quoted in Mulder and Mortensen (eds.), *Among the Mormons*, 328.

39. It should be noted that Freemasons were rarely accused of sexual crimes, owing perhaps to their greater degree of integration within American society, and to their conformity to the dominant pattern of monogamy. They were sometimes attacked, however, for excluding women from their Order, and for swearing not to violate the chastity of wives, sisters, and daughters of fellow Masons. Why, anti-Masons asked, was such an oath not extended to include *all* women? David Bernard, *Light on Masonry: A Collection of all the Most Important Documents on the Subject* (Utica, 1829), 62 n.

40. Anthony Gavin, *A Master-Key to Popery, Giving a Full Account of All the Customs of the Priests and Friars, and the Rites and Ceremonies of Popish Religion* (n.p., 1812), 70-72. Such traditional works of European anti-Catholicism were frequently reprinted and imitated in America.

41. *Cloven Foot*, 224. The Mormons were also alleged to regard the wives of infidels "lawful prey to any believer who can win them." Beadle, *Life in Utah*, 233.

42. Hogan, *Auricular Confession*, 289.

43. Ann Eliza Young, *Wife No. 19: or, the Story of a Life in Bondage, Being a Complete Expose of Mormonism* (Hartford, 1875), 433, 440-41, 453.

44. Maria Ward, *Female Life among the Mormons: A Narrative of Many Years' Personal Experience, By the Wife of a Mormon Elder, Recently Returned from Utah*

(New York, 1857), 24; Beadle, *Life in Utah, 339.*

45. Ward, *Female Life among the Mormons,* 68, 106, 374.

46. The Mormons, for instance, were imagined to engage in the most licentious practices in the Endowment House ceremonies. See Nelson W. Green (ed.), *Fifteen Years among the Mormons: Being the Narrative of Mrs. Mary Ettie V. Smith* (New York,1857), 44-51.

47. Hogan, *Auricular Confession,* 254-55; *Cloven Foot,* 301-304.

48. This point is ably discussed by Kimball Young, *Isn't One Wife Enough?* (New York,1954) ,26-27.

49. *Ibid.,* 311.

50. Quoted in Mulder and Mortensen (eds.),*Among the Mormons,* 274-78.

51. George Bourne, *Lorette: The History of Louise, Daughter of a Canadian Nun, Exhibiting the Interior of Female Convents* (New York, 1834), 176-77; Hogan, *Auricular. Confession,*271; Frances Stenhouse, *A Lady's Life among the Mormons: A Record of Personal Experience as One of the Wives of a Mormon Elder* (New York, 1872), 77.

52. *Anti.-Masonic Review,* I (December, 1828),24 if.; *Cloven Foot,* 325-42, 357-58; Froiseth (ed.), *Women of Mormonism,* 317-18; Ward, *Female Life among the Mormons,* 428-29.

53. Armstrong, *Masonry, 22.*

54. *Free Masonry: A Poem,* p. iv.

55. *Ibid .,* pp. iii, 51 ; Hopkins, *Renunciation of Free Masonry,* 5, 9-11; *Anti-Masonic Almanac, 1830,* pp. 28-29; Bernard, *Light on Masonry,* p. iii.

56. Stenhouse, *Lady's Life among the Mormons,* 142-43.

57. Hogan, *Auricular Confession,* 226-29, 233, 296-97.

In this wide ranging and abstract analysis, Simmel attempts to describe the ways in which secrecy binds and separates individuals within society. In his own words, he seeks to limn "the significance of secrecy for the structure of human reciprocities."

Like many sociologists working at the end of the nineteenth century, Simmel was particularly interested in the ways in which modernity, especially urbanization and industrialization, were reshaping Western societies. In this work, the author's concern with this topic is reflected in his discussion of the individual's integration into, or differentiation from, society. Simmel condescendingly refers repeatedly to Native Americans, Africans, and tribal groups as "nature people," thus signaling the cultural superiority claimed by Europeans at the advent of the twentieth century.

Albion W. Small, who translated this work into English, has occasionally retained Simmel's original German words within parentheses in the text to assist readers in grasping the intended meaning.

THE SOCIOLOGY OF SECRECY AND OF SECRET SOCIETIES[1]
Georg Simmel
1906
American Journal of Sociology. 11 (4)(Jan. 1906), 441-498.

ALL relationships of people to each other rest, as a matter of course, upon the precondition that they know something about each other. The merchant knows that his correspondent wants to buy at the lowest price and to sell at the highest price. The teacher knows that he may credit to the pupil a certain quality and quantity of information. Within each social stratum the individual knows approximately what measure of culture he has to presuppose in each other individual. In all relationships of a personally differentiated sort there develop, as we may affirm with obvious reservations, intensity and shading in the degree in which each unit reveals himself to the other through word and deed. How much error and sheer prejudice may lurk in all this knowing is immaterial. Just as our apprehension of external nature, along with its elusions and its inaccuracies, still attains that degree of truth which is essential for the life and progress of our species, so each knows the other with whom he has to do, in a rough and ready way, to the degree necessary in order that the needed kinds of intercourse may proceed. That we shall know with whom we have to do, is the first precondition of having anything to do with another. The customary reciprocal presentation, in the case of any somewhat protracted conversation, or in the case of contact upon the same social plane, although at first sight an empty form, is an excellent symbol of that reciprocal apprehension which is the presumption of every social relationship. The fact is variously concealed from consciousness, because, in the case of a very large number of relationships, only the quite typical tendencies and qualities need to be reciprocally recognized. Their necessity is usually observed only when they happen to be wanted. It would be a profitable scientific labor to investigate the sort and degree of reciprocal apprehension which is needed for the various relationships between human beings. It would be worth while to know how the general psychological presumptions with which each approaches each are interwoven with the special experiences with reference to the individual who is in juxtaposition with us; how in many ranges of association the reciprocal apprehension does or does not need to be equal, or may or may not be permitted to be equal; how conventional relationships are determined in their development only through that reciprocal or unilateral knowledge developing with reference to the other party. The investigation should finally proceed in the opposite direction; that is, it should inquire how our objectively psychological picture of others is influenced by the real relationships of practice and of sentiment between us. This latter problem by no means has reference to falsification. On the contrary, in a quite legitimate fashion, the theoretical conception of a given individual varies with the standpoint from which it is formed, which standpoint is given by the total relationship of the knower to the known. Since one never can absolutely know another, as this would mean knowledge of every particular thought and feeling; since we must rather form a conception of a personal unity out of the fragments of another person in which alone he is accessible to us, the unity so formed necessarily depends upon that portion of the other which our standpoint toward him permits us to see. These differences, however, by no means spring merely from differences in the quantity of the apprehension. No psychological knowledge is a mere mechanical echo of its object. It is rather, like knowledge of external nature, dependent upon the forms that the knowing mind brings to it, and in which it takes up the data. When we are concerned with apprehension of individual by individual, these forms are individually differentiated in a very high degree. They do not arrive at the scientific generality and super-subjective conclusiveness which are attainable in our knowledge of external nature, and of the typically individual psychic processes. If A has a different conception of M from that of B, this does not necessarily mean incompleteness or deception. On the contrary, the personality of A and the total circumstances of his relation to M being what they are, his picture of M is for him true, while for B a picture differing somewhat in its content may likewise be true. It is by no means correct to say that, over and above these two pictures, there is the objectively correct apprehension of M, by which the two are to be corrected according to, the measure of their agreement with it. Rather is the ideal truth which, to be sure, the actual picture of M in the conception of A approaches only asymptotically, that is as ideal, something different from that of B. It contains, as integrating organizing precondition, the psychical peculiarity of A and the special relationship into which A and M are brought, by virtue of their characteristics and their fortunes. Every relationship between persons causes a picture of each to take form in the mind of the other, and this picture evidently is in reciprocal relationship with that personal relationship. While this latter constitutes the presupposition, on the basis of which the conceptions each of the other take shape so and so, and with reference to which these conceptions possess actual truth for the given case, on the other hand the actual reciprocity of the individuals is based upon the picture which they derive of each other. Here we have one of the deep circuits of the intellectual life, inasmuch as one element presupposes a second, but the second presupposes the first. While this is a fallacy within narrow ranges, and thus makes the whole involved intellectual process unreliable, in more general and fundamental application it is the unavoidable expression of the unity in which these two elements coalesce, and which cannot be expressed in our forms of thought except as a building of the first upon the second, and at the same time of the second upon the first. Accordingly, our situations develop themselves upon the basis of a reciprocal knowledge of each other, and this knowledge upon the basis of actual situations, both inextricably interwoven, and, through their alternations within the reciprocal sociological process, designating the latter as one of the points at which reality and idea make their mysterious unity empirically perceptible.

In the presence of the total reality upon which our conduct is founded, our knowledge is characterized by peculiar limitations and aberrations. We cannot say in principle that "error is life and knowledge is death," because a being involved in persistent errors would continually act wide of the purpose, and would thus inevitably perish. At the same time, in view of our accidental and defective adaptations to our life-conditions, there is no doubt that we cherish not only so much truth, but also so much nescience, and attain to so much error as is useful for our practical purposes. We may call to mind in this connection the vast sums of human knowledge that modify human life, which, however, are overlooked or disregarded if the total cultural situation does not make these modifications possible and useful. At the other extreme, we may refer to the *Lebenslüge* of the individual, so often in need of illusion as to his powers and even as to his feelings, of superstition with reference to God as well as men, in order to sustain himself in his being and in his potentialities. In this psycho-biological respect error is co-ordinated with truth. The utilities of the external, as of the subjective, life provide that we get from the one as well as from the other precisely that which constitutes the basis of the conduct which is essential for us. Of course, this proposition holds only in the large, and with a wide latitude for variations and defective adaptations.

But there is within the sphere of objective knowledge, where there is room for truth and illusion, a definite segment in which both truth and illusion may take on a character nowhere else observed. The subjective, internal facts of the person with whom we are in contact present this area of knowledge. Our fellow-man either may voluntarily reveal to us the truth about himself, or by dissimulation he may deceive us as to the truth. No other object of knowledge can thus of its own initiative, either enlighten us with reference to itself or conceal itself, as a human being can. No other knowable object modifies its conduct from consideration of its being understood or misunderstood. This modification does not, of course, take place throughout the whole range of human relations. In many ways our fellow-man is also in principle only like a fragment of nature, which our apprehension, so to speak, holds fast in its grasp. In many respects, however, the situation is different, and our fellow-man of his own motion gives forth truth or error with reference to himself. Every lie, whatever its content, is in its essential nature a promotion of error with reference to the mendacious subject; for the lie consists in the fact that the liar conceals from the person to whom the idea is conveyed the true conception which he possesses. The specific nature of the lie is not exhausted in the fact that the person to whom the lie is told has a false conception of the fact. This is a detail in common with simple error. The additional trait is that the person deceived is held in misconception about the true intention of the person who tells the lie. Veracity and mendacity are thus of the most far-reaching significance for the relations of persons with each other. Sociological structures are most characteristically differentiated by the measure of mendacity that is operative in them. To begin with, in very simple relationships a lie is much more harmless for the persistence of the group than in complex associations. Primitive man, living in communities of restricted extent, providing for his needs by his own production or by direct co-operation, limiting his spiritual interests to personal experience or to simple tradition, surveys and controls the material of his existence more easily and completely than the man of higher culture. In the latter case life rests upon a thousand presuppositions which the individual can never trace back to their origins, and verify; but which he must accept upon faith and belief. In a much wider degree than people are accustomed to realize, modern civilized life -- from the economic system which is constantly becoming more and more a credit-economy, to the pursuit of science, in which the majority of investigators must use countless results obtained by others, and not directly subject to verification -- depends upon faith in the honor of others. We rest our most serious decisions upon a complicated system of conceptions, the majority of which presuppose confidence that we have not been deceived. Hence prevarication in modern circumstances becomes something much more devastating, something placing the foundations of life much more in jeopardy, than was earlier the case. If lying appeared today among us as a sin as permissible as among the Greek divinities, the Hebrew patriarchs, or the South Sea Islanders; if the extreme severity of the moral law did not veto it, the progressive up-building of modern life would be simply impossible, since modern life is, in a much wider than the economic sense, a "credit-economy." This relationship of the times recurs in the case of differences of other dimensions. The farther third persons are located from the center of our personality, the easier can we adjust ourselves practically, but also subjectively, to their lack of integrity. On the other hand, if the few persons in our immediate environment lie to us, life becomes intolerable. This banality must, nevertheless, be brought out to view, because it shows that the ratios of truthfulness and mendacity, which are reconcilable with the continuance of situations, form a scale that registers the ratios of the intensity of these relationships.

In addition to this relative sociological permissibility of lying in primitive conditions, we must observe a positive utility of the same. In cases where the first organization, stratification, and centralization of the group are in question, the process is accomplished by means of subjection of the weaker to the physically and mentally superior. The lie that succeeds - that is, which is not seen through - is without doubt a means of bringing mental superiority to expression, and of enabling it to guide and subordinate less crafty minds. It is a spiritual fist-law, equally brutal, but occasionally quite as much in place, as the physical species; for instance, as a selective agency for the breeding of intelligence; as a means of enabling a certain few, for whom others must labor, to secure leisure for production of the higher cultural good; or in order to furnish a means of leadership for the group forces. The more these purposes are accomplished by means which have fewer disagreeable consequences, the less is lying necessary, and the more room is made for consciousness of its ethical unworthiness. This process is by no means completed. The small trader still thinks that he cannot dispense with a certain amount of mendacious recommendations of his wares, and he acts accordingly without compunctions of conscience. Wholesale and retail trade on a large scale have passed this stadium, and they are accordingly able to act in accordance with complete integrity in marketing their goods. So soon as the methods of doing business among small traders, and those of the middle class, have reached a similar degree of perfection, the exaggerations and actual falsifications, in advertising and recommending goods, which are today in general not resented in those kinds of business, will fall under the same ethical condemnation which is now passed in the business circles just referred to. Commerce built upon integrity will be in general the more advantageous within a group, in the degree in which the welfare of the many rather than that of the few sets the group standard. For those who are deceived -- that is, those placed at a disadvantage by the lie -- will always be in the majority as compared with the liar who gets his advantage from the lie. Consequently that enlightenment which aims at elimination of the element of deception from social life is always of a democratic character.

Human intercourse rests normally upon the condition that the mode of thought among the persons associated has certain common characteristics; in other words, that objective spiritual contents constitute the common material, which is developed in its individual phases in the course of social contacts. The type and the most essential vehicle of this community of spiritual content is common language. If we look a little closer, however, the common basis here referred to consists by no means exclusively of that which all equally know, or, in a particular case, of that which the one accepts as the spiritual content of the other; but this factor is shot through by another, viz., knowledge which the one associate possesses, while the other does not. If there were such a thing as complete reciprocal transparency, the relationships of human beings to each other would be modified in a quite unimaginable fashion. The dualism of human nature, by reason of which every manifestation of it has its sources in numerous origins that may be far distant from each other, and every quantity is estimated at the same time as great or small, according as it is contemplated in connection with littleness or greatness, makes it necessary to think of sociological relationships in general dualistically; that is, concord, harmony, mutuality, which count as the socializing forces proper, must be interrupted by distance, competition, repulsion, in order to produce the actual configuration of society. The strenuous organizing forms which appear to be the real constructors of society, or to construct society as such, must be continually disturbed, unbalanced, and detached by individualistic and irregular forces, in order that their reaction and development may gain vitality by alternate concession and resistance. Relationships of an intimate character, the formal vehicle of which is psycho-physical proximity, lose the charm, and even the content, of their intimacy, unless the proximity includes, at the same time and alternately, distance and intermission. Finally — and this is the matter with which we are now concerned — the reciprocal knowledge, which is the positive condition of social relationships, is not the sole condition. On the contrary, such as those relationships are, they actually presuppose also a certain nescience, a ratio, that is immeasurably variable to be sure, of reciprocal concealment. The lie is only a very rude form, in the last analysis often quite self-contradictory, in which this necessity comes to the surface. However frequently lying breaks up a social situation, yet, so long as it existed, a lie may have been an integrating element of its constitution. We must take care not to be misled, by the ethically negative value of lying, into error about the direct positive sociological significance of untruthfulness, as it appears in shaping certain concrete situations. Moreover, lying in connection with the elementary sociological fact here in question -- viz., the limitation of the knowledge of one associate by another -- is only one of the possible means, the positive and aggressive technique, so to speak, the purpose of which in general is obtained through sheer secrecy and concealment. The following discussion has to do with these more general and negative forms. Before we come to the question of secrecy as consciously willed concealment, we should notice in what various degrees different circumstances involve disregard of reciprocal knowledge by the members of associations. Among those combinations which involve some degree of direct reciprocity on the part of their members, those which are organized for a special purpose are first in eliminating this element of reciprocal knowledge. Among these purposeful organizations, which in principle still involve direct reciprocity, the extreme in the present particular is represented by those in which utterly objective performances of the members are in view. This situation is best typified by the cases in which the contribution of so much cash represents the participation of the individuals in the activities of the group. In such instances reciprocity, coherence, and common pursuit of the purpose by no means rest upon psychological knowledge of the one member by the others. As member of the group the individual is exclusively the agent of a definite performance; and whatever individual motive may impel him to this activity, or whatever may be the total characteristics of his conduct as a whole, is in this connection a matter of complete indifference. The organization for a special purpose (*Zweckverband*) is the peculiarly discreet sociological formation; its members are in psychological respects anonymous; and, in order to form the combination, they need to know of each other only that they form it. Modern culture is constantly growing more objective. Its tissues grow more and more out of impersonal energies, and absorb less and less the subjective entirety of the individual. In this respect the hand laborer and the factory laborer furnish the antithesis which illustrates the difference between past and present social structure. This objective character impresses itself also upon sociological structure, so that combinations into which formerly the entire and individual person entered, and which consequently demanded reciprocal knowledge beyond the immediate content of the relationship, are now founded exclusively on this content in its pure objectivity.

By virtue of the situation just noticed, that antecedent or consequent form of knowledge with reference to an individual -- viz., confidence in him, evidently one of the most important synthetic forces within society -- gains a peculiar evolution. Confidence, as the hypothesis of future conduct, which is sure enough to become the basis of practical action, is, as hypothesis, a mediate condition between knowing and not knowing another person. The possession of full knowledge does away with the need of trusting, while complete absence of knowledge makes trust evidently impossible.[2] Whatever quantities of knowing and not knowing must commingle, in order to make possible the detailed practical decision based upon confidence, will be determined by the historic epoch, the ranges of interests, and the individuals. The objectification of culture referred to above has sharply differentiated the amounts of knowing and not knowing essential as the condition of confidence. The modern merchant who enters into a transaction with another, the scholar who undertakes an investigation with another, the leader of a political party who makes an agreement with the leader of another party with reference to an election, or the handling of a proposed bill -- all these, with exceptions and modifications that need not be further indicated, know, with reference to their associates, precisely what it is necessary to know for the purposes of the relationship in question. The traditions and institutions, the force of public opinion, and the circumscription of the situation, which unavoidably prejudice the individual, are so fixed and reliable that one only needs to know certain externalities with reference to the other in order to have the confidence necessary for the associated action. The basis of personal qualities, from which in principle a modification of attitude within the relationship could spring, is eliminated from consideration. The motivation and the regulation of this conduct has become so much a matter of an impersonal program that it is no longer influenced by that basis, and confidence no longer depends upon knowledge of that individual element. In more primitive, less differentiated relationships, knowledge of one's associates was much more necessary in personal respects, and much less in respect to their purely objective reliability. Both factors belong together. In order that, in case of lack in the latter respect, the necessary confidence may be produced, there is need of a much higher degree of knowledge of the former sort.

That purely general objective knowledge of a person, beyond which everything that is strictly individual in his personality may remain a secret to his associates, must be considerably reinforced in the knowledge of the latter, whenever the organization for a specific purpose to which they belong possesses an essential significance for the total existence of its members. The merchant who sells grain or oil to another needs to know only whether the latter is good for the price. The moment, however, that he associates another with himself as a partner, he must not merely know his standing as to financial assets, and certain quite general qualities of his make-up, but he must see through him very thoroughly as a personality; he must know his moral standards, his degree of companionability, his daring or prudent temperament; and upon reciprocal knowledge of that sort must depend not merely the formation of the relationship, but its entire continuance, the daily associated actions, the division of functions between the partners, etc. The secret of personality is in such a case sociologically more restricted. On account of the extent to which the common interest is dependent upon the personal quality of the associates, no extensive self-existence is in these circumstances permitted to the personality of the individual.

Beyond the organizations for distinct purposes, but in like manner beyond the relationships rooted in the total personality, stands the relationship, highly significant sociologically, which is called, in the higher strata of culture, "acquaintance." That persons are "acquainted" with each other signifies in this sense by no means that they know each other reciprocally; that is, that they have insight into that which is peculiarly personal in the individuality. It means only that each has, so to speak, taken notice of the existence of the other. As a rule, the notion of acquaintanceship in this sense is associated only with mere mentioning of the name, the "presentation." Knowledge of the *that*, not of the *what*, of the personality distinguishes the "acquaintanceship." In the very assertion that one is acquainted with a given person, or even well acquainted with him, one indicates very distinctly the absence of really intimate relationships. In such case one knows of the other only his external characteristics. These may be only those that are on exhibit in social functions, or they may be merely those that the other chooses to exhibit to us. The grade of acquaintanceship denoted by the phrase "well acquainted with another" refers at the same time not to the essential characteristics of the other, not to that which is most important in his inmost nature, but only to that which is characteristic in the aspect presented to the world. On that account, acquaintanceship in this polite sense is the peculiar seat of "discretion." This attitude consists by no means merely in respect for the secret of the other - that is, for his direct volition to conceal from us this or that. It consists rather in restraining ourselves from acquaintance with all of those facts in the conditions of another which he does not positively reveal. In this instance the particulars in question are not in principle distinctly defined as forbidden territory. The reference is rather to that quite general reserve due to the total personality of another, and to a special form of the typical antithesis of the imperatives; viz.: what is not forbidden is permitted, and, what is not permitted is forbidden. Accordingly, the relationships of men are differentiated by the question of knowledge with reference to each other: what is not concealed may be known, and what is not revealed may yet not be known. The last determination corresponds to the otherwise effective consciousness that an ideal sphere surrounds every human being, different in various directions and toward different persons; a sphere varying in extent, into which one may not venture to penetrate without disturbing the personal value of the individual. Honor locates such an area. Language indicates very nicely an invasion of this sort by such phrases as "coming too near" (*zu nahe treten*). The radius of that sphere, so to speak, marks the distance which a stranger may not cross without infringing upon another's honor. Another sphere of like form corresponds to that which we designate as the "significance" (*Bedeutung*) of another personality. Towards the "significant" man there exists an inner compulsion to keep one's distance. Even in somewhat intimate relationships with him this constraint does not disappear without some special occasion; and it is absent only in the case of those who are unable to appreciate the "significance." Accordingly, that zone of separation does not exist for the valet, because for him there is no "hero." This, however, is the fault, not of the hero, but of the valet. Furthermore, all intrusiveness is bound up with evident lack of sensitiveness for the scale of significance among people. Whoever is intrusive toward a significant personality does not, as it might superficially appear, rate that person high or too high; but on the contrary, he gives evidence of lacking capacity for appropriate respect. As the painter often emphasizes the significance of one figure in a picture that includes many persons, by grouping the rest at a considerable distance from the important figure, so, there is a sociological parallel in the significance of distance, which holds another outside of a definite sphere filled by the personality with its power, its will, and its greatness. A similar circuit, although quite different in value, surrounds the man in the setting of his affairs and his qualities. To penetrate this circuit by curiosity is a violation of his personality. As material property is at the same time an extension of the ego -- property is precisely that which obeys the will of the possessor, as, in merely graduated difference, the body is our first "property" (*Besitz*) -- and as on that account every invasion of this possession is resented as a violation of the personality; so there is a spiritual private property, to invade which signifies violation of the ego, at its center. Discretion is nothing other than the sense of justice with respect to the sphere of the intimate contents of life. Of course, this sense is various in its extension in connection with different personalities, just as the sense of honor and of personal property has a quite different radius with reference to the persons in one's immediate circle from that which it has toward strangers and indifferent persons. In the case of the above-mentioned social relationships in the narrower sense, as most simply expressed in the term "acquaintanceship," we have to do immediately with a quite typical boundary, beyond which perhaps no guarded secrets lie; with reference to which, however, the outside party, in the observance of conventional discretion, does not obtrude by questions or otherwise.

The question where this boundary lies is, even in principle, by no means easy to answer. It leads rather into the finest meshes of social forms. The right of that spiritual private property just referred to can no more be affirmed in the absolute sense than that of material property. We know that in higher societies the latter, with reference to the three essential sides, creation, security, and productiveness, never rests merely upon the personal agency of the individual. It depends, also upon the conditions and powers of the social environment; and consequently its limitations, whether through the prohibitions that affect the mode of acquiring property, or through taxation, are from the beginning the right of the whole. This right, however, has a still deeper basis than the principle of service and counter-service between society and the individual. That basis is the much more elementary one, that the part must subject itself to so much limitation of its self-sufficiency as is demanded by the existence and purposes of the whole. The same principle applies to the subjective sphere of personality. In the interest of association, and of social coherence, each must know certain things with reference to the other; and this other has not the right to resist this knowledge from the moral standpoint, and to demand the discretion of the other; that is, the undisturbed possession of his being and consciousness, in cases in which discretion would prejudice social interests. The business man who enters into a contractual obligation with another, covering a long future; the master who engages a servant; and, on the other hand, this latter, before he agrees to the servile relationship; the superintendent who is responsible for the promotion of a subordinate; the head of a household who admits a new personality into her social circle -- all these must have the right to trace out or to combine everything with reference to the past or the present of the other parties in question, with reference to their temperament, and their moral make-up, that would have any relation to the conclusion or the rejection of the proposed relationship. These are quite rough cases in which the beauty of discretion -- that is, of refraining from knowledge of everything which the other party does not voluntarily reveal to us-- must yield to the demands of practical necessity. But in finer and less simple form, in fragmentary passages of association and in unuttered revelations, all commerce of men with each other rests upon the condition that each knows something more of the other than the latter voluntarily reveals to him; and in many respects this is of a sort the knowledge of which, if possible, would have been prevented by the party so revealed. While this, judged as an individual affair, may count as indiscretion, although in the social sense it is necessary as a condition for the existing closeness and vitality of the interchange, yet the legal boundary of this invasion upon the spiritual private property of another is extremely difficult to draw. In general, men credit themselves with the right to know everything which, without application of external illegal means, through purely psychological observation and reflection, it is possible to ascertain. In point of fact, however, indiscretion exercised in this way may be quite as violent, and morally quite as unjustifiable, as listening at keyholes and prying into the letters of strangers. To anyone with fine psychological perceptions, men betray themselves and their inmost thoughts and characteristics in countless fashions, not only in spite of efforts not to do so, but often for the very reason that they anxiously attempt to guard themselves. The greedy spying upon every unguarded word; the boring persistence of inquiry as to the meaning of every slight action, or tone of voice; what may be inferred from such and such expressions; what the blush at the mention of a given name may betray -- all this does, not overstep the boundary of external discretion; it is entirely the labor of one's own mind, and therefore apparently within the unquestionable rights of the agent. This is all the more the case, since such misuse of psychological superiority often occurs as a purely involuntary procedure. Very often it is impossible for us to restrain our interpretation of another, our theory of his subjective characteristics and intentions. However positively an honorable person may forbid himself to practice such cogitation with reference to the unrevealed traits of another, and such exploiting of his lack of foresight and defenselessness, a knowing process often goes on with reference to another so automatically, its result often presents itself so suddenly and unavoidably, that the best intention can do nothing to prevent it. Where the unquestionably forbidden may thus be so unavoidable, the division line between the permitted and the non-permitted is the more indefinite. To what extent discretion must restrain itself from mental handling "of all that which is its own," to what extent the interests of intercourse, the reciprocal interdependence of the members of the same group, limits this duty of discretion -- this is a question for the answer to, which neither moral tact, nor survey of the objective relationships and their demands, can alone be sufficient, since both factors must rather always work together. The nicety and complexity of this question throw it back in a much higher degree upon the responsibility of the individual for decision, without final recourse to any authoritative general norm, than is the case in connection with a question of private property in the material sense.

In contrast with this preliminary form, or this attachment of secrecy, in which not the attitude of the person keeping the secret, but that of a third party, is in question, in which, in view of the mixture of reciprocal knowledge or lack of knowledge, the emphasis is on the amount of the former rather than on that of the latter -- in contrast with this, we come to an entirely new variation; that is, in those relationships which do not, like those already referred to, center around definitely circumscribed interests; but in relationships which, at least in their essential idea, rest upon the whole extension of the personalities concerned. The principal types in this category are friendship and marriage. The ideal of friendship that has come down from antique tradition, and singularly enough has been developed directly in the romantic sense, aims at absolute spiritual confidence, with the attachment that material possession also shall be a resource common to the friends. This entrance of the entire undivided ego into the relationship may be the more plausible in friendship than in love, for the reason that, in the case of friendship, the one-sided concentration upon a single element is lacking, which is present in the other case on account of the sensuous factor in love. To be sure, through the circumstance that in the totality of possible grounds of attachment one assumes the headship, a certain organization of the relationship occurs, as is the case in a group with recognized leadership. A single strong factor of coherence often blazes out the path along which the others, otherwise likely to have remained latent, follow; and undeniably in the case of most men, sexual love opens the doors of the total personality widest; indeed, in the case of not a few, sexuality is the sole form in which they can give their whole ego; just as, in the case of the artist, the form of his art, whatever it may be, furnishes the only possibility of presenting his entire nature. This is to be observed with special frequency among women -- to be sure, the same thing is to be asserted in the case of the quite different "Christian love "-- namely, that they not only, because they love, devote their life and fortune without reserve; but that this at the same time is chemically dissolved in love, and only and entirely in its coloring, form, and temperature flows over upon the other. On the other hand, however, where the feeling of love is not expansive enough, where the other contents of the soul are not flexible enough, it may take place, as I indicated, that the predominance of the erotic nexus may suppress not only the practically moral, but also the spiritual, contacts that are outside of the erotic group. Consequently friendship, in which this intensity, but also this inequality of devotion, is lacking, may more easily attach the whole person to the whole person, may more easily break up the reserves of the soul, not indeed by so impulsive a process, but throughout a wider area and during a longer succession. This complete intimacy of confidence probably becomes, with the changing differentiation of men, more and more difficult. Perhaps the modern man has too much to conceal to make a friendship in the ancient sense possible; perhaps personalities also, except in very early years, are too peculiarly individualized for the complete reciprocality of understanding, to which always so much divination and productive phantasy are essential. It appears that, for this reason, the modern type of feeling inclines more to differentiated friendships; that is, to those which have their territory only upon one side of the personality at a time, and in which the rest of the personality plays no part. Thus a quite special type of friendship emerges. For our problem, namely, the degree of intrusion or of reserve within the friendly relationship, this type is of the highest significance. These differentiated friendships, which bind us to one man from the side of sympathy, to another from the side of intellectual community, to a third on account of religious impulses, to a fourth because of common experiences, present, in connection with the problem of discretion, or self-revelation and self-concealment, a quite peculiar synthesis. They demand that the friends reciprocally refrain from obtruding themselves into the range of interests and feelings not included in the special relationship in each case. Failure to observe this condition would seriously disturb reciprocal understanding. But the relationship thus bounded and circumscribed by discretion nevertheless has its sources at the center of the whole personality, in spite of the fact that it expresses itself only in a single segment of its periphery. It leads ideally toward the same depths of sentiment, and to the same capacity to sacrifice, which undifferentiated epochs and persons associate only with a community of the total circumference of life, with no question about reserves and discretions.

Much more difficult is measurement of self-revelation and reserve, with their correlates intrusiveness and discretion, in the case of marriage. In this relationship these forms are among the universal problems of the highest importance for the sociology of intimate associations. We are confronted with the questions, whether the maximum of reciprocality is attained in a relationship in which the personalities entirely resign to each other their separate existence, or quite the contrary, through a certain reserve -- whether they do not in a certain qualitative way belong to each other more if they belong to each other less quantitatively. These questions of ratio can of course, at the outset, be answered only with the further question: How is the boundary to be drawn, within the whole area of a person's potential communicability, at which ultimately the reserve and the respect of another are to begin? The advantage of modern marriage -- which, to be sure, makes both questions answerable only one case at a time -- is that this boundary is not from the start determined, as was the case in earlier civilizations. In these other civilizations marriage is, in principle, as a rule, not an erotic phenomenon, but merely a social-economic institution. The satisfaction of the instincts of love is only accidentally connected with it. With certain exceptions, the marriage is not on grounds of individual attraction, but rather of family policy, labor relationships, or desire for descendants. The Greeks, for example, carried this institution to the most extreme differentiation. Thus Demosthenes said: "We have *hetaerae* for our pleasure, concubines for our daily needs, but wives to give us lawful children and to care for the interior of the house." The same tendency to exclude from the community of marriage, *a priori*, certain defined life-contents, and by means of super-individual provisions, appears in the variations in the forms of marriage to be found in one and the same people, with possibility of choice in advance on the part of those contracting marriages. These forms are differentiated in various ways with reference to the economic, religious, legal, and other interests connected with the family. We might cite many nature-peoples, the Indians, the Romans, etc. No one will, of course, fail to observe that, also within modern life, marriage is, probably in the majority of cases, contracted from conventional or material motives; nevertheless, entirely apart from the frequency of its realization, the sociological idea of modern marriage is the community of all life-contents, in so far as they immediately, and through their effects, determine the value and the destiny of the personalities. Moreover, the prejudice of this ideal demand is by no means ineffective. It has often enough given place and stimulus for developing an originally very incomplete reciprocation into an increasingly comprehensive attachment. But, while the very indeterminateness of this process is the vehicle of the happiness and the essential vitality of the relationship, its reversal usually brings severe disappointments. If, for example, absolute unity is from the beginning anticipated, if demand and satisfaction recognize no sort of reserve, not even that which for all fine and deep natures must always remain in the hidden recesses of the soul, although they may think they open themselves entirely to each other — in such cases the reaction and disillusionment must come sooner or later.

In marriage, as in free relationships of analogous types, the temptation is very natural to open oneself to the other at the outset without limit; to abandon the last reserve of the soul equally with those of the body, and thus to lose oneself completely in another. This, however, usually threatens the future of the relationship. Only those people can without danger give themselves entirely to each other who *cannot possibly* give themselves entirely, because the wealth of their soul rests in constant progressive development, which follows every devotion immediately with the growth of new treasures. Complete devotion is safe only in the case of those people who have an inexhaustible fund of latent spiritual riches, and therefore can no more alienate them in a single confidence than a tree can give up the fruits of next year by letting go what it produces at the present moment. The case is quite different, however, with those people who, so to speak, draw from their capital all their betrayals of feeling and the revelations of their inner life; in whose case there is no further source from which to derive those elements which should not be revealed, and which are not to be disjoined from the essential ego. In such cases it is highly probable that the parties to the confidence will one day face each other empty-handed; that the Dionysian free-heartedness may leave behind a poverty which — unjustly, but not on that account with less bitterness — may so react as even to charge the enjoyed devotion with deception. We are so constituted that we not merely, as was remarked, need a certain proportion of truth and error as the basis of our life, but also a similar mixture of definiteness and indefiniteness in the picture of our life-elements. That which we can see through plainly to its last ground shows us therewith the limit of its attraction, and forbids our phantasy to do its utmost in adding to the reality. For this loss no literal reality can compensate us, because the action of the imagination of which we are deprived is self-activity, which cannot permanently be displaced in value by any receptivity and enjoyment. Our friend should not only give us a cumulative gift, but also the possibility of conferring gifts upon him, with hopes and idealizations, with concealed beauties and charms unknown even to himself. The manner, however, in which we dispose of all this, produced by ourselves, but for his sake, is the vague horizon of his personality, the intermediate zone in which faith takes the place of knowledge. It must be observed that we have here to do by no means with mere illusions, or with optimistic or infatuated self-deception. The fact is rather that, if the utmost attractiveness of another person is to be preserved for us, it must be presented to us in part in the form of vagueness or impenetrability. This is the only substitute which the great majority of people can offer for that attractive value which the small minority possess through the inexhaustibility of their inner life and growth. The mere fact of absolute understanding, of having accomplished psychological exhaustion of the contents of relationship with another, produces a feeling of insipidity, even if there is no reaction from previous exaltation; it cripples the vitality of the relationship, and gives to its continuance an appearance of utter futility. This is the danger of that unbroken, and in a more than external sense shameless, dedication to which the unrestricted possibilities of intimate relationships seduce, which indeed is easily regarded as a species of obligation in those relationships. Because of this absence of reciprocal discretion, on the side of receiving as well as of giving, many marriages are failures. That is, they degenerate into vulgar habit, utterly bereft of charm, into a matter-of-course which retains no room for surprises. The fruitful depth of relationships which, behind every latest revelation, implies the still unrevealed, which also stimulates anew every day to gain what is already possessed, is merely the reward of that tenderness and self-control which, even in the closest relationship, comprehending the whole person, still respect the inner private property, which hold the right of questioning to be limited by a right of secrecy.

All these combinations are characterized sociologically by the fact that the secret of the one party is to a certain extent recognized by the other, and the intentionally or unintentionally concealed is intentionally or unintentionally respected. The intention of the concealment assumes, however, a quite different intensity so soon as it is confronted by a purpose of discovery. Thereupon follows that purposeful concealment, that aggressive defense, so to speak, against the other party, which we call secrecy in the most real sense. Secrecy in this sense— i.e., which is effective through negative or positive means of concealment— is one of the greatest accomplishments of humanity. In contrast with the juvenile condition in which every mental picture is at once revealed, every undertaking is open to everyone's view, secrecy procures enormous extension of life, because with publicity many sorts of purposes could never arrive at realization. Secrecy secures, so to speak, the possibility of a second world alongside of the obvious world, and the latter is most strenuously affected by the former. Every relationship between two individuals or two groups will be characterized by the ratio of secrecy that is involved in it. Even when one of the parties does not notice the secret factor, yet the attitude of the concealer, and consequently the whole relationship, will be modified by it. The historical development of society is in many respects characterized by the fact that what was formerly public passes under the protection of secrecy, and that, on the contrary, what was formerly secret ceases to require such protection and proclaims itself. This is analogous with that other evolution of mind in which movements at first executed consciously become unconsciously mechanical, and, on the other hand, what was unconscious and instinctive rises into the light of consciousness. How this development is distributed over the various formations of private and public life, how the evolution proceeds toward better-adapted conditions, because, on the one hand, secrecy that is awkward and undifferentiated is often far too widely extended, while, on the other hand, in many respects the usefulness of secrecy is discovered very late; how the quantum of secrecy has variously modified consequences in accordance with the importance or indifference of its content -- all this, merely in its form as questions, throws a flow of light upon the significance of secrecy for the structure of human reciprocities. In this connection we must not allow ourselves to be deceived by the manifold ethical negativeness of secrecy. Secrecy is a universal sociological form, which, as such, has, nothing to do with the moral valuations of its contents. On the one hand, secrecy may embrace the highest values: the refined shame of the lofty spirit, which covers up precisely its best, that it may not seem to seek its reward in praise or wage; for after such payment one retains the reward, but no longer the real value itself. On the other hand, secrecy is not in immediate interdependence with evil, but evil with secrecy. For obvious reasons, the immoral hides itself, even when its content encounters no social penalty, as, for example, many sexual faults. The essentially isolating effect of immorality as such, entirely apart from all primary social repulsion, is actual and important. Secrecy is, among other things, also the sociological expression of moral badness, although the classical aphorism, "No one is so bad that he also wants to seem bad," takes issue with the facts. Obstinacy and cynicism may often enough stand in the way of disguising the badness. They may even exploit it for magnifying the personality in the judgment of others, to the degree that sometimes immoralities which do not exist are seized upon as material for self-advertising. The application of secrecy as a sociological technique, as a form of commerce without which, in view of our social environment, certain purposes could not be attained, is evident without further discussion. Not so evident are the charms and the values which it possesses over and above its significance as a means, the peculiar attraction of the relation which is mysterious in form, regardless of its accidental content. In the first place, the strongly accentuated exclusion of all not within the circle of secrecy results in a correspondingly accentuated feeling of personal possession. For many natures possession acquires its proper significance, not from the mere fact of having, but besides that there must be the consciousness that others must forego the possession. Evidently this fact has its roots in our stimulability by contrast. Moreover, since exclusion of others from a possession may occur especially in the case of high values, the reverse is psychologically very natural, viz., that what is withheld from the many appears to have a special value. Accordingly, subjective possessions of the most various sorts acquire a decisive accentuation of value through the form of secrecy, in which the substantial significance of the facts concealed often enough falls into a significance entirely subordinate to the fact that others are excluded from knowing them. Among children a pride and self-glory often bases itself on the fact that the one can say to the others: "I know something that you don't know." This is carried to such a degree that it becomes a formal means of swaggering on the one hand, and of de-classing on the other. This occurs even when it is a pure fiction, and no secret exists. From the narrowest to the widest relationships, there are exhibitions of this jealousy about knowing something that is concealed from others. The sittings of the English Parliament were long secret, and even in the reign of George III reports of them in the press were liable to criminal penalties as violations of parliamentary privilege. Secrecy gives the person enshrouded by it an exceptional position; it works as a stimulus of purely social derivation, which is in principle quite independent of its casual content, but is naturally heightened in the degree in which the exclusively possessed secret is significant and comprehensive. There is also in this connection an inverse phenomenon, analogous with the one just mentioned. Every superior personality, and every superior performance, has, for the average of mankind, something mysterious. To be sure, all human being and doing spring from inexplicable forces. Nevertheless, within levels of similarity in quality and value, this fact does not make the one person a problem to another, especially because in respect to this equality a certain immediate understanding exists which is not a special function of the intellect. If there is essential inequality, this understanding cannot be reached, and in the form of specific divergence the general mysteriousness will be effective — somewhat as one who always lives in the same locality may never encounter the problem of the influence of the environment, which influence, however, may obtrude itself upon him so soon as he changes his environment, and the contrast in the reaction of feeling upon the life-conditions calls his attention to this causal factor in the situation. Out of this secrecy, which throws a shadow over all that is deep and significant, grows the logically fallacious, but typical, error, that everything secret is something essential and significant. The natural impulse to idealization, and the natural timidity of men, operate to one and the same end in the presence of secrecy; viz., to heighten it by phantasy, and to distinguish it by a degree of attention that published reality could not command.

Singularly enough, these attractions of secrecy enter into combination with those of its logical opposite; viz., treason or betrayal of secrets, which are evidently no less sociological in their nature. Secrecy involves a tension which, at the moment of revelation, finds its release. This constitutes the climax in the development of the secret; in it the whole charm of secrecy concentrates and rises to its highest pitch— just as the moment of the disappearance of an object brings out the feeling of its value in the most intense degree. The sense of power connected with possession of money is most completely and greedily concentrated for the soul of the spendthrift at the moment at which this power slips from his hands. Secrecy also is sustained by the consciousness that it *might be* exploited, and therefore confers power to modify fortunes, to produce surprises, joys, and calamities, even if the latter be only misfortunes to ourselves. Hence the possibility and the temptation of treachery plays around the secret, and the external danger of being discovered is interwoven with the internal danger of self-discovery, which has the fascination of the brink of a precipice. Secrecy sets barriers between men, but at the same time offers the seductive temptation to break through the barriers by gossip or confession. This temptation accompanies the psychical life of the secret like an overtone. Hence the sociological significance of the secret, its practical measure, and the mode of its workings must be found in the capacity or the inclination of the initiated to, keep the secret to himself, or in his resistance or weakness relative to the temptation to, betrayal. From the play of these two interests, in concealment and in revelation, spring shadings and fortunes of human reciprocities throughout their whole range. If, according to our previous analysis, every human relationship has, as one of its traits, the degree of secrecy within or around it, it follows that the further development of the relationship in this respect depends on the combining proportions of the retentive and the communicative energies— the former sustained by the practical interest and the formal attractiveness of secrecy as such, the latter by inability to, endure longer the tension of reticence, and by the superiority which is latent, so to speak, in secrecy, but which is actualized for the feelings only at the moment of revelation, and often also, on the other hand, by the joy of confession, which may contain that sense of power in negative and perverted form, as self-abasement and contrition.

All these factors, which determine the sociological role of secrecy, are of individualistic nature, but the ratio, in which the qualities and the complications of personalities form secrets depends at the same time upon the social structure upon which its life rests. In this connection the decisive element is that the secret is an individualizing factor of the first rank, and that in the typical double role; i.e., social relationships characterized by a large measure of personal differentiation permit and promote secrecy in a high degree, while, conversely, secrecy serves and intensifies such differentiation. In a small and restricted circuit, construction and preservation of secrets are technically difficult from the fact that each is too close to the circumstances of each, and that the frequency and intimacy of contacts carry with them too great temptation to disclose what might otherwise be hidden. But in this case there is no need of secrecy in a high degree, because this social formation usually tends to level its members, and every peculiarity of being, acting, or possessing the persistence of which requires secrecy is abhorrent to it. That all this changes to its opposite in case of large widening of the circle is a matter-of-course. In this connection, as in so many other particulars, the facts of monetary relationships reveal most distinctly the specific traits of the large circle. Since transfers of economic values have occurred principally by means of money, an otherwise unattainable secrecy is possible in such transactions. Three peculiarities of the money form of values are here important: first, its compressibility, by virtue of which it is possible to, make a man rich by slipping into his hand a check without attracting attention; second, its abstractness and absence of qualitative character, in consequence of which numberless sorts of acquisitions and transfers of possessions may be covered up and guarded from publicity in a fashion impossible so long as values could be possessed only as extended, tangible objects; third, its long-distance effectiveness, by virtue of which we may invest it in the most widely removed and constantly changing values, and thus withdraw it utterly from the view of our nearest neighbors. These facilities of dissimulation which inhere in the degree of extension in the use of money, and which disclose their dangers particularly in dealings with foreign money, have called forth, as protective provisions, publicity of the financial operations of corporations. This points to a closer definition of the formula of evolution discussed above; viz., that throughout the form of secrecy there occurs a permanent in- and out-flow of content, in which what is originally open becomes secret, and what was originally concealed throws off its mystery. Thus we might arrive at the paradoxical idea that, under otherwise like circumstances, human associations require a definite ratio of secrecy which merely changes its objects; letting go of one, it seizes another, and in the course of this exchange it keeps its quantum unvaried. We may even fill out this general scheme somewhat more exactly. It appears that with increasing telic characteristics of culture the affairs of people at large become more and more public, those of individuals more and more secret. In less developed conditions, as observed above, the circumstances of individual persons cannot protect themselves in the same degree from reciprocal prying and interfering as within modern types of life, particularly those that have developed in large cities, where we find a quite new degree of reserve and discretion. On the other hand, the public functionaries in undeveloped states envelop themselves in a mystical authority, while in maturer and wider relations, through extension of the range of their prerogatives, through the objectivity of their technique, through the distance that separates them from most of the individuals, a security and a dignity accrue to them which are compatible with publicity of their behavior. That earlier secrecy of public functions, however, betrayed its essential contradictoriness in begetting at once the counter-movements of treachery, on the one hand, and of espionage, on the other. As late as the seventeenth and eighteenth centuries, governments most anxiously covered up the amounts of public debts, the conditions of taxation, and the size of their armies. In consequence of this, ambassadors often had nothing better to do than to act as informers, to get possession of the contents of letters, and to prevail upon persons who were acquainted with valuable facts, even down to servants, to tattle their secrets.[3] In the nineteenth century, however, publicity takes possession of national affairs to such an extent that the governments themselves publish the official data without concealing, which no government would earlier have thought possible. Accordingly, politics, administration, justice, have lost their secrecy and inaccessibility in precisely the degree in which the individual has gained possibility of more complete privacy, since modern- life has elaborated a technique for isolation of the affairs of individuals, within the crowded conditions of great cities, possible in former times only by means of spatial separation.

To what extent this development is to be regarded as advantageous depends upon social standards of value. Democracies are bound to regard publicity as the condition desirable in itself. This follows from the fundamental idea that each should be informed about all the relationships and occurrences with which he is concerned, since this is a condition of his doing his part with reference to them, and every community of knowledge contains also the psychological stimulation to community of action. It is immaterial whether this conclusion is entirely binding. If an objective controlling structure has been built up, beyond the individual interests, but nevertheless to their advantage, such a structure may very well, by virtue of its formal independence, have a rightful claim to carry on a certain amount of secret functioning without prejudice to its *public* character, so far as real consideration of the interests of all is concerned. A logical connection, therefore, which would necessitate the judgment of superior worth in favor of the condition of publicity, does not exist. On the other hand, the universal scheme of cultural differentiation puts in an appearance here: that which pertains to the public becomes more public, that which belongs to the individual becomes more private. Moreover, this historical development brings out the deeper real significance: that which in its nature is public, which in its content concerns all, becomes also externally, in its sociological form, more and more public; while that which in its inmost nature refers to the self alone -- that is, the centripetal affairs of the individual -must also gain in sociological position a more and more private character, a more decisive possibility of remaining secret.

While secrecy, therefore, is a sociological ordination which characterizes the reciprocal relation of group elements, or rather in connection with other forms of reaction constitutes this total relation, it may further, with the formation of "secret societies," extend itself over the group as a whole. So long as the being, doing, and having of an individual persist as a secret, his general sociological significance is isolation, antithesis, egoistic individualization. In this case the sociological meaning of the secrecy is external; as relationship of him who has the secret to him who does not have it. So soon, however, as a group as such seizes upon secrecy as its form of existence, the sociological meaning of the secrecy becomes internal.

It now determines the reciprocal relations of those who possess the secret in common. Since, however, that relation of exclusion toward the uninitiated exists here also with its special gradations, the sociology of secret societies presents the complicated problem of ascertaining the immanent forms of a group which are determined by attitudes of secrecy on the part of the same toward other elements. I do not preface this part of the discussion with a systematic classification of secret societies, which would have only an external historical interest. The essential categories will appear at once.

The first internal relation that is essential to a secret society is the reciprocal *confidence* of its members. This element is needed in a peculiar degree, because the purpose of maintaining the secrecy is, first of all, protection. Most radical of all the protective provisions is certainly that of invisibility. At this point the secret society is distinguished in principle from the individual who seeks the protection of secrecy. This can be realized only with respect to specific designs or conditions; as a whole, the individual may hide himself temporarily, he may absent himself from a given portion of space; but, disregarding wholly abstruse combinations, his existence cannot be a secret. In the case of a societary unity, on the contrary, this is entirely possible. Its elements may live in the most frequent commerce, but that they compose a society -- a conspiracy, or a band of criminals, a religious conventicle, or an association for sexual extravagances -- may remain essentially and permanently a secret. This type, in which not the individuals but their combination is concealed, is sharply distinguished from the others, in which the social formation is unequivocally known, but the membership, or the purpose, or the special conditions of the combination are secrets; as, for instance, many secret bodies among the nature peoples, or the Freemasons. The form of secrecy obviously does not afford to the latter types the same unlimited protection as to the former, since what is known about them always affords a point of attack for further intrusion. On the other hand, these *relatively* secret societies always have the advantage of a certain variability. Because they are from the start arranged on the basis of a certain degree of publicity, it is easier for them to accommodate themselves to further betrayals than for those that are as societies entirely unavowed. The first discovery very often destroys the latter, because their secret is apt to face the alternative, whole or not at all. It is the weakness of secret societies that secrets do not remain permanently guarded. Hence we say with truth: "A secret that two know is no longer a secret." Consequently, the protection that such societies afford is in its nature, to be sure, absolute, but it is only temporary, and, for contents of positive social value, their commitment to the care of secret societies is in fact a transitional condition, which they no longer need after they have developed a certain degree of strength. Secrecy is finally analogous only with the protection which one secures by evading interruptions. It consequently serves only provisionally, until strength may be developed to cope with interruptions. Under these circumstances the secret society is the appropriate social form for contents which are at an immature stage of development, and thus in a condition peculiarly liable to injury from opposing interests. Youthful knowledge, religion, morality, party, is often weak and in need of defense. Hence each may find a recourse in concealment. Hence also there is a predestination of secret societies for periods in which new life-contents come into existence in spite of the opposition of the powers that be. The eighteenth century affords abundant illustrations. For instance, to cite only one example, the elements of the liberal party were present in Germany at that time. Their emergence in a permanent political structure was postponed by the power of the civic conditions. Accordingly, the secret association was the form in which the germs could be protected and cultivated, as in the case of the orders of the *Illumninati*. The same sort of protection which secrecy affords to ascending movements is also secured from it during their decline. Refuge in secrecy is a ready resort in the case of social endeavors and forces that are likely to be displaced by innovation. Secrecy is thus, so to speak, a transition stadium between being and not-being. As the suppression of the German communal associations began to occur, at the close of the Middle Ages, through the increasing power of the central governments, a wide-reaching secret life developed within these organizations. It was characterized by hidden assemblies and conferences, by secret enforcement of law, and by violence -- somewhat as animals seek the protection of concealment when near death. This double function of secrecy as a form of protection, to afford an intermediate station equally for progressing and for decaying powers, is perhaps most obvious in the case of religious movements. So long as the Christian communities were persecuted by the state, they were often obliged to withdraw their meetings, their worship, their whole existence, from public view. So soon, however, as Christianity had become the state religion, nothing was left for the adherents of persecuted, dying paganism than the same hiding of its cultus which it had previously forced upon the new faith. As a general proposition, the secret society emerges everywhere as correlate of despotism and of police control. It acts as protection alike of defense and of offense against the violent pressure of central powers. This is true, not alone in political relations, but in the same way within the church, the school, and the family.

Corresponding with this protective character of the secret society, as an external quality, is, as already observed, the inner quality of reciprocal confidence between the members. This is, moreover, a quite specific type of confidence, viz., in the ability to preserve silence. Social unities may rest, so far as their content is concerned, upon many sorts of presumption about grounds of confidence. They may trust, for example, to the motive of business interest, or to religious conviction, to courage, or to love, to the high moral tone, or − in the case of criminal combinations -- to the radical break with moral imperatives. When the society becomes secret, however, there is added to the confidence determined by the peculiar purposes of the society the further formal confidence in ability to keep still -- evidently a faith in the personality, which has, sociologically, a more abstract character than any other, because every possible common interest may be subsumed under it. More than that, exceptions excluded, no kind of confidence requires so unbroken subjective renewal; for when the uncertainty in question is faith in attachment or energy, in morality or intelligence, in sense of honor or tact, facts are much more likely to be observable which will objectively establish the degree of confidence, since they will reduce the probability of deception to a minimum. The probability of betrayal, however, is subject to the imprudence of a moment, the weakness or the agitation of a mood, the perhaps unconscious shading of an accentuation. The keeping of the secret is something so unstable, the temptations to betrayal are so manifold, in many cases such a continuous path leads from secretiveness to indiscretion, that unlimited faith in the former contains an incomparable preponderance of the subjective factor. For this reason those secret societies whose rudimentary forms begin with the secret shared by two, and whose enormous extension through all times and places has not even yet been appreciated, even quantitatively -- such societies have exerted a highly efficient disciplinary influence upon moral accountability among men. For there resides in confidence of men toward each other as high moral value as in the companion fact that this confidence is justified. Perhaps the former phenomenon is freer and more creditable, since a confidence reposed in us amounts almost to a constraining prejudice, and to disappoint it requires badness of a positive type. On the contrary, we "give" our faith in another. It cannot be delivered on demand, in the same degree in which it can be realized when spontaneously offered.

Meanwhile the secret societies naturally seek means psychologically to promote that secretiveness which cannot be directly forced. The oath, and threats of penalties, are here in the foreground and need no discussion. More interesting is the frequently encountered technique for teaching novices the art of silence. In view of the above-suggested difficulties of guarding the tongue absolutely, in view especially of the tell-tale connection which exists on primitive social planes between thought and expression -- among children and many nature peoples thinking and speaking are almost one -- there is need at the outset of learning silence once for all, before silence about any particular matter can be expected. Accordingly, we hear of a secret order in the Molucca Islands in which not merely silence about his experiences during initiation is enjoined upon the candidate, but for weeks he is not permitted to exchange a word on any subject with anybody, even in his own family. In this case we certainly have the operation not only of the educational factor of entire silence, but it corresponds with the psychical undifferentiation of this cultural level, to forbid speech in general in a period in which some particular silence must be insured. This is somewhat analogous with the fact that immature peoples easily employ the death penalty, where later for partial sins a partial punishment would be inflicted, or with the fact that similar peoples are often moved to offer a quite disproportionate fraction of their possessions for something that momentarily strikes their fancy. It is the specific "incapacity" (*Ungeschicklichkeit*) which advertises itself in all this; for its essence consists in its incompetence to undertake the particular sort of inhibition appropriate to endeavors after a strictly defined end. The unskilled person moves his whole arm where for his purpose it would be enough to move only two fingers, the whole body when a precisely differentiated movement of the arm would be indicated. In like manner, in the particular types of cases which we are considering, the preponderance of psychical commerce, which can, be a matter of logical and actual thought-exchange only upon a higher cultural level, both enormously increases the danger of volubility, and, on the other hand, leads far beyond prohibition of the specific act which would embarrass its purposes, and puts a ban on the whole function of which such act would be an incident. When, on the other hand, the secret society of the Pythagoreans prescribed silence for the novice during a number of years, it is probable that the aim went beyond mere pedagogical discipline of the members in the art of silence, not, however, with special reference to the clumsiness just alluded to, but rather with the aim of extending the differentiated purpose in its own peculiar direction; that is, the aim was not only to secure silence about specific things, but through this particular discipline the adept should acquire power to control himself in general. The society aimed at severe self-discipline and schematic purity of life, and whoever succeeded in keeping silence for years was supposed to be armed against seductions in other directions.

Another means of placing reticence upon an objective basis was employed by the Gallic druids. The content of their secrets was deposited chiefly in spiritual songs, which every druid had to commit to memory. This was so arranged, however — especially by prohibition of putting the songs in writing-- that an inordinate period was necessary for the purpose, in some cases twenty years. Through this long duration of pupilage, before anything considerable could be acquired which could possibly be betrayed, there grew up a gradual habit of reticence. The undisciplined mind was not suddenly assailed by the temptation to divulge what it knew. There was opportunity for gradual adaptation to the duty of reticence. The other regulation, that the songs should not be written down, had much more thorough-going sociological structural relations. It was more than a protective provision against revelation of the secrets. The necessity of depending upon tradition from person to person, and the fact that the spring of knowledge flowed only from within the society, not from an objective piece of literature -- this attached the individual member with unique intimacy to the community. It gave him the feeling that if he were detached from this substance, he would lose his own, and would never recover it elsewhere. We have perhaps not yet sufficiently observed to what extent, in a more advanced cultural stage, the objectifications of intellectual labors affect the capacity of the individual to assert independence. So long as direct tradition, individual instruction, and more than all the setting up of norms by personal authorities, still determine the spiritual life of the individual, he is solidly merged in the environing, living group. This group alone gives him the possibility of a fulfilled and spiritual existence. The direction of those connective tissues through which the contents of his life come to him, run perceptibly at every moment only between his social *milieu* and himself. So soon, however, as the labor of the group, has capitalized its out-put in the form of literature, in visible works, and in permanent examples, the former immediate flow of vital fluid between the actual group and the individual member is interrupted. The life-process of the latter no longer binds him continuously and without competition to the former. Instead of that, he can now sustain himself from objective sources, not dependent upon the actual presence of former authoratative persons. There is relatively little efficacy in the fact that this now accumulated stock has come from the processes of the social mind. In the first place, it is often the labor of far remote generations quite unconnected with the individual's feeling of present values, which is crystallized in that supply. But, more than that, it is before all else the form of the objectivity of this supply, its detachment from the subjective personality, by virtue of which there is opened to the individual a super-social natural source, and his mental content becomes much more notably dependent, in kind and degree, upon his powers of appropriation than upon the conventionally furnished ideas. The peculiar intimacy of association within the secret society, of which more must be said later, and which gets its place among the categories of the feelings from the traits of the specific "confidence" (*Vertrauen*) characteristic of the order, in consequence of what has been said very naturally avoids committing the contents of its mysteries to writing, when tradition of spiritual contents is the minor aim of the association.

In connection with these questions about the technique of secrecy, it is not to be forgotten that concealment is by no means the only means under whose protection promotion of the material interests of the community is attempted. The facts are in many ways the reverse. The structure of the group is often with the direct view to assurance of keeping certain subjects from general knowledge. This is the case with those peculiar types of secret society whose substance is an esoteric doctrine, a theoretical, mystical, religious gnosis. In this case secrecy is the sociological end-unto-itself. The issue turns upon a body of doctrine to be kept from publicity. The initiated constitute a community for the purpose of mutual guarantee of secrecy. If these initiates were merely a total of personalities not interdependent, the secret would soon be lost. Socialization affords to each of these individuals a psychological recourse for strengthening him against temptations to divulge the secret. While secrecy, as I have shown, works toward isolation and individualization, socialization is a counteractive factor. If this is in general the sociological significance of the secret society, its most clear emergence is in the case of those orders characterized above, in which secrecy is not a mere sociological technique, but socialization is a technique for better protection of the secrecy, in the same way that the oath and total silence, that threats and progressive initiation of the novices, serve the same purpose. All species of socialization shuffle the individualizing and the socializing needs back and forth within their forms, and even within their contents, as though promotion of a stable combining proportion were satisfied by introduction of quantities always qualitatively changing. Thus the secret society counterbalances the separatistic factor which is peculiar to, every secret by the very fact that it is society.

Secrecy and individualistic separateness are so decidedly correlatives that with reference to secrecy socialization may play two quite antithetical roles. It can, in the first place, as just pointed out, be directly sought, to the end that during the subsequent continuance of the secrecy its isolating tendency may be in part counteracted, that *within* the secret order the impulse toward community may be satisfied, while it is vetoed with reference to the rest of the world. On the other hand, however, secrecy in principle loses relative significance in cases where the particularization is in principle rejected. Freemasonry, for example, insists that it purposes to become the most universal society, "the union of unions," the only one that repudiates every particularistic character and aims to appropriate as its material exclusively that which is common to all good men. Hand in hand with this increasingly definite tendency there grows up indifference toward the element of secrecy on the part of the lodges, its restriction to the merely formal externalities. That secrecy is now promoted by socialization, and now abolished by it, is thus by no means a contradiction. These are merely diverse forms in which its connection with individualization expresses itself— somewhat as the interdependence of weakness and fear shows itself both in the fact that the weak seek social attachments in order to protect themselves, and in the fact that they avoid social relations when they encounter greater dangers within them than in isolation.

The above-mentioned gradual initiation of the members belongs, moreover, to a very far-reaching and widely ramifying division of sociological forms, within which secret societies are marked in a special way. It is the principle of the hierarchy, of graded articulation, of the elements of a society. The refinement and the systematization with which secret societies particularly work out their division of labor and the grading of their members, go along with another trait to be discussed presently; that is, with their energetic *consciousness* of their life. This life substitutes for the organically more instinctive forces an incessantly regulating will; for growth from within, constructive purposefulness. This rationalistic factor in their upbuilding cannot express itself more distinctly than in their carefully considered and clear-cut architecture. I cite as example the structure of the Czechic secret order, *Omladina,* which was organized on the model of a group of the *Carbonari,* and became known in consequence of a judicial process in 1893. The leaders of the *Omladina* are divided into "thumbs" and "fingers." In secret session a "thumb" is chosen by the members. He selects four "fingers." The latter then choose another "thumb," and this second "thumb" presents himself to the first "thumb." The second "thumb" proceeds to choose four more "fingers"; these, another "thumb;" and so the articulation continues. The first "thumb" knows all the other "thumbs," but the remaining "thumbs" do not know each other. Of the "fingers" only those four know each other who are subordinate to one and the same "thumb." All transactions of the *Omladina* are conducted by the first "thumb," the "dictator." He informs the other "thumbs" of all proposed under-takings. The "thumbs" then issue orders to their respective subordinates, the "fingers." The latter in turn instruct the members of the *Omladina* assigned to each. The circumstance that the secret society must be built up, from its base by calculation and conscious volition evidently affords free play for the peculiar passion which is the natural accompaniment of such arbitrary processes of construction, such foreordaining programs. All schematology — of science, of conduct, of society— contains a reserved power of compulsion. It subjects a material which is outside of thought to a form which thought has cast. If this is true of all attempts to organize groups according to *a priori* principles, it is true in the highest degree of the secret society, which does not grow, which is built by design, which has to reckon with a smaller quantum of ready-made building material than any despotic or socialistic scheme. Joined to the interest in making plans, and the constructive impulse, which are in themselves compelling forces, we have in the organization of a society in accordance with a preconceived outline, with fixed positions and ranks, the special stimulus of exercising a decisive influence over a future and ideally submissive circle of human beings. This impulse is decisively separated sometimes from every sort of utility, and revels in utterly fantastic construction of hierarchies. Thus, for example, in the "high degrees" of degenerate Freemasonry. For purposes of illustration I call attention to merely a few details from the "Order of the African Master-Builders." It came into existence in Germany and France after the middle of the eighteenth century, and although it was constructed according to the principles of the Masonic order, it aimed to destroy Freemasonry. The government of the very small society was administered by fifteen officials: summus register, summi locum tenentes, prior, sub-prior, magister, etc. The degrees of the order were seven: the Scottish Apprentices, the Scottish Brothers, the Scottish Masters, the Scottish Knights, the Eques Regii, the Eques de Secta Consueta, the Eques Silentii Regii; etc., etc.

Parallel with the development of the hierarchy, and with similar limitations, we observe within secret societies the structure of the ritual. Here also their peculiar emancipation from the prejudices of historical organizations permits them to build upon a self-laid basis extreme freedom and opulence of form. There is perhaps no external tendency which so decisively and with such characteristic differences divides the secret from the open society, as the valuation of usages, formulas, rites, and the peculiar preponderance and antithetic relation of all these to, the body of purposes which the society represents. The latter are often guarded with less care than the secret of the ritual. Progressive Freemasonry emphasizes expressly that it is not a secret combination; that it has no occasion to conceal the roll of its members, its purposes, or its acts; the oath of silence refers exclusively to the forms of the Masonic rites. Thus the student order of the *Amicisten*, at the end of the eighteenth century, has this characteristic provision in sec. I of its statutes:

> The most sacred duty of each member is to preserve the profoundest silence with reference to such things as concern the well-being of the order. Among these belong: symbols of the order and signs of recognition, names of fraternity brothers, ceremonies, etc.

Later in the same statute the purpose and character of the order are disclosed and precisely specified! In a book of quite limited size which describes the constitution and character of the *Carbonari*, the account of the ceremonial forms and usages, at the reception of new members and at meetings, covers seventy-five pages! Further examples are needless. The role of the ritual in secret societies is sufficiently well known, from the religio-mystical orders of antiquity, on the one hand, to the *Rosenkreutzer* of the eighteenth century, and the most notorious criminal bands. The sociological motivations of this connection are approximately the following.

That which is striking about the treatment of the ritual in secret societies is not merely the precision with which it is observed, but first of all the anxiety with which it is guarded as a secret - as though the unveiling of it were precisely as fatal as betrayal of the purposes and actions of the society, or even the existence of the society altogether. The utility of this is probably in the fact that, through this absorption of a whole complex of external forms into the secret, the whole range of action and interest occupied by the secret society becomes a well-rounded unity. The secret society must seek to create among the categories peculiar to itself, a species of life-totality. Around the nucleus of purposes which the society strongly emphasizes, it therefore builds a structure of formulas, like a body around a soul, and places both alike under the protection of secrecy, because only so can a harmonious whole come into being, in which one part supports the other. That in this scheme secrecy of the external is strongly accentuated, is necessary, because secrecy is not so much a matter of course with reference to these superficialities, and not so directly demanded as in the case of the real interests of the society. This is not greatly different from the situation in military organizations and religious communities. The reason why, in both, schematism, the body of forms, the fixation of behavior, occupies so large space, is that, as a general proposition, both the military and the religious career demand the whole man; that is, each of them projects the whole life upon a special plane; each composes a variety of energies and interests, from a particular point of view, into a correlated unity. The secret society usually tries to do the same. One of its essential characteristics is that, even when it takes hold of individuals only by means of partial interests, when the society in its substance is a purely utilitarian combination, yet it claims the whole man in a higher degree, it combines the personalities more in their whole compass with each other, and commits them more to reciprocal obligations, than the same common purpose would within an open society. Since the symbolism of the ritual stimulates a wide range of vaguely bounded feelings, touching interests far in excess of those that are definitely apprehended, the secret society weaves these latter interests into an aggregate demand upon the individual. Through the ritual form the specific purpose of the secret society is expanded into a comprehensive unity and totality, both sociological and subjective. Moreover, through such formalism, just as through the hierarchical structure above discussed, the secret society constitutes itself a sort of counterpart of the official world with which it places itself in antithesis. Here we have a case of the universally emerging sociological norm; viz., structures, which place themselves in opposition to and detachment from larger structures in which they are actually contained, nevertheless repeat in themselves the forms of the greater structures. Only a structure that in some way can count as a whole is in a situation to hold its elements firmly together. It borrows the sort of organic completeness, by virtue of which its members are actually the channels of a unifying life-stream, from that greater whole to which its individual members were already adapted, and to which it can most easily offer a parallel by means of this very imitation.

The same relation affords finally the following motive for the sociology of the ritual in secret societies. Every such society contains a measure of freedom, which is not really provided for in the structure of the surrounding society. Whether the secret society, like the *Vehme*, complements the inadequate judicature of the political area; or whether, as in the case of conspiracies or criminal bands, it is an uprising against the law of that area; or whether, as in the case of the "mysteries," they hold themselves outside of the commands and prohibitions of the greater area -- in either case the apartness (*Heraussonderung*) which characterizes the secret society has the tone of a freedom. In exercise of this freedom a territory is occupied to which the norms of the surrounding society do not apply. The nature of the secret society as such is autonomy. It is, however, of a sort which approaches anarchy. Withdrawal from the bonds of unity which procure general coherence very easily has as consequences for the secret society a condition of being without roots, an absence of firm touch with life (*Lebensgefühl*), and of restraining reservations. The fixedness and detail of the ritual serve in part to counterbalance this deficit. Here also is manifest how much men need a settled proportion between freedom and law; and, furthermore, in case the relative quantities of the two are not prescribed for him from a single source, how he attempts to reinforce the given quantum of the one by a quantum of the other derived from any source whatsoever, until such settled proportion is reached. With the ritual the secret society voluntarily imposes upon itself a formal constraint, which is demanded as a complement by its material detachment and self-sufficiency. It is characteristic that, among the Freemasons, it is precisely the Americans— who enjoy the largest political freedom — of whom the severest unity in manner of work, the greatest uniformity of the ritual of all lodges, are demanded; while in Germany -- where the otherwise sufficient quantum of bondage leaves little room for a counter-demand in the direction of restrictions upon freedom — more freedom is exercised in the manner in which each individual lodge carries on its work. The often essentially meaningless, schematic constraint of the ritual of the secret society is therefore by no means a contradiction of its freedom bordering on anarchy, its detachment from the norms of the circle which contains it. Just as widespread existence of secret societies is, as a rule, a proof of public unfreedom, of a policy of police regulation, of police oppression; so, conversely, ritual regulation of these societies from within proves a freedom and enfranchisement in principle for which the equilibrium of human nature produces the constraint as a counter-influence.

These last considerations have already led to the methodological principle with reference to which I shall analyze the still outstanding traits of secret societies. The problem is, in a word, to what extent these traits prove to be in essence quantitative modifications of the typical traits of socialization in general. In order to establish this manner of representing secret societies, we must again review their status in the whole complex of sociological forms.

The secret element in societies is a primary sociological fact, a definite mode and shading of association, a formal relationship of quality in immediate or mediate reciprocity with other factors which determine the habit of the group-elements or of the group. The secret society, on the other hand, is a secondary structure; i.e., it arises always only within an already complete society. Otherwise expressed, the secret society is itself characterized by its secret, just as other societies, and even itself, are characterized by their superiority and subordination, or by their offensive purposes, or by their initiative character. That they can build themselves up with such characteristics is possible, however, only under the presupposition of an already existing society. The secret society sets itself as a special society in antithesis with the wider association included within the greater society. This antithesis, whatever its purpose, is at all events intended in the spirit of exclusion. Even the secret society which proposes only to render the whole community a definite service in a completely unselfish spirit, and to dissolve itself after performing the service, obviously regards its temporary detachment from that totality as the unavoidable technique for its purpose. Accordingly, none of the narrower groups which are circumscribed by larger groups are compelled by their sociological constellation to insist so strongly as the secret society upon their formal self-sufficiency. Their secret encircles them like a boundary, beyond which there is nothing but the materially, or at least formally, antithetic, which therefore shuts up the society within itself as a complete unity. In the groupings of every other sort, the *content* of the group-life, the actions of the members in the sphere of rights and duties, may so fill up their consciousness that within it the formal fact of socialization under normal conditions plays scarcely any role. The secret society, on the other hand, can on no account permit the definite and emphatic consciousness of its members that they constitute a society to escape from their minds. The always perceptible and always to-be-guarded pathos of the secret lends to the form of union which depends upon the secret, as contrasted with the content, a predominant significance, as compared with other unions.

In the secret society there is complete absence of organic growth, of the character of instinct in accumulation, of all unforced matter of course with respect to belonging together and forming a unity. No matter how irrational, mystical, impressionistic (*gefühlsmässig*) their contents, the way in which they are constructed is always conscious and intentional. Throughout their derivation and life *consciousness of being a society* is permanently accentuated. The secret society is, on that account, the antithesis of all genetic (*triebhaft*) societies, in which the unification is more or less only the expression of the natural growing together of elements whose life has common roots. Its socio-psychological form is invariably that of the teleological combination (*Zweckverbacnd*). This constellation makes it easy to understand that the specifications of form in the construction of secret societies attain to peculiar definiteness, and that their essential sociological traits develop as mere quantitative heightenings of quite general types of relationship.

One of these latter has already been indicated; viz., the characterization and the coherence of the society through closure toward the social environment. To this end the often complicated signs of recognition contribute. Through these the individual offers credentials of membership in the society. Indeed, in the times previous to the general use of writing, such signs were more imperative for this use than later. At present their other sociological uses overtop that of mere identification. So long as there was lack of documentary credentials, an order whose sub-divisions were in different localities utterly lacked means of excluding the unauthorized, of securing to rightful claimants only the enjoyment of its benefits or knowledge of its affairs, unless these signs were employed. These were disclosed only to the worthy, who were pledged to keep them secret, and who could use them for purposes of legitimation as members of the order wherever it existed. This purpose of drawing lines of separation very definitely characterizes the development manifested by certain secret orders among the nature peoples, especially in Africa and among the Indians. These orders are composed of men alone, and pursue essentially the purpose of magnifying their separation from the women. The members appear in disguises, when they come upon the stage of action as members, and it is customary to forbid women, on pain of severe penalties, to approach them. Still, women have occasionally succeeded in penetrating their veil of secrecy sufficiently to discover that the horrible figures are not ghosts, but their own husbands. When this occurred, the orders have often lost their whole significance, and have fallen to the level of a harmless masquerade. The undifferentiated sensuous conceptions of nature people cannot form a more complete notion of the separateness which orders of this sort wish to emphasize, than in the concealment, by disguise or otherwise, of those who have the desire and the right thus to abstract themselves. That is the rudest and externally most radical mode of concealment; viz., covering up not merely the special act of the person, but at once the whole person obscures himself; the order does not do anything that is secret, but the totality of persons comprising it makes itself into a secret. This form of the secret society corresponds completely with the primitive intellectual plane in which the whole agent throws himself entire into each specific activity; that is, in which the activity is not yet sufficiently objectified to give it a character which less than the whole man can share. Hence it is equally explicable that so soon as the disguise-secret is broken through, the whole separation becomes ineffective, and the order, with its devices and its manifestations, loses at once its inner meaning.

In the case in question the separation has the force of an expression of value. There is separation from others because there is unwillingness to give oneself a character common with that of others, because there is desire to signalize one's own superiority as compared with these others. Everywhere this motive leads to the formation of groups which are obviously in sharp contrast with those formed in pursuit of material (*sachlich*) purposes. As a consequence of the fact that those who want to distinguish themselves enter into combination, there results an aristocracy which strengthens and, so to speak, expands the self-consciousness of the individuals through the weight of their sum. That exclusiveness and formation of groups are thus bound together by the aristocracy-building motive gives to the former in many cases from the outset the stamp of the "special" in the sense of value. We may observe, even in school classes, how small, closely attached groups of comrades, through the mere formal fact that they form a special group, come to consider themselves an élite, compared with the rest who are unorganized; while the latter, by their enmity and jealousy, involuntarily recognize that higher value. In these cases secrecy and pretense of secrecy (*Geheimnistnerei*) are means of building higher the wall of separation, and therein a reinforcement of the aristocratic nature of the group.

This significance of secret associations, as intensification of sociological exclusiveness in general, appears in a very striking way in political aristocracies. Among the requisites of aristocratic control secrecy has always had a place. It makes use of the psychological fact that the unknown as such appears terrible, powerful, and threatening. In the first place, it employs this fact in seeking to conceal the numerical insignificance of the governing class. In Sparta the number of warriors was kept so far as possible a secret, and in Venice the same purpose was in view in the ordinance prescribing simple black costumes for all the *nobili*. Conspicuous costumes should not be permitted to make evident to the people the petty number of the rulers. In that particular case the policy was carried to complete concealment of the inner circle of the highest rulers. The names of the three state inquisitors were known only to the Council of Ten who chose them. In some of the Swiss aristocracies one of the most important magistracies was frankly called "the secret officials" (*die Heimlichen*), and in Freiburg the aristocratic families were known as *die heimlichen Geschlechter*. On the other hand, the democratic principle is bound up with the principle of publicity, and, to the same end, the tendency toward general and fundamental laws. The latter relate to an unlimited number of subjects, and are thus in their nature public. Conversely, the employment of secrecy within the aristocratic regime is only the extreme exaggeration of that social exclusion and exemption for the sake of which aristocracies are wont to oppose general, fundamentally sanctioned laws.

In case the notion of the aristocratic passes over from the politics of a group to the disposition (*Gesinnung*) of an individual, the relationship of separation and secrecy attains to a plane that is, to outward appearance, completely changed. Perfect distinction (*Vornehmheit*) in both moral and mental respects despises all concealment, because its inner security makes it indifferent to what others know or do not know about us, whether their estimate of us is true or false, high or low. From the stand-point of such superiority, secrecy is a concession to outsiders, a dependence of behavior upon consideration of them. Hence the "mask" which so many regard as sign and proof of their aristocratic soul, of disregard of the crowd, is direct proof of the significance that the crowd has for such people. The mask of those whose distinction is real is that the many can at best not understand them, that they do not see them, so to speak, even when they show themselves without disguise.

The bar against all external to the circle, which, as universal sociological form-fact, makes use of secrecy as a progressive technique, gains a peculiar coloring through the multiplicity of degrees, through which initiation into the last mysteries of secret societies is wont to occur, and which threw light above upon another sociological trait of secret societies. As a rule, a solemn pledge is demanded of the novice that he will hold secret everything which he is about to experience, before even the first stages of acceptance into the society occur. Therewith is the absolute and formal separation which secrecy can effect, put into force. Yet, since under these conditions the essential content or purpose of the order is only gradually accessible to the neophyte -- whether the purpose is the complete purification and salvation of the soul through the consecration of the mysteries, or whether it is the absolute abolition of all moral restraint, as with the *Assassins* and other criminal societies -- the separation in material respects is otherwise ordered; i.e., it is made more continuous and more relative. When this method is employed, the initiate is in a condition nearer to that of the outsider. He needs to be tested and educated up to the point of grasping the whole or the center of the association. Thereby, however, a protection is obviously afforded to the latter, an isolation of it from the external world, which goes beyond the protection gained from the entrance oath. Care is taken— as was incidentally shown by the example of the druids— that the still untried shall also have very little to betray if he would, inasmuch as, within the secret principle which surrounds the society as a whole, graduated secrecy produces at the same time an elastic zone of defense for that which is inmost and essential. The antithesis of the exotic and the esoteric members, as we have it in the case of the Pythagoreans, is the most striking form of this protective arrangement. The circle of the only partially initiated constitutes to a certain extent a buffer area against the totally uninitiated. As it is everywhere the double function of the "mean" to bind and to separate— or, rather, as it plays only *one* role, which we, however, according to our apperceptive categories, and according to the angle of our vision, designate as uniting and separating— so in this connection the unity of activities which externally clash with each other appears in the clearest light. Precisely because the lower grades of the society constitute a mediating transition to the actual center of the secret, they bring about the gradual compression of the sphere of repulsion around the same, which affords more secure protection to it than the abruptness of a radical standing wholly without or wholly within could secure.

Sociological self-sufficiency presents itself in practical effect as group-egoism. The group pursues its purposes with the same disregard of the purposes of the structure external to itself, which in the case of the individual is called egoism. For the consciousness of the individual this attitude very likely gets a moral justification from the fact that the group-purposes in and of themselves have a super-individual, objective character; that it is often impossible to name any individual who would directly profit from the operation of the group egoism; that conformity to this group program often demands unselfishness and sacrifice from its promoters. The point at issue here, however, is not the ethical valuation, but the detachment of the group, from its environments, which the group egoism effects or indicates. In the case of a small group, which wants to maintain and develop itself within a larger circle, there will be certain limits to this policy, so long as it has to be pursued before all eyes. No matter how bitterly a public society may antagonize other societies of a larger organization, or the whole constitution of the same, it must always assert that realization of its ultimate purposes would redound to the advantage of the whole, and the necessity of this ostensible assertion will at all events place some restraint upon the actual egoism of its action. In the case of secret societies this necessity is absent, and at least the possibility is given of a hostility toward other societies, or toward the whole of society, which the open society cannot admit, and consequently cannot exercise without restrictions. In no way is the detachment of the secret society from its social environment so decisively symbolized, and also promoted, as by the dropping of every hypocrisy or actual condescension which is indispensable in co-ordinating the open society with the teleology of the environing whole.

In spite of the actual quantitative delimitation of every real society, there is still a considerable number the inner tendency of which is: Whoever is not excluded is included. Within certain political, religious, and class peripheries, everyone is reckoned as of the association who satisfies certain conditions, mostly involuntary, and given along with his existence. Whoever, for example, is born within the territory of a state, unless peculiar circumstances make him an exception, is a member of the highly complex civic society. The member of a given social class is, as a matter of course, included in the conventions and forms of attachment pertaining to the same, if he does not voluntarily or involuntarily make himself an outsider. The extreme is offered by the claim of a church that it really comprehends the totality of the human race, so that only historical accidents, sinful obduracy, or a special divine purpose excludes any persons from the religious community which ideally anticipates even those not in fact within the pale. Here is, accordingly, a parting of two ways, which evidently signify a differentiation in principle of the sociological meaning of societies in general, however they may be confused, and their definiteness toned down in practice. In contrast with the fundamental principle: Who so is not expressly excluded is included, stands the other: Whoever is not expressly included is excluded. The latter type is presented in the most decisive purity by the secret societies. The unlimited character of their separation, conscious at every step of their development, has, both as cause and as effect, the rule that whoever is not expressly adopted is thereby expressly excluded. The Masonic fraternity could not better support its recently much emphasized assertion that it is not properly a secret order, than through its simultaneously published ideal of including all men, and thus of representing humanity as a whole.

Corresponding with intensification of separateness from the outer world, there is here, as elsewhere, a similar access of coherence within, since these are only the two sides or forms of manifestation of one and the same sociological attitude. A purpose which stimulates formation of a secret union among men as a rule peremptorily excludes such a preponderating portion of the general social environment from participation that the possible and actual participants acquire a scarcity value. These must be handled carefully, because, *ceteris paribus*, it is much more difficult to replace them than is the case in an ordinary society. More than that, every quarrel within the secret society brings with it the danger of betrayal, to avoid which in this case the motive of self-preservation in the individual is likely to co-operate with the motive of the self-preservation off the whole. Finally, with the defection of the secret societies from the environing social syntheses, many occasions of conflict disappear. Among all the limitations of the individual, those that come from association in secret societies always occupy an exceptional status, in contrast with which the open limitations, domestic and civic, religious and economic, those of class and of friendship, however manifold their content, still have a quite different measure and manner of efficiency. It requires the comparison with secret societies to make clear that the demands of open societies, lying so to speak in one plane, run across each other. As they carry on at the same time an open competitive struggle over the strength and the interest of the individual, within a single one of these spheres, the individuals come into sharp collision, because each of them is at the same time solicited by the interests of other spheres. In secret societies, in view of their sociological isolation, such collisions are very much restricted. The purposes and programs of secret societies require that competitive interests from that plane of the open society should be left outside the door. Since the secret society occupies a plane of its own -- few individuals belonging to more than one secret society -- it exercises a kind of absolute sovereignty over its members. This control prevents conflicts among them which easily arise in the open type of co-ordination. The "King's peace" (*Burgfriede*) which should prevail within every society is promoted in a formally unsurpassed manner within secret societies through their peculiar and exceptional limitations. It appears, indeed, that, entirely apart from this more realistic ground, the mere form of secrecy as such holds the associates safer than they would otherwise be from disturbing influences, and thereby make concord more feasible. An English statesman has attempted to discover the source of the strength of the English cabinet in the secrecy which surrounds it. Everyone who has been active in public life knows that a small collection of people may be brought to agreement much more easily if their transactions are secret.

Corresponding with the peculiar degree of cohesion within secret societies is the definiteness of their centralization. They furnish examples of an unlimited and blind obedience to leaders, such as occurs elsewhere of course; but it is the more remarkable here, in view of the frequent anarchical and negative character toward all other law. The more criminal the purposes of a secret society, the more unlimited is likely to be the power of the leaders, and the more cruel its exercise. The *Assassins* in Arabia; the *Chauffeurs*, a predatory society with various branches that ravaged in France, particularly in the eighteenth century; the *Gardunas* in Spain, a criminal society that, from the seventeenth to the beginning of the nineteenth century, had relations with the Inquisition -- all these, the nature of which was lawlessness and rebellion, were under one commander, whom they sometimes set over themselves, and whom they obeyed without criticism or limitation. To this result not merely the correlation of demand from freedom and for union contributes, as we have observed it in case of the severity of the ritual, and in the present instance it binds together the extremes of the two tendencies. The excess of freedom, which such societies possessed with reference to all otherwise valid norms, had to be offset, for the sake of the equilibrium of interests, by a similar excess of submissiveness and resigning of the individual will. More essential, however, was probably the necessity of centralization, which is the condition of existence for the secret society, and especially when, like the criminal band, it lives off the surrounding society, when it mingles with this society in many radiations and actions, and when it is seriously threatened with treachery and diversion of interests the moment the most invariable attachment to one center ceases to prevail. It is consequently typical that the secret society is exposed to peculiar dangers, especially when, for any reasons whatever, it does not develop a powerfully unifying authority. The Waldenses were in nature not a secret society. They became a secret society in the thirteenth century only, in consequence of the external pressure, which made it necessary to keep themselves from view. It became impossible, for that reason, to hold regular assemblages, and this in turn caused loss of unity in doctrine. There arose a number of branches, with isolated life and development, frequently in a hostile attitude toward each other. They went into decline because they lacked the necessary and reinforcing attribute of the secret society, viz., constantly efficient centralization. The fact that the dynamic significance of Freemasonry is obviously not quite in proportion with its extension and its resources is probably to be accounted for by the extensive autonomy of its parts, which have neither a unified organization nor a central administration. Since their common life extends only to fundamental principles and signs of recognition, these come to be virtually only norms of equality and of contact between man and man, but not of that centralization which holds together the forces of the elements, and is the correlate of the apartness of the secret society.

It is nothing but an exaggeration of this formal motive when, as is often the case, secret societies are led by unknown chiefs. It is not desirable that the lower grades should know whom they are obeying. This occurs primarily, to be sure, for the sake of guarding the secret, and with this in view the device is carried to the point of constructing such a secret society as that of the Welfic Knights in Italy. The order operated at the beginning of the nineteenth century in the interest of Italian liberation and unification. At each of its seats it had a supreme council of six persons, who were not mutually acquainted, but dealt with each other only through a mediator who was known as "The Visible." This, however, is by no means the only utility of the secret headship. It means rather the most extreme and abstract sublimation of centralized coherence. The tension between adherent and leader reaches the highest degree when the latter withdraws from the range of vision. There remains the naked, merciless fact, so to speak, modified by no personal coloring, of obedience pure and simple, from which the superordinated subject has disappeared. If even obedience to an impersonal authority, to, a mere magistracy, to the representative of an objective law, has the character of unbending severity, this obedience mounts still higher, to the level of an uncanny absoluteness, so soon as the commanding personality remains in principle hidden. For if, along with the visibility of the ruler, and acquaintance with him, it must be admitted that individual suggestion, the force of the personality, also vanish from the commanding relationship; yet at the same time there also disappear from the relationship the limitations, i.e., the merely relative, the "human," so to speak, which are attributes of the single person who can be encountered in actual experience. In this case obedience must be stimulated by the feeling of being subject to an intangible power, not strictly defined, so far as its boundaries are concerned; a power nowhere to be seen, but for that reason everywhere to be expected.

The sociologically universal coherence of a group through the unity of the commanding authority is, in the case of the secret society with unknown headship, shifted into a *focus imaginarius*, and it attains therewith its most distinct and intense form.

The sociological character of the individual elements of the secret society, corresponding with this centralized subordination, is their individualization. In case the society does not have promotion of the interests of its individual members as its immediate purpose, and, so to speak, does not go outside of itself, but rather uses its members as means to externally located ends and activities— in such case the secret society in turn manifests a heightened degree of self-abnegation, of leveling of individuality, which is already an incident of the social state in general, and with which the secret *society* outweighs the above-emphasized individualizing and differentiating character of the *secrecy*. This begins with the secret orders of the nature peoples, whose appearance and activities are almost always in connection with use of disguises, so that an expert immediately infers that wherever we find the use of disguises (*Masken*) among nature peoples, they at least indicate a probability of the existence of secret orders. It is, to be sure, a part of the essence of the secret order that its members conceal themselves, as such. Yet, inasmuch as the given man stands forth and conducts himself quite unequivocally as a member of the secret order, and merely does not disclose which otherwise known individuality is identical with this member, the disappearance of the personality, as such, behind his role in the secret society is most strongly emphasized. In the Irish conspiracy which was organized in America in the seventies under the name Clan-na-gael, the individual members were not designated by their names, but only by numbers. This, of course, was with a view to the practical purpose of secrecy. Nevertheless, it shows to what extent secrecy suppresses individuality. Among persons who figure only as numbers, who perhaps -- as occurs at least in analogous cases -- are scarcely known to the other members by their personal names, leadership will proceed with much less consideration, with much more indifference to individual wishes and capacities, than if the union includes each of its members as a personal being. Not less effective in this respect are the extensive role and the severity of the ritual. All of this always signifies that the object mold has become master over the personal in membership and in activity. The hierarchical order admits the individual merely as agent of a definite role; it likewise holds in readiness for each participant a conventional garb, in which his personal contour disappears. It is merely another name for this effacement of the differentiated personality, when secret societies cultivate a high degree of relative equality among the members. This is so far from being in contradiction of the despotic character of their constitutions that in all sorts of other groupings despotism finds its correlate in the leveling of the ruled. Within the secret society there often exists between the members a fraternal equality which is in sharp and purposeful contrast with their differences in all the other situations of their lives. Typical cases in point appear, on the one hand, in secret societies of a religio-ethical character, which strongly accentuate the element of brotherhood; on the other hand, in societies of an illegal nature. Bismarck speaks in his memoirs of a widely ramified pederastic organization in Berlin, which came under his observation as a young judicial officer; and he emphasizes "the equalizing effect of co-operative practice of the forbidden vice through all social strata." This depersonalizing, in which the secret society carries to an excessive degree a typical relationship between individual and society, appears finally as the characteristic irresponsibility. In this connection, too, physical disguise (*Maske*) is the primitive phenomenon. Most of the African secret orders are alike in representing themselves by a man disguised as a forest spirit. He commits at will upon whomsoever he encounters any sort of violence, even to robbery and murder. No responsibility attaches to him for his outrages, and evidently this is due solely to the disguise. That is the somewhat unmanageable form under which such societies cause the personality of their adherents to disappear, and without which the latter would undoubtedly be over-taken by revenge and punishment. Nevertheless, responsibility is quite as immediately joined with the ego — philosophically, too, the whole responsibility problem is merely a detail of the problem of the ego — in the fact that removing the marks of identity of the person has, for the naive understanding in question, the effect of abolishing responsibility. Political finesse makes no less use of this correlation. In the American House of Representatives the real conclusions are reached in the standing committees, and they are almost always ratified by the House. The transactions of these committees, however, are secret, and the most important portion of legislative activity is thus concealed from public view. This being the case, the political responsibility of the representatives seems to be largely wiped out, since no one can be made responsible for proceedings that cannot be observed. Since the shares of the individual persons in the transactions remain hidden, the acts of committees and of the House seem to be those of a super-individual authority. The irresponsibility is here also the consequence or the symbol of the same intensified sociological de-individualization which goes with the secrecy of group-action. In all directorates, faculties, committees, boards of trustees, etc., whose transactions are secret, the same thing holds. The individual disappears as a person in the anonymous member of the ring, so to speak, and with him the responsibility, which has no hold upon him in his intangible special character.

Finally, this one-sided intensification of universal sociological traits is corroborated by the danger with which the great surrounding circle rightly or wrongly believes itself to be threatened from the secret society. Wherever there is an attempt to realize strong centralization, especially of a political type, special organizations of the elements are abhorred, purely as such, entirely apart from their content and purposes. As mere unities, so to speak, they engage in competition with the central principle. The central power wants to reserve to itself the prerogative of binding the elements together in a form of common unity. The jealous zeal of the central power against every special society (*Sonderbund*) runs through all political history. A characteristic type is presented by the Swiss convention of 1481, according to which no separate alliances were to be formed between any of the ten confederated states. Another is presented by the persecution of the associations of apprentices by the despotism of the seventeenth and eighteenth centuries. A third appears in the tendency to disfranchise local political bodies, so often manifested by the modern state. This danger from the special organization for the surrounding whole appears at a high potency in the case of the secret society. Men seldom have a calm and rational attitude toward strangers or persons only partially known. The folly which treats the unknown as the non-existent, and the anxious imaginativeness which inflates the unknown at once into gigantic dangers and horrors, are wont to take turns in guiding human actions. Accordingly, the secret society seems to be dangerous simply because it is secret. Since it cannot be surely known that any special organization whatever may not some day turn its legally accumulated powers to some undesired end, and since on that account there is suspicion in principle on the part of central powers toward organizations of subjects, it follows that, in the case of organizations which are secret in principle, the suspicion that their secrecy conceals dangers is all the more natural. The societies of Orangemen, which were organized at the beginning of the nineteenth century in England for the suppression of Catholicism, avoided all public discussion, and operated only in secret, through personal bonds and correspondence. But this very secrecy gave them the appearance of a public danger. The suspicion arose "that men who shrank from appealing to public opinion meditated a resort to force." Thus the secret society, purely on the ground of its secrecy, appears dangerously related to conspiracy against existing powers. To what extent this is a heightening of the universal political seriousness of special organizations, appears very plainly in such an occurrence as the following: The oldest Germanic guilds afforded to their members an effective legal protection, and thus to that extent were substitutes for the state. On the one hand, the Danish kings regarded them as supports of public order, and they consequently favored them. On the contrary, however, they appeared, for the same reason, to be direct competitors with the state. For that reason the Frankish capitularies condemned them, and the condemnation even took the form of branding them as *conspiracies*. The secret association is in such bad repute as enemy of central powers that, conversely, every politically disapproved association must be accused of such hostility!

ENDNOTES

1. Translated by Albion W. Small

2. There is, to be sure, still another type of confidence, which our present discussion has nothing to do with, since it is a type that falls outside the bounds either of knowing or not knowing. It is the type which we call faith of one person in another. It belongs in the category of religious faith. Just as no one has ever believed in the existence of God on grounds of proof, but these proofs are rather subsequent justifications or intellectual reflections of a quite immediate attitude of the affections; so we have faith in another person, although this faith may not be able to justify itself by proofs of the worthiness of the person, and it may even exist in spite of proofs of his unworthiness. This

confidence, this subjective attitude of unreservedness toward a person, is not brought into existence by experiences or by hypotheses, but it is a primary attitude of the soul with respect to another. This condition of faith, in a perfectly pure form, detached from every sort of empirical consideration, probably occurs only within the sphere of religion. In order that it may be exercised toward men it probably always needs a stimulus or a sanction from the knowledge or the inference above referred to. On the other hand, it is probable that in those social forms of confidence, however exact or intellectually sanctioned they may seem to be, an element of that sentimental and even mystical " faith " of man toward man is hidden. Perhaps the type of attitude here indicated is a fundamental category of human conduct, resting back upon the metaphysical meaning of our relationship, and realized only empirically, accidentally, and partially through the special conscious grounds of confidence.

3. This counter-movement occurs also in the reverse direction. It has been observed, in connection with the history of the English court, that the actual court cabals, the secret whisperings, the organized intrigues, do not spring up under despotism, but only after the king has constitutional advisers, when the government is to that extent a system open to view. After that time -- and this applies especially since Edward II-- the king begins to form an unofficial, and at the same time subterranean, circle of advisers, in contrast with the ministers somehow forced upon him. This body brings into existence, within itself, and through endeavors to join it, a chain of concealments and conspiracies.

While other authors address the size and popularity of fraternal organizations and discuss their function within American society, Noel P. Gist analyzes the cultural factors which define fraternalism. In this essay, Gist asserts that the ceremonies of American fraternal organizations at the beginning of the twentieth century shared characteristics and thus formed a "cultural pattern." From an examination of the rituals of seventy organizations, the author concludes that in undergoing a fraternal ceremony, an initiate commonly undertakes a symbolic journey, faces an ordeal, is sworn to an oath, and experiences an allegorical death and rebirth.

CULTURE PATTERNING IN SECRET SOCIETY CEREMONIALS
Noel P. Gist
University of Missouri
1936
Social Forces, 14 (4) (May 1936), 497-505. [1]

ORGANIZED secrecy has been a feature of many civilizations. In primitive cultures secret organizations frequently attain a position which makes them of major importance in the social life of the people. Among the early Mediterranean civilizations the Ancient Mysteries played an important part in cultural development. During the Middle Ages, when knighthood and feudalism flourished on European soil, secret societies functioned as an important part of the social order, frequently as military or revolutionary brotherhoods. Later, as the Industrial Revolution dawned, new types of esoteric groups sprang up to meet the social and economic needs of a people whose mode of life had been affected by the change from agrarianism to industrialism. The Friendly Societies of England and various craft guilds of Britain and other lands are examples of secret fraternities constructed to harmonize with the socio-economic conditions of the time.

Secret fraternalism in its totality represents one of the major patterns of American civilization, a vast complex of material and non-material traits which have been woven into a distinctive cultural scheme. In 1800 there were but a few thousand members of the secret brotherhoods, but during the following century over six hundred societies sprang up or were introduced from abroad. Although adequate data are not at hand to show the exact number of fraternities or fraternalists, it was estimated in 1927 that there were approximately 800 different orders having a combined membership of 30 million persons. Fraternalism and the notions pertaining to it have penetrated almost every segment of society, influencing alike old and young, male and female, rich and poor. In this paper the proposition is presented that these societies are characterized by major culture patterns or configurations which bear conspicuous resemblances both in their structural and functional aspects. The problem, then, resolves itself mainly into the task of describing these patterns and indicating the extent to which they are typical of the secret society complex. It is recognized, of course, that while a common cultural thread appears to run through the whole of fraternalism, specific societies have effected innumerable variations of the pattern which serve to give each group a certain individuality within the larger fraternal complex. The study is thus necessarily concerned not only with the uniformities but also with deviations from the basic configurations. The present discussion will be limited to a consideration of secret society ceremonies.

THE CONCEPT OF CULTURE PATTERN

It is well at this point to consider briefly the theoretical aspects of the culture pattern concept as it is here used. The term may be defined as the design or gestalt which any combination of culture traits (culture complex) may assume in a given culture. In the patterning process the various cultural elements tend to arrange themselves in certain combinations according to the actual functions the traits perform. The culture pattern may therefore be said to be a sort of cultural frame to which disparate elements may be added and molded to harmonize with the prevailing design. The patterns of a whole culture constitute in their totality what might be called the configuration of that culture, which distinguishes it from other civilizations. This distinction becomes all the more apparent when it is realized that many cultures are oriented in terms of some dominant *motif*. Thus the total configuration, focussed as it is likely to be toward some definite concept or objective, is no less real than the dominant style characterizing the art or music of a people.

In any culture the patterning of a given complex appears to be fairly uniform from group to group and from locality to locality. If the culture is homogeneous, as in the case of a primitive group, relatively few aberrations from the established norm are sanctioned. In western culture, with its extreme differentiation and its multiplicity of values, deviations from the recognized patterns are likely to be characteristic of cultural development. Each group is not only separate from others in space; it also has its own distinctive history as well as its own functions and needs. Consequently it is reasonable to expect that within a culture complex would appear numerous variations in patterning. A study of any major complex of our own culture would undoubtedly reveal certain basic patterns and also multifarious variations of a minor character. In different groups new elements are introduced and woven into the existing pattern, while others are modified or dropped altogether; so that in the final analysis each local manifestation of the pattern tends to become somewhat different from the others, although still preserving the basic design. Organized Christianity is a case in point. The numerous sects and denominations in this country represent an infinite number of aberrational patterns. Yet these divergent groupings preserve with considerable fidelity the basic concepts and ideas of the Christian religion. This same tendency may be noted in the secret society complex of contemporary American culture.

In their psychological aspects culture patterns may be said to exert a compulsive force in human behavior and personality. In a sense these culture patterns represent the objective side of personality; they are, as Benedict points out, the individual "thrown large upon the screen, given gigantic proportions and a long-term span."[2] Just as the total configurations of a culture may take a distinctive shape and become so oriented as to provide a definite channel for the individual tendencies of the members of that particular society, so may any of the patterns which make up the culture assume a consistent form and serve to channelize the thought and conduct of individuals.

THE NATURE OF ESOTERIC CEREMONIALS

It is proposed here to describe patterns of secret society ceremonials and to indicate the extent to which the patterning process as manifest by cultural uniformities is exhibited. These ritualistic activities represent a sort of sub-complex, with the various traits, that is, symbolic acts and objects, dovetailed together into a pattern which, in its broad outlines, appears to be more or less common to fraternal societies. Ritual in general tends to be dramatic in character; in secret orders the dramatic features are conspicuously apparent. Ordinarily these ceremonialized dramas or pageants are founded on some fable, allegory, myth, legend, or historical event. Most of the fraternal ceremonials have dramas that contain simple narrative plots in which the members and neophytes play appropriate dramatic roles. These dramas are invariably moralistic in tone, being designed to convey the dogmas and doctrines which characterize the ideological framework of the orders. In most instances the "moral lesson" of the ceremonials is so obvious as to leave little for the imagination of even the most unimaginative novitiate or member.

SOURCE OF CEREMONIAL THEMES

So far as the themes of ceremonial dramas are concerned, the Bible seems to be the most common source of ideas. Biblical legends have been dramatized to suit the purposes of the fraternity employing them and have been woven into the rituals in a fashion deemed appropriate for the occasion. The Masonic lodge, for example, centers much of its ritualistic drama on Biblical lore relating to King Solomon and his temple. Two famous legendary friendships, that of Jonathan and David and the one between Damon and Pythias, are used as thematic materials for several fraternities. The story of the Good Samaritan has also been found appropriate for ceremonial dramatization. But variations in these themes appear. The Improved Order of Red Men, for instance, has a dramatic ritual which is intended to be representative of Indian life and customs. The Forestry organizations, of which there are several, have built a ceremonial drama on the legendary experiences of Robin Hood. In the Ku Klux Klan the dramatic ceremony has for its theme the naturalization of aliens. For the Knights of the Golden Eagle the theme is drawn from the traditions and history of the Crusaders; for the Homesteaders it centers around frontier life. In some instances the dramas take the form of allegories in which members impersonate certain "vices," "evils," and "truths." The recently-formed Utopian Society of

California has a drama representing the struggle of the down-trodden masses and their final discovery of a society in which "reason is ascendant." The drama is presented in five "cycles," and concludes in a truly American manner with the unemployed finding prosperity and security in a Utopian world and living happily ever after.

THE ROLE OF THE NOVICE

One of the most characteristic aspects of the ceremonial patterns is the dramatic role of the novitiate. In the process of leading the novice from the "profane" world into the realm of mystery the individual is usually given a special symbolic role to perform. Ordinarily this role is such as to impress upon the candidate certain doctrines or principles which the society seeks to impart and to heighten the person's awareness of his own status of subordination as a newcomer from the outside. These candidatorial roles bear striking resemblances to each other, with each society, of course, varying the details of the part to conform harmoniously with the *motif* of the ceremony.

The common procedure is for the novitiate to play the role of a stranger. He may be a "weary traveller in the wilderness," a "pilgrim in search of light," an "alien far from his own shores," an "intruder," or a "spy." In the Ancient Arabic Order of Nobles of the Mystic Shrine, for instance, the candidates are greeted as "poor sons of the desert, who are weary of the hot sands and the burning sun of the plains and humbly crave shelter and the protecting dome of the Temple." The Modern Samaritans present the novice as a weary stranger going down the road from Jerusalem to Jericho. In the Ku Klux Klan the members refer to the neophyte as an "alien" who is seeking citizenship in the Invisible Empire, in the Utopian Society he is a "pilgrim," in the Knights of Pythias he is a "stranger who desires to be inducted into the mysteries of the rank of Page," while in the Modern Woodmen of America he is a "stranger, without friends, in a strange land." Certain variations from this common pattern may be noted. The ritual of the Grange (Patrons of Husbandry) refers in the first degree to the candidates as "laborers" and "maids" (both sexes are admitted to the organization); in the second degree they represent "cultivators" and "shepherdesses"; in the third degree, "harvesters" and "gleaners"; and in the fourth, "husbandmen" and "'matrons."

THE SYMBOLIC JOURNEY

As a correlative feature of the candidatorial role of stranger or travellers is the journey of the novice. Always these "journeys" are symbolic in character; they may symbolize a sojourn "through the wilderness," "over hot sands," across swollen streams," "over rough and uneven roads," or in the "land of the enemy"; they may perhaps be symbolical of mere wandering in search of "light," "truth," or "protection." As the ritual-drama unfolds, with the novice playing the leading role, the members, in their respective parts, explain for his benefit the symbolic content of the "journey" and endeavor to link it up with some moral precept or principle to which they as representatives of the order subscribe. Sometimes obstacles are placed in front of the blindfolded candidate to make his journey more realistic. Often he is manhandled by members posing as "robbers" or "ruffians," or is challenged by someone who wants to know his mission and perhaps his password.

As noted in the following concrete examples, the ceremonial journey tends to conform fairly closely to a common pattern. In the Improved Order of Red Men, for example, the candidate is divested of clothing, blindfolded, given a bow of arrows, and started on a "difficult journey" over a "rough and treacherous path." During the course of the journey (which consists of perambulations around the lodge room) the conductor interprets for the novice the meaning of this phase of the drama. The Royal Purple Degree of Odd Fellowship has a similar dramatization. Here the candidate is referred to as a pilgrim making a journey through the wilderness. As he is conducted around the room he is stopped at different stations to receive "lectures" by different officials on the dangers and pitfalls of his sojourn. During the course of the "journey" the candidate and his conductor hear the clash of arms as if a battle is under way; they pass the ruins of a castle, face an approaching storm, and finally come to a deep and muddy river which they must cross. The initiated members try to make this symbolic journey as realistic as possible.

In the Modern Woodmen of America the candidate and his escort take the role of impoverished beggars wandering in the "forests" and "city streets." The neophyte in the Independent Order of Foresters is escorted into the lodge room where he is addressed by one of the officials as a "Forester journeying through the forest of life." In the ritual of the Ku Klux Klan the candidates are admitted to "our Klavern to journey through the mystic cave in quest of citizenship in the Invisible Empire," whereupon the Exalted Cyclops instructs one of the officials to "afford them a safe journey from the world of selfishness and fraternal alienation to the sacred altar of the empire of chivalry, industry, honor, and love." The novitiate in the Order of the Rainbow, a Masonic affiliate for young girls, is conducted on a "journey" to the "end of the rainbow." At each of the series of stations the novice is halted to receive an interpretation of the color-symbols of the order.

THE CEREMONIAL ORDEAL

Ritualistic ordeals as a feature of initiatory rites in secret societies are a common practice among peoples of varying cultures. In primitive esoteric societies the ordeal is frequently found in rigorous and even brutal ceremonies ostensibly designed to test the courage and endurance of novices who are to be inducted into the mystic realms. These ordeals undoubtedly serve a double function: first, to satisfy the members of the constancy and suitability of the initiates, and, second, through the severity and sometimes horror of initiatory experiences, to impress the neophyte with the seriousness of the steps he is taking in entering the society. Primitive ordeals are sometimes "so severe as to ruin the health, and even to cause the death of the weaker novices--an outcome which is always defended by the old men on well-known Darwinian principles."[3] Flogging, knocking out of teeth, scarification, nose, lip and ear-boring, tattooing, sprinkling with human blood-these are some of the forms of ordeals which are employed to inculcate the "tribal virtues of bravery, obedience, and self-control."[4] The rather fragmentary literature of the Ancient Mysteries indicates that the ordeal was also a feature of the ceremonialism of those organizations.

Practices of these societies are mentioned because of the extent to which they parallel the ceremonials of contemporary fraternities. But in modern society there appears to be a tendency toward the refinement and symbolization of the primordial rites. These ceremonial ordeals function partly as a device for testing the candidate's suitability for full membership in the order, although this is probably not so significant, and partly as an instrument for indoctrinating the novice with the accepted dogmas of esoteric fraternalism. They seem to be characteristic chiefly of men's organizations rather than societies for women.

The ordeal is commonly a part of the symbolic drama, with the novice, as previously noted, playing the role of an untested and unconfirmed outsider. The candidate is accordingly given what is called a test of loyalty or fortitude, or is subjected to some humiliating or disconcerting experience. Sometimes the ordeal assumes the character of a threat. But instead of the novitiate being forced to undergo some terrifying physical experience he usually becomes the center of a dramatic episode having something of the character of an ordeal. These symbolic ordeals are commonly built around what might be called "spy" or "intruder" situations. Lighting and noise effects are also included to give a touch of reality to dramatic events that might otherwise border too closely on the fringe of puerility. During the course of the dramatic ritual the candidate is confronted with some situation that gives the appearance of a fidelity test.

In the Improved Order of Red Men, for example, the novice, taking the role of a "pale face," is seized as a spy and trespasser. After due consideration and much make-believe haggling he is ordered burned at the stake to test his courage. The faggots are lighted, the "braves" circle about him performing a scalp dance, and there is much excitement. At the proper moment the "prophet" rushes into the group, scatters the faggots, releases the thongs that bind the candidate, and proceeds to denounce the persecutors for trying to execute a man merely on suspicion. Much the same procedure is followed in the Independent Order of Foresters. The ordeal in this organization takes the form of a "test of fidelity" administered by the members. Before the candidate is permitted to enter the "realm of the purple cross" he is given a key which he is told to keep regardless of what may happen to him. On his "journey" he is "attacked" by "robbers," who declare that they are going to take the key from him whether he be "dead or alive." At this point of the ritual-drama one of the officers gives the fraternal sigh of distress, the members rush up and disperse the "robbers," and the candidate and his escort are permitted to continue their journey. At the conclusion of the sojourn he is congratulated by the presiding officer on his loyalty and faithfulness in refusing to yield to the threats of his attackers.

The "temptation situations" sometimes take the form of an allegory, with the member-actors impersonating certain ideas or fictitious characters such as Poverty, Indolence, and the Devil. The Knights of the Holy Cross, an auxiliary of the Methodist church, has a ritual in which the novice is "tempted" by the Flesh, the World, and the Devil. On the symbolic journey the candidate is accosted by these three characters, who invite him to come along with them so that they may all "eat, drink, and be merry." If he refuses, as he is supposed to do, they seize him and attempt to drag him along, but a member intervenes to save him from their clutches. Frequently the orders institute "tests of fortitude." In the Shrine the candidate is subjected to what is known in Shriner parlance as the "Moslem test of courage." Blindfolded, and with hands tied behind him, the candidate is started on the "journey over hot sands" with the warning that "those who die in the faith will be resurrected in glory.'" As he goes around the room he is punched and beaten with sabers, and during the course of the ceremonies he is subjected to humiliating and embarrassing experiences that border on the burlesque. In the ritual of one of the Masonic degrees the narrator relates the Biblical story found in Chronicles. When he comes to the description of the slaying of two young men by the Chaldees the members in the room imitate the noise of battle by stamping, yelling, groaning, clashing swords, overturning benches and chairs, and creating a bedlam in general. Then the candidates are "attacked," bound hand and foot, and carried into the preparation room as "captives taken at the siege of Jerusalem."

Perhaps more primitive in their character are the burlesque ordeals which usually precede the serious initiatory rites. While these initiatory caricatures most assuredly test the individual's powers of mental and physical endurance as well as his disposition, they are probably employed less as proof of the individual's suitability as fraternal timber than as an expression of certain sadistic tendencies of the fraternalists themselves. This feature of fraternal ritualism, it may be noted, has lost some of the vogue it apparently held among men's societies in earlier days, although collegians frequently employ it as a prelude to formal initiation. In many fraternities the burlesque is limited to pre-initiation bantering indulged in for its psychological effects on the initiate and the satisfaction it appears to afford the regular members.

THE CEREMONIAL OBLIGATION

It is common knowledge that secret societies make use of the ceremonial oath to further the cohesiveness of the group by guaranteeing the loyalty and support of the members. In its modern form the obligation is something more than a mere verbal promise to protect the secrets and observe the principles of the order. It involves action -- prescribed bodily posture, gestures, and formal ritualized expressions. Frequently it is accompanied by prayer, by chanting, or by special lighting effects to add impressiveness to the situation. In most instances the candidate is conducted to the altar in the center of the room to receive the obligation. Frequently he is required to perform some symbolic act as kissing an open Bible or kneeling before a coffin. These acts themselves reflect the religious, or at least quasi-religious, character of esoteric fraternalism, and are illustrative of the way in which the culture patterns of strictly religious organizations tend to be dovetailed into the patterns of secret societies.

It is observed that the obligation serves not only to guarantee the preservation of the ritualistic secrets of the fraternal order but also to define the individual's conduct according to the moral principles emphasized by the group. The entering novice promises in proper ceremonial fashion to render assistance to fellow-members who may be in distress, to observe the principles of honesty in his financial dealings with other members, to propose for membership only persons whose impeccable character is unquestioned, to obey the orders of his superior officers, to obey all signs and summons, and, if a man, never to violate the chastity of a wife, sister, or daughter of a member of the society. The definitions of conduct, however, are restricted to relations between members within the order rather than to relations between members and non-members. While it is undoubtedly true that fraternal orders do not sanction or encourage unprincipled conduct outside the fraternal circle, such definitions of behavior ordinarily go unmentioned in the obligations. Illicit sexual conduct, for example, is narrowed down to relations of a member with the female relatives or dependents of another member; beyond this there are no explicitly stated taboos. It is a good example of in-group morality.

A portion of the ritualistic obligation of the Order of the Star of

Bethlehem may be cited in this connection:

> I ... do solemnly promise that I will never reveal the secrets that are about to be committed to my keeping.... I will not indite, paint, print, stain, engrave, hew, mark, or cause to be done, any syllable, word, or sentence, upon anything under the heavens, which will tend to expose the secret work of this order or any part of it.

The resemblances of this obligation to that of one of the Masonic degrees is most pronounced:

> I. . . of my own free will and accord, in the presence of Almighty God . .. most solemnly and sincerely promise and swear that I will always hail, ever conceal, and never reveal any of the secret arts, parts, or points of the hidden mysteries of Free-masonry which may have beenheretofore, shall be at this time or any future period, communicated to me as such, to any person or   persons whomsoever .... I furthermore promise and swear that I will not write, print, paint, stamp, stain, cut, carve, mark, or engrave them, nor cause the same to be done on anything movable or immovable, capable of receiving the least impression of a word, syllable, letter, or character, whereby the same may become legible or intelligible to any person or persons under the canopy of heaven...

Certain fraternal organizations have proceeded to put "'teeth" in the obligation by incorporating within it what may be called the "self-threat." In the ceremonial self-threat the candidate, at the conclusion of the formal oath, wishes upon himself some terrible calamity or excruciating experience should he ever betray the secrets entrusted to him. In the Benevolent Order of American Scouts, a supervised juvenile organization of a patriotic nature, the candidate is given an obligation which concludes with the following self-threat:

> And should I fall so low as to violate this part of my solemn and binding obligation may I be denied the fellowship of men and driven to the haunts of the oathsome (sic) reptile, or perish in the sand of the desert and forever spurned and despised by all worthy Scouts and citizens, driven from cover to cover as the renegade who betrays his kind.

Similarly, the candidate in the Knights of the Holy Cross swears to keep the secrets of the order, asking that his hair be torn from his scalp, his scalp torn from his body, and his body burned to ashes and "scattered to the four winds of heaven" should he ever betray his obligation. In the United Order of Friendship, a Negro society, the novice asks that "lightning from the west" tear him limb from limb and the "four winds" scatter his remains so that his grave may never be found. The novitiate in one of the Masonic degrees obligates himself "under no less a penality than that of having my throat cut across, my tongue torn out by its roots and buried in the rough sands of the sea at low-water mark where the tide ebbs and flows once in twenty-four hours" should he ever violate his solemn oath. For the novice who is more credulous than critical such a self-threat, while more or less meaningless, may produce a definite emotional reaction. There is some reason to believe that this device is an effective means of regulating the behavior of members who take fraternalism seriously. Not all societies feature the self-threat, but a sufficient number have this phase of the oath to make it an important aspect of fraternal ritualism.

CEREMONIAL DEATH AND RESURRECTION

Another striking pattern of the ritualistic drama is the ceremonial death and resurrection. In primitive secret societies the initiatory rites almost universally include a mimic death and resurrection of the novice. The ancient Mithraic cult, according to Phythian-Adams, included a symbolic murder of the neophyte and his resurrection as a spiritualized being.[5] Frazer relates that in the rituals of Adonis, Attis, and Osiris the ceremonial death and rebirth of these mythological personalities was staged in the form of a dramatization of the myths current at the time.[6] In contemporary fraternalism the death and resurrection *motif* is less common than other features of esoteric ceremonialism. One notable version of the theme is to be found in the famous Hiramic Legend of Freemasonry. The dramatized legend deals with the conspiracy against the skilled workman of Solomon's Temple, his violent death and burial, the attempted escape of the conspirators and their capture, the finding of the grave, and the resurrection. The candidate, assigned the role of the murdered Hiram in this part of the drama, is resurrected from a make-believe grave in the lodge room. Ceremonial deaths and resurrections in certain other lodges are so strikingly similar to the one featured in the Masonic ritual as to suggest actual copying. Variations in death scenes are noted in different rituals. In one patriotic organization, for instance, the novice is placed in a coffin draped with an American flag and carried in a procession around the room to the "grave," where a funeral eulogy is delivered. Skeletons and other objects symbolizing death are employed in the ceremonies and allusions are frequently made to the imminence of death. The purpose of the death theme in the ceremonials is ostensibly to impress the candidate not only with the seriousness of the ritual itself but also with the reality of death and immortality. This aspect of ritualism seems to be especially appropriate for organizations having insurance provisions or sick and death benefits.

It has been mentioned that the ceremonials function chiefly as devices for the dissemination and inculcation of cherished fraternal ideologies. Lest the ritualistic dramas themselves be inadequate as instruments of indoctrination the rituals are supplemented by what is known in fraternal parlance as lectures. These formalized sermons, delivered usually for the benefit of the newcomer, are both explanatory and hortatory in character -- explanatory in that they are presumed to explain for the candidate the moral lesson of the ritual-drama, and hortatory in that they exhort him as to the way he as a member shall be expected to act. It is in these lectures also that the general political, economic, patriotic, religious, and racial creeds of the various organizations are expounded.

CONCLUSION

This method of analysis indicates a similar patterning process in other fraternal ceremonials. The burial rituals, the installation and founding services, the opening and closing ceremonies, the ceremonial balloting, all these tend to conform more or less closely to a common pattern or design. By the same token, the same approach may be utilized in an analysis of other aspects of secret fraternalism. In the character of organizational structure, in the methods of selection and control of members, in the ideological framework, in the general character of origin myths, and in the content and character of fraternal symbols the fraternities have tended to develop according to a rather uniform basic design. The presence of these cultural similarities would suggest that diffusion has been an important factor in producing this phenomenon, and historical data would tend to bear out such an assumption. The significant point of the whole matter for this discussion is, however, the fact that these cultural patterns do exist, that they may be described with some degree of accuracy, and that in their totality they constitute an institutional framework which functions as a social matrix to determine certain outlines of human thought and conduct.

ENDNOTES

1. This study of ceremonialism is part of a more inclusive study of secret societies. Data for this paper are based on the rituals of seventy representative fraternities.

2. Ruth Bendedict, "Configurations of Culture in North America," *American Anthropologist, XXXIV* (1929), p. 24.

3. Hutton Webster, *Primitive Secret Societies*, p. 34.

4. *Ibid.*

5. W. J. Phythian-Adams, *Mithraism*, p. 83.

6. Jame G. Frazer, *Adonis, Attis, Osiris*, pp. 125-35; 163-72; 211-18.

Noel P. Gist's second article on fraternalism appeared in the journal Social Forces *two years after his initial treatment of the subject. In this analysis, Gist suggests a system of classification of secret societies based upon their social function. An analysis of the form manifested by oath-bound organizations comprises the main substance of this piece. Fraternalism, Gist asserts, is characterized by "constellations" of related groups, graduated memberships, and hierarchical systems of governance.*

STRUCTURE AND PROCESS IN SECRET SOCIETIES
Noel P. Gist
University of Missouri
1938
Social Forces 16(3) (Mar. 1938), 349-357.

Used by permission of the publisher. www.uncpress.unc.edu

SECRET societies constitute one of the important culture patterns both of primitive and of modern civilizations. Anthropological literature is replete with systematic descriptions and analyses of organized secrecy among primitive peoples, and historical evidence is not lacking to indicate the role of esoteric fraternalism in more complex cultures. The Ancient Mysteries of the early Mediterranean civilizations, the military orders of knighthood of the Middle Ages, the Friendly Societies and other craft guilds of England during the Industrial Revolution, the revolutionary societies of nineteenth century Europe, and the numerous benevolent and protective societies of the United States bear witness to the social significance of institutionalized secrecy in the western world. For reasons that are not altogether apparent, this country has been especially productive of secret societies. At the beginning of the nineteenth century there were only a few thousand members of the secret brotherhoods, but by 1927, according to an estimate by Merz, there were approximately eight hundred different societies of recognized standing having a combined membership of thirty million persons.[1]

CLASSIFICATION OF SECRET SOCIETIES
While this analysis is concerned primarily with the structural and processual patterns of secret orders, it seems appropriate by way of introduction to present a classification according to their dominant functional characteristics. Some societies are so

conspicuously earmarked with certain functional traits that they can be catalogued without difficulty; the entire organization is built around some idea or function that figures prominently in the complex of traits. But for many the classification is hardly so simple. There may be a number of important functional characteristics, and to select the dominant function is not always an easy task. While it may be quite a simple matter to place in a given category a society that is avowedly and passionately devoted to the idea of patriotism, it may be quite another matter to determine if melioristic activities or religious inculcation are the paramount traits of a different order. Thus the French and Polish Catholic societies may represent a combination of nationalistic, economic, and religious activities, while the Knights of Pythias may at the same time be benevolent, recreational, and patriotic in character. Yet in most instances a careful study of the society reveals certain features which provide a fairly adequate basis for a functional classification. While frankly recognizing these difficulties, a tentative classificatory scheme is offered: benevolent, beneficial, and philanthropic societies; revolutionary and reformist societies; patriotic societies; professional and occupational societies; mystical and occult societies; religious orders; military societies and orders of knighthood; collegiate "social" and recreational societies; honor societies; abstinence societies; convivial societies; criminal societies.

Whatever may be the defects of such a classificatory arrangement, it may readily be seen that a wide variety of functions do exist. Naturally one may expect also that these rather widely differentiated functions, overlapping as they do in many instances, profoundly influence the structural framework of the organizations and affect the processes of change that take place within them. It is almost axiomatic in sociological theory to say that function influences structure and that in turn structure places certain limitations on functional activities. In secret societies there exists structural differentiation just as there exists a differentiation of functions. Indeed, fraternal orders, like many other forms of social organization, may be characterized quite as much by their structural differences as by their likenesses. This divergent patterning of esoteric societies has taken numerous forms; yet these organizations, like the family or church, have shown a propensity to retain certain skeletal outlines of structure that show marked resemblances to each other.

THE FRATERNAL CONSTELLATION

One of the significant structural patterns of fraternalism is the secret society constellation. As an accompaniment of the process of differentiation has come a tendency for esoteric fraternities to form clusters having as their characteristic configuration a dominant nuclear society and related subordinate groupings. These fraternal constellations are composed of organizations whose inter-relationships are sufficiently distinctive to set them off from other orders. The secret societies forming a fraternal constellation, while differentiated in numerous ways, are usually related to each other by marital ties or bonds of blood kinship between the various members. The most familiar manifestation of this phenomenon is the superior-subordinate relationship pattern between an original nuclear group composed of males and ancillary groupings composed of women or children who are related to the men by marriage or blood. But variations of this pattern occur: some auxiliary organizations admit persons who are unrelated to the members of the dominant societies as well as those who are related; some admit only males who have attained a certain rank in the nuclear societies, or women whose husbands, fathers, or brothers have attained such rank; others are open to members of the central orders who otherwise qualify by their occupational affiliations, their social acceptability, or their interests in certain recreational, melioristic, or military activities.

As a mechanism for increasing the solidarity, stability, and permanence of secret societies the fraternal constellation has undoubtedly been effective. Wives, mothers, and sisters of male fraternalists have identified themselves with societies under the aegis of a particular order and have therefore become interested not only in the organizations to which they themselves belong but also in the men's complementary organization to which they owe a sort of allegiance. Supervised juvenile societies, organized by members of adult fraternities, become "feeders" for the orders to which their elders belong, thereby providing a more or less steady inflow of new recruits who are carefully selected and conditioned for membership in the higher realms. Furthermore, the close relationship between the various societies within a fraternal constellation results in an interpenetration of culture traits and consequently close parallels in ritualism, symbols, ideology, and aspects of formal structural organization. The pattern of the central order is unmistakably stamped upon the auxiliary societies that come within its sphere of influence and therefore upon the whole complex. Thus there exist fraternal constellations for the Masonic order, the Independent Order of Odd Fellows, the Knights of Pythias, and numerous other societies of a similar character. Something fairly comparable to this arrangement is found in college Greek-letter societies, which have alumni organizations, parents' clubs, boards of trustees, and other appendant groups centering around a given organization.

It would appear that the larger the fraternity and the more numerous are its members, the greater is the tendency for satellite societies to develop. A large membership means, ordinarily, a heterogeneous membership: different races, occupations, and religions may be represented, sectionalism may spring up, and members may otherwise be differentiated in attitudes, interests, and points of view. Such a divergent membership is therefore likely to find expression in fraternal groupings or sub-groupings which carry with them many of the traits and much of the philosophy of the central group with which they are affiliated.

Perhaps the most impressive fraternal constellation in this country revolves around the Masonic order. At least thirty different organizations, both secret and non-secret, are affiliated with the Masonic lodge. But almost all societies of any note exhibit this structural pattern. The following examples represent the extent to which this process has worked itself out in two contemporary fraternities:

THE MASONIC CONSTELLATION

Orders of Knighthood. Knights Templar; Knights of the Red Cross of Constantine; Royal Order of Scotland.

Convivial Societies: Ancient Arabic Order, Nobles of the Mystic Shrine; Royal Order of Jesters (a Shrine sub-auxiliary); Mystic Order of the Veiled Prophets of the Enchanted Realm; Tall Cedars of Lebanon; Egyptian Order of Sciots; Order of Rameses.

Women's Auxiliary Societies: Daughters of the Nile; Mysterious Witches of Salem; Order of the Eastern Star; White Shrine of Jerusalem; Heroines of Jericho; Order of the Amaranth; True Kindred; Order of Beauceant.

Collegiate Societies: Acacia; Square and Compass; Scimitar; Gamma Alpha Phi; Phi Omega Phi (women).

Juvenile Societies: Order of De Molay; Order of Builders; Order of

Chivalry; Order of the Rainbow; Job's Daughters.
Non-secret Masonic Clubs: National Sojourners' Club; High Twelve Club.
Honorary: Order of High Priesthood.

THE MOOSE CONSTELLATION

Loyal Order of Moose (central organization for men);Mooseheart Legion of the World (men's auxiliary); Women of the Mooseheart Legion (women's auxiliary); Home Chapter (women's auxiliary); Moose Veterans' Association (men's honorary auxiliary); Mooseheart Alumni Association; Junior Order of Moose (young men's auxiliary); Junior Legion (children's auxiliary).

Where racial or cultural cleavages are so pronounced as to mean the exclusion of certain groups from fraternal membership, individuals who are objects of discrimination sometimes organize fraternities of their own which are patterned closely after the societies denying them admittance. These societies may also be considered a segment of the fraternal constellation, although there is seldom if ever any official connection between them and the "authentic" orders. In this country Negroes are rarely admitted to white secret societies, but in order to overcome this difficulty colored fraternalists have developed their own organizations, which, in many instances, are veritable facsimiles of the white associations. Among the Negroes there are orders of Shriners, Elks, Foresters, Pythians, Masons, and Woodmen; and although these societies are legitimate in the sense that they are patterned in structure and function after the white fraternities, they are usually labeled as "clandestine," "spurious," or "imitative." Disputes over the use of names, symbols, or fraternal paraphernalia have in some instances led to litigation between Negro and white fraternities. In order to avoid illegal infringement on white territory, the Negroes have made certain alterations in the names or other features of their organizations. The Negro Pythians, for example, have named their order the Knights of Pythias of North and South America, Europe, Asia, and Africa; the name of the Elk fraternity has been changed to the Improved Benevolent and Protective Order of Elks; and the Odd Fellow lodge is now the Grand United Order of Odd Fellows.

SCHISMATIC DIFFERENTIATION

Another extra-legal feature of the fraternal constellation is the schismatic society. Not infrequently have fraternal orders been torn by internal dissensions which have culminated in the complete secession of disgruntled and rebellious factions. These schismatic or secessionist orders bear much the same relation to the parent organization as religious sects do to the older bodies from which they have separated. In general the secessionists have tended to take over most of the characteristic features of the original order, frequently preserving the name with slight modifications. So far as the functions and the structural patterns are concerned the societies remain much the same.

This process of schismatic differentiation has been characteristic of the development of a number of important contemporary societies. Both Freemasonry and Odd Fellowship, according to one fraternal historian,[2] had turbulent careers during the early days in England. Stevens traces no less than twenty-seven Odd Fellow organizations which represented factional cleavages at one time or another.[3] Indeed, he observes that the separation of English Odd Fellowship went even farther than the formation of independent Odd Fellow societies, "in many instances giving birth to like organizations but with entirely different names, among them Foresters, Druids, Shepherds, and Free Gardeners." Today Odd Fellowship in this country is fairly well unified, but in England there are a number of independent branches existing alongside each other.

The growth of a number of Forestry societies is still further illustrative of the process of schismatic differentiation and the formation of legal and extra-legal fraternal constellations. The parent order of the Forestry organizations was the Royal Order of Foresters, founded in England in 1790. From this original society sprang the Ancient Order of Foresters, which in turn has produced, directly or indirectly, a number of schismatic organizations. Among the Forestry societies in this country are the American branch of the Ancient Order of Foresters, the Irish National Order of Foresters, the Foresters of America, the Bohemian American Foresters, and *les Forestiers Franco-Américains*. Both the Independent Order of Foresters and the Foresters of America are direct offshoots of the Ancient Order of Foresters. In addition may be mentioned the Canadian Order of Foresters and the United Order of Americans, formerly the United

Order of Foresters. There are probably other schismatic Forestry organizations whose names conceal their relationship to the original orders. One other illustration of this schismatic development may be given. The Order of Chosen Friends, founded in 1879, gave birth to the Independent Order of Chosen Friends, the United Friends of Michigan, the Canadian Order of Chosen Friends, the Order of United Friends, and the United League of America, the latter organization formed by German Friends of Chicago.

The reasons for the growth of these separatist organizations are probably legion. *Les Forestiers Franco-Américans*, for example, came into existence when the French members of the Foresters of America protested unavailingly against an official decree providing for the exclusive use of the English language in all fraternal activities. Other splits no doubt have occurred when members differed over matters of ideology and official policy. While the seceding fraternalists have usually striven for a certain amount of individuality in the organizations which they have set up, the similarities are certainly more impressive than the differences.

PATTERNS OF STRATIFICATION

Another important structural pattern is the system of internal stratification which has developed among the more highly institutionalized societies. In accordance with this scheme, the individual, as an outsider, proceeds to the inner realms of the secret group by means of a succession of steps known in fraternal parlance as degrees. This graduated process of admission, as Simmel was wont to call it,[4] may be pictured graphically as a series of concentric circles, the outer-most circle representing the first stage and the inner circle representing the final stage in fraternal membership. In the peripheral zone is the neophyte, the newcomer, the uninitiated, occupying a marginal position between the world of mystery which he is about to enter and the "profane" world from which he has come. It is a period of testing, of apprenticeship, and the novice, as yet untried and unproved, is given an opportunity to display the traits which the society deems desirable for complete membership. But between the outer and inner "circles" may be other zones— numerous in some instances— through which the member must pass before he is finally awarded the distinction that goes with the completion of full membership requirements or a long record of unstinted service. To attain that honor may require diligence, perseverance, and sustained interest in fraternal activities, especially if the degrees are numerous and the ritualistic requirements complicated, as they are in some orders.

While this process of graduated admission in different societies varies as to the amount of time and money involved, the principles of social selectivity tend to be much the same: the unworthy, the uninterested, the unpatriotic, or the unreliable fall by the wayside and are culled out in the winnowing process. Insofar as this process becomes selective in character, then, it is a protective feature for the fraternity and a guarantee of stability and permanence. But the sifting process works also to another end, namely, the tendency to produce a homogeneous membership within the order. It is a fairly common observation, and perhaps a fairly accurate one, that the members of esoteric fraternities tend to run to "types," and the stratifying scheme intensifies and accelerates this type-forming process.

The highly-touted democracy of secret brotherhoods is somewhat offset by the formation of social layers within the organization. At the bottom of the ladder are the novitiates, marginal members who are still "in darkness" and who must perforce demonstrate their fraternal worthiness before they are admitted to a higher social level. Becoming to their low station are an attitude of meekness and a manifestation of respect and reverence for things fraternal. At the pinnacle of the pyramid is the honorary member who has passed the various grades and who by virtue of his loyalty and diligence has been awarded a special honorary degree as an expression of the esteem of his fellow-fraternalists. Between them are other positions representing different social levels and indicating varying social distances between the members.

This stratification is not without its value in the unification of the group and the development of *esprit de corps* among the members. The fraternity itself is a sort of miniature open-class social order whose vertical channels are open to those who possess the proper qualities and who by dint of perseverance have shown themselves capable of "rising from the ranks." The higher degrees, then, become an important goal whose attainment means added prestige for those who achieve it and a quickening of the competitive process for those who aspire to such heights. They represent important devices for social control.

There is a rather wide variation in the number of stages or ranks that characterize this system of stratification. Perhaps the most highly stratified society in this country is the Masonic order, with thirty-two degrees and an additional honorary rank. At the other end of the scale, however, are a number of organizations with only one "degree." Even among collegiate societies this pattern of stratification is exhibited in a somewhat simplified way in the relationships between senior members, junior members, and pledges, the latter occupying a somewhat marginal position of quasi-membership. For societies of the lodge type, at least, the average number of degrees would probably be around three. The following representative societies are illustrative of the range of degrees:

Knights of Malta	14
Independent Order of Odd Fellows	7
National Grange	7
United Brothers of Friendship (Negro)	6
Loyal Orange Institution	5
United American Mechanics	5
Knights of the Mystic Chain	4
Knights of the Golden Seal	4
Order of Owls	4
Ancient Order of Druids	4
Improved Order of Red Men	4
Ladies of the Royal League	3
Independent Order of Foresters	3
Knights of Pythias	3
Ancient Order of United Workmen	3
Modern Woodmen of America	2
Patriotic Order of Americans	2
Sons of Herman	1
Sons of Norway	1

THE GOVERNMENTAL STRUCTURE

Since most fraternities are national or at least regional in scope, it becomes necessary for them to have some plan of control and coordination of the various local bodies if any semblance of unity is to be maintained. In their governmental structure these orders show striking parallels, a hierarchical arrangement not unlike that of the Roman Catholic Church, or perhaps better still, the Russian Soviet, being the commonly accepted pattern. Local or subordinate lodges are organized under the direction and supervision of state lodges, which in turn are controlled by supreme lodges or councils. But even with this centralization of government the orders are inclined toward democratic rather than autocratic principles, at least in the matter of representation. State organizations are composed of representatives from the subordinate lodges, while the national council is ordinarily made up, at least in part, of representatives from state organizations and representatives selected on a proportional basis according to the membership in each state jurisdiction. Variations in the manner of representation, however, occur in different societies.

Usually supreme authority is vested in the national organization. In the Knights of Malta, for example, the "supreme grand commandery" possesses the "sole and supreme authority to rule, guide, and govern" the subordinary chapters. It is the final arbiter in all disputed matters, the "repository and guardian of the symbols and mysteries of the order," and the sole authority in matters of taxation, charters, and general welfare. The supreme council of the Knights of Columbus delegates to itself complete authority to "make, alter, and repeal all laws, rules, and regulations for the government, management, discipline, and control of the fraternity or any division of it, and to enforce the rules it has instituted." Similar functions of the national organization are to be found in other societies. In the Knights of Pythias the "supreme government" is divided into legislative, judicial, and executive departments, patterned after the triangular plan of the federal government at Washington. Ordinarily the duties and responsibilities of the officers of the supreme or national councils are carefully defined by the constitutions of the orders. Membership in the national organization is usually honorary in nature, although the officials whose duties are numerous are on a salaried basis.

Subordinate to the national plenary councils are the "grand" organizations whose jurisdiction is limited to a definite state or territory. These state bodies are somewhat similar in function to the national bodies. Usually they are created only after a specified number of subordinate organizations have been formed. The Patriotic Order of Americans, for example, requires that twenty local "camps" must exist before a state organization can be formed. For the Foresters of America and the Knights of Pythias a minimum of ten "courts" is necessary, while for the Royal Arcanum a thousand members are required before a "grand council" is set up.

The state bodies have direct supervision over the subordinate chapters in their respective territories. Each state organization has its judicial, executive, and legislative functions, and its authoritative position is unchallenged unless its actions conflict with the national or supreme council. These functions customarily involve the power to amend the constitution or alter existing rule and regulations, to establish subordinate councils, to enact new laws for the government of local bodies, to have general supervisory power within a given territory, to order the trial of recalcitrant members, to assess penalties against convicted members, and to raise revenue and make expenditures.

At the bottom of the pyramid are the subordinate chapters which carry on most of the work of the fraternities. Ordinarily a membership of twenty or thirty persons is required before a charter will be granted by the state organization, although in some instances as few as ten members are necessary. Each local organization has its own officers whose titles and duties correspond to those of other subordinate lodges. It conducts its own ritualistic activities, administers insurance funds or otherwise engages in welfare activities, and sponsors recreational programs for the members.

HISTORIC FACTORS IN THE PATTERNING PROCESS

The presence of these structural uniformities naturally leads to the inquiry concerning the developmental processes which have resulted in their formation. Granted that Goldenweiser's theory of limited possibilities has some application here,[5] there still remain certain historic events which strongly suggest the diffusion of specific traits if not of whole complexes. A systematic examination of esoteric ceremonialism reveals the extent to which this patterning process has been carried in fraternal rituals.[6]

The first secret societies in this country were imported from Europe along with other culture complexes. Freemasonry was introduced within a decade after the formation of the first grand lodge in England in 1717. Some time later the Independent Order of Odd Fellows, the Ancient Order of Druids, the Ancient Order of Foresters, the Ancient Order of Hibernians, the Independent Order of Rechabites (an abstinence society), the Loyal Orange Institution, and the Order of Illuminati were introduced from abroad. These early orders of European extraction undoubtedly served as models for the patterns of fraternalism in this country. To what extent the imported societies themselves were copied directly from Freemasonry there can be no way of knowing, but it is reasonable to suppose that Masonic influence was significant.

Be that as it may, the familiar phenomenon of "interlocking memberships" in American fraternal societies has undoubtedly intensified the patterning tendency in the same way that the process of schismatic differentiation, mentioned above, has facilitated it. The facts of history indicate that esoteric fraternities have, in many instances, been founded by individuals who were at the time members of one or more secret orders. While the founders may have striven for originality and distinctiveness, it is not surprising that they grafted upon the new organizations many of the practices and usages with which they were already familiar. The Modern Woodmen of America, for instance, was founded by a man who was also a prominent Mason, Odd Fellow, Pythian, and United Workman. This same founder was also active in the establishment of the Woodmen of the World. The original organizer of the Mystic Workers of the World was a member of the Masonic order, Modern Woodmen, Maccabees, and Woodmen of the World. The founder of the Knights of Pythias was also a Mason and a member of the Improved Order of Red Men.

Thus the system of American fraternalism makes multiple membership a possibility; in fact, fraternalists in this country frequently participate as members in a number of different orders. It is reasonable to suppose, therefore, that this arrangement not only tends to strengthen fraternalism in general but also to diffuse more widely the prevailing fraternity patterns.

Another historic factor which may have contributed to the patterning process is the opposition which esoteric societies have received. The wide publicity given to secret orders in the form of exposes and propaganda has left little to be learned of their ceremonials and organizational features. Anti-Masonic agitation growing out of the famous Morgan case in the nineteenth century may have retarded fraternal development for a time, but in the end it probably served to sharpen the curiosities and stimulate the interests of many who might otherwise have been indifferent to fraternity life. Such sectarian bodies as the National Christian Association and the Catholic and Lutheran churches are still committed to a policy of opposition to fraternalism, and have spared no little effort to expose the secrets of societies, which they regard as "unchristian."[7]

By way of summary, then, it may be stated that institutionalized secrecy constitutes an important feature of American civilization. Secret societies may logically be classified according to their paramount functional activities. Although differentiated structural patterns may be observed, there appears to be a basic skeletal configuration that characterizes most of the organizations, particularly those of the lodge type. One of these patterns is the fraternal constellation, which consists of a number of secret orders clustered around some nuclear society. Another pattern is the system of stratification or graduated membership which characterizes the more highly institutionalized organizations. A third is the hierarchical character of the governmental structure. Such factors as schismatic differentiation, interlocking memberships, and organized opposition to fraternalism have probably accounted in part for this trend of development.

ENDNOTES

1. Charles Merz, "Sweet Land of Secrecy," Harper's Magazine, CLIV (1927), p. 329. *(Ed's note: Reprinted in this volume.)*

2. Albert C. Stevens, *Cyclopedia of Fraternities* (New York, 1907), p. 22. *Ed's note: An essay by Stevens is reprinted in this volume.*

3. *Ibid.*, p. 250.

4. Georg Simmel, "The Sociology of Secrecy," *American Journal of Sociology*, XI (1906), pp. 488-489. *Ed's note: Reprinted in this volume.*

5. Alexander Goldenweiser, "Principle of Limited Possibilities," *Journal of American Folklore*, XXVI (1913), p. 270-273

6. See especially my article, "Culture Patterning in Secret Society Ceremonials," *Social Forces,* XIV (1936), pp- 497-505. *Ed's note: Reprinted in this volume.*

7. *The Christian Cynosure*, a monthly journal published at Chicago by the National Christian Association, is devoted primarily to the cause of anti-fraternalism.

The first decade of the twentieth century in the United States was characterized by progressive reform. Throughout American society, experts identified problems (including poverty, drunkenness, and tainted food) and proposed solutions (such as improved education, prohibition, and government regulation). In this piece, B. H. Meyer explores the fraternal insurance industry which developed at the end of the nineteenth century and finds it largely praiseworthy, but does identify several weaknesses which he claims border on the "criminal." As a Progressive, Meyer proposes solutions including greater government oversight and self-regulation through new organizations such as the National Fraternal Congress and the American Fraternal Congress.

FRATERNAL BENEFICIARY SOCIETIES IN THE UNITED STATES[1]
B. H. Meyer
University of Wisconsin
1901
The Amercian Journal of Sociology 6(5) (Mar. 1901),
646-661.

WE are fond of saying that there is nothing new under the sun. Men less wise than Solomon, if they will but look and see, may discover that the world itself is new. The elements which compose land and water have remained unchanged, and the natural laws which they obey are eternal. But the relations which mankind bears to the animate and inanimate world surrounding it are continually changing. It is in these changed relations that one may discover the newness of the present world, and it is also in these changed relations that every significant political and social question of the present has taken its rise. Most of the earlier economic, political, and religious systems were based upon the principles of authority and dependence. The banner of independence was carried high by the leaders of the revolutions which one by one broke up the old systems. The eras of revolutions -- religious, political, and industrial - were transitional in their nature, and paved the way for a system of society having for its watchword neither dependence nor independence, but interdependence. Present society had its beginnings in dependence; its intermediary was independence; and the keynote of the future will probably always remain interdependence.

Interdependence is the prime characteristic of the new world of which we are a part. Old institutions have been modified, the "cake of custom" has been broken, and new institutions have been created to bring about a proper readjustment among men in these changed relations. Among the institutions which have performed and are performing services in this respect, the network of fraternal beneficiary societies in the United States deserves full recognition. The social history of the United States cannot be written without taking notice of a system which includes one out of every fifteen of our population, and which involves the expenditure of millions of dollars annually. These societies constitute a complex of organizations which embraces in its scope the most diverse elements with respect to race affinity, material possessions, religious beliefs, political affiliations, intellectual attainment, and social position. The thread of fraternity joins them all in one great round table of equality and democracy.

Fraternal beneficiary societies, as the name suggests, are dual in their nature. Because they are both fraternal and beneficiary, these societies are really composed of two organizations each: a fraternity and an insurance company. The National Fraternal Congress declares the following to be the distinctive features of a fraternal beneficiary society: (1) the lodge system; (2) representative government; (3) ritualistic work; (4) fraternal assistance to living members in sickness and destitution; (5) the payment of benefits to living members for total physical disability; (6) the payment of benefits at the death of members to the families, heirs, blood-relatives, or dependents of such deceased members. In other words, a typical fraternal society rests upon three things: *first,* voluntary organization on a basis of equality; *second,* some ritualistic system; and *third,* a system of benefits. These three are united in different proportions in different societies, and in not a few of them a struggle for predominance is taking place between the first and third. This is the battle between "fraternalism and commercialism." No such antagonism should exist, for some system of relief is a natural outgrowth of the idea of fraternity. As a matter of fact, it does not exist except where the benefit features are made so prominent that the fraternal element is lost from sight, and the fraternal society becomes an insurance company, perhaps wrapping the fraternal mantle about the decrepit body of a tottering insurance scheme.

The lodge system characteristic of fraternal societies goes hand in hand with the representative form of government. The term "lodge" may be used to designate the lowest unit of organization; in it direct representation is the rule, while indirect representation prevails in the higher lodges, usually termed grand (state) and supreme (national) lodges. Elementary lodges, or lodges of the first degree, have various names in different fraternal societies. There are camps, castles, chapters, clans, colonies, conclaves, divisions, rulings, hives, and tents. Lodges of the higher order generally have the same name, modified by some syllable, word, or phrase; such as high, superior, supreme, grand. Other societies have adopted special terms for their compound lodges. The higher bodies customarily exercise some supervision over the lower, and are legally responsible as principals of the latter.

The highest lodges usually meet biennially, the intermediate ones annually, and the local lodges weekly, biweekly, or monthly. Numerically the biweekly meetings appear to prevail. At the local meetings routine business is transacted in a manner similar to that in which any other society would do its business. Initiations and the granting of degrees are accompanied by ritualistic exercises. The rituals of fraternal societies are based upon sacred as well as secular themes, the latter being rather the exception. Among the former may be mentioned: the story of the cross, the building of the temple, David and Jonathan, Joseph, Maccabaeus, Ben Hur. Facts of United States history, the life of the nomad, the friendship between Damon and Pythias, are employed by other societies for their rituals. It has been said that most rituals are the very quintessence of dryness. In reply it may be urged that rituals are not to be read in one's study, but that they must be seen and heard in order to be appreciated. The ritual aims to reach the human soul through both the avenues of sight and hearing. By appealing to two senses at the same time the impression is likely to be much more abiding. Ritualism cultivates certain attitudes of mind and leads the participant mentally through scenes and experiences associated with lofty themes. It arouses the imagination and teaches objectively what many a learner through ritual could scarcely acquire through private reading, even if he possessed both ability and time, neither of which is probable. The value of ritualistic exercises can be properly estimated only when we take into consideration the multitudes to whom such ceremonies appeal with all the force of reality. Other features of the programs of fraternal societies are essentially similar to those of literary clubs -- readings, essays, debates, musical selections, etc. In addition, fraternal solicitude and the work which grows out of it find a permanent place in these meetings. It is customary in several great orders for the presiding officer to open the meeting with the question, "Does any brother know of a brother or a brother's family in need?" or words to that effect. Other societies adopt analogous forms. This is a truly beautiful custom, which can hardly fail to teach that in modern society vital relations exist among men, and that, *in* a sense at least, every man is every other man's keeper. The unobtrusive manner in which relief is given affords practical illustrations of true charity, in which every piece of silver is accompanied by golden, loving words and more loving deeds.

The relief work of some of the orders is magnificent, as the following statistics, recording the activity of a single society for the last year, will testify: brothers relieved, 87,546; weeks' benefits paid, 568,094; widowed families relieved, 5,685; brothers buried, 8,997; paid for the relief of brothers, $2,111,646.26; paid for the relief of widowed families, $124,836.81; paid for the relief of orphans, $33,130.46; paid for the education of orphans, $6,823.33; paid for burying the dead, $583,556.96; special relief, $259,131.65; total relief, $3,119,125.47. While this order pays small death benefits, it by no means belongs to the insurance type of fraternal societies; yet it is expending nearly $8,500 per day, over $350 per hour, and approximately $6 per minute. Surely this kind of charity is more than "sounding brass or a tinkling cymbal."

Relief work of this kind is not to be confused with the systems of "benefits" adopted by the great majority of the newer, societies, and which differ in name only, but not in substance, from mutual insurance. There exists much opposition among some fraternal societies to the use of such "old-line" terms as "premium," "policy," "reserve," etc. They prefer the terms "contribution," "certificate," "emergency fund," etc. Nevertheless, whenever a definite sum of money is promised at the end of a fixed period of time in return for specified contributions, an insurance contract is entered into, and the transaction is insurance. No amount of sophistry can cover an escape from this conclusion, and such a contract must ultimately rest upon the same fundamental principles upon which all other insurance contracts rest. There are fraternal societies whose beneficiary system stands as firm as the pyramids of Egypt, and the fraternal spirit of which has not been dwarfed in consequence. There is no fundamental antagonism between the noblest aspirations of fraternity and the demands for absolute safety and permanency on part of benefit features of fraternal societies; indeed, without the latter the former may become an illusion capable of drawing multitudes into bitter disappointments, if not worse.

There are in the neighborhood of six hundred fraternal beneficiary societies in the United States, with an aggregate membership of five and a half millions, two and a quarter of which are included in the three greatest and oldest and most purely fraternal orders - the Independent Order of Odd Fellows, the Freemasons, and the Knights of Pythias -- two and a half millions in the forty-seven which together form the National Fraternal Congress, and the remaining membership is distributed among the five hundred or more smaller societies. Collectively these societies have an annual income of sixty millions and carry certificates -- insurance policies -- aggregating nearly five thousand millions of dollars. About 5 percent of their income is derived from admission fees and other dues, and the remainder is raised by assessments and annual dues. Fees for admission vary from $1 to $50 in different societies, $5 being most common; and annual dues usually range between $2 and $10 and over, depending upon the amount of benefit carried. Only "benefit" members pay all the dues. "Social" members, constituting about 14 per cent of the aggregate membership of the societies in which such a class is maintained, generally pay the regular admission fees, dues, etc., but do not contribute for benefits, except, perhaps, to relief, widows' and orphans', and similar charity funds. "Honorary" and "invited" members are commonly exempt from financial obligations to the society.

The weakest spot of the fraternal beneficiary system is found in its protective features. Not that there are no fraternal societies whose systems of benefits are not thoroughly reliable, for there are such; but rather that there are so many of them that persistently and consciously ignore those fundamental and elementary principles without which anything in the nature of insurance can never endure. So often has this been done that the whole fraternal system of benefits has fallen into disrepute among many thinking people, and will require radical reforms and heroic work on the part of its friends to dispel the cloud which has been hanging over it. A brilliant Frenchman has said that people will not learn from experience unless this experience is repeated *on a large scale* through successive generations. The history of benefit systems of fraternal societies lends support to the generalization of the Frenchman. It would be neither agreeable nor very profitable to rehearse the many tales of disaster connected with the history of fraternal societies. However, it is worth our while to take a brief survey of the plans which are at present pursued by many of them in operating their benefit departments.

A speaker before the National Fraternal Congress, in 1899, presented the following statistics, illustrating the many different rates charged by different societies for the same amount of protection at the same age:

At age 30: $0.25, .35, .37 1/2 , .44, .45, .46, .50, .55, .56, .60, .62, .64, .65, .69, .70, .80, .82, .84, .85, .90, .92, 1.00, 1.04, 1.10, 1.11, 1.14, 1.16, 1.19, 1.21, 1.22, 1.40.

At age 50: $0.65, .75, .80, .85, .90, 1.00, 1.10, 1.16, 1.20, 1.25, 1.33, 1.38, 1.40, 1.42, 1.45, 1.50, 1.53, 1.55, 1.58, 1.60, 1.65, 1.72, 1.78, 1.80, 1.85, 1.86, 1.90, 1.96, 2.00, 2.07, 2.08, 2.15, 2.35, 2.45, 2.52, 2.56, 2.86, 2.90, 3.00, 3.30, 3.80.

These figures tell their own story. The speaker also found that there were twenty-one orders charging less at age fifty than another order charges for age thirty. When large numbers of men are considered, health experiences are as certain, although not as definite, as the laws of natural science, and any system of benefits which ignores this fact cannot be sound. It seems almost incredible that in this late day men should be found who deny the certainty of mortality experience, yet in fraternal literature one may find proof thereof. In justice to those who, it is hoped, constitute a majority among fraternalists, it should be said that notes of warning from within the ranks have not been wanting. They have been sounded loud and clear in unmistakable tones. The National Fraternal Congress has taken the bull by the horns by repudiating the hand-to-mouth "levy" schemes and elaborating a table of level rates, step-rates, and of two modified step-rate plans. These tables have been recommended to members by successive congresses. The table of level rates is approximately one-sixth lower than the net premiums (*i. e.,* premiums including only the mortuary and reserve elements, but not the "loading" or expense) based on the American Experience Table at 4 per cent interest, for corresponding ages up to thirty-five; and nearly 10 per cent below the same above age thirty-five. Whatever may be said with respect to the adequacy or inadequacy of the rates recommended by the Fraternal Congress, it must at least be admitted that it shows a conscious attempt on part of influential fraternal societies to base rates of contributions on actual experiences in health and expense items. One fraternal society has adopted for its basis of rates the combined experience tables of four great orders, and intends to continue on this basis until it has accumulated experience of its own adequate for the formulation of reliable tables. This is a rational method of procedure. If fraternal societies can furnish protection at lower rates than those which have hitherto seemed possible, they should have an opportunity to do so, provided that the experiment does not involve inevitable ruin. Experimentation is justifiable, both ethically and socially considered, only within certain limits. We may encourage a man to become an expert marksman, but we have no right to condemn his fellow-beings to serve as targets, nor should our statutes permit him to go unpunished in case he persists in continuing such target practice. Some societies are doing business today at rates less than one half and one-third of those recommended by the congress. This is nothing short of criminal. There is something radically wrong somewhere when a small organization can slide along in a happy-go-lucky fashion with its liabilities half a million in excess of its assets; yet such is the case today. To wipe out so large an unfavorable balance requires special assessments. These are unpopular and threaten to reduce membership. The infusion-of-new-blood hobby is held up as an encouragement to the faithful members, until the inevitable must be faced. Relatively few fraternalists seem to realize that the only safe way is to charge whatever is necessary to cover the risk at whichever age a person may enter; in other words, that the only way to do an insurance business is to conduct the same in accordance with well-established principles and business methods. If the standard mortality tables used by old-line companies are too high for the experience of fraternal societies, let their own experience serve as a guide; but until experience tables of individual societies have been actually established the use of some other reliable tables should be made compulsory. If fraternal societies can bring about a more favorable health experience, they should have an opportunity to do so. If they can reduce the cost of insurance, they will benefit society by extending the blessings of protection to ever-widening circles. If the expense element is at present too high, let them have free rein, consistent with safety, to demonstrate that it can be reduced. Their present weaknesses should not lead us into intolerance.

These remarks in regard to the safety of benefit systems apply only to those societies which promise a fixed sum to beneficiaries in certain contingencies. Although the exact number could not be ascertained, a careful estimate places the number of societies which will be excluded by this last limitation at from one-third to one-half of the whole number, so that approximately only 50 per cent of the fraternal societies will be directly affected by radical changes in protective features. The original fraternal idea was to have members contribute equal sums in specified contingencies, and the proceeds of such contributions, not exceeding a certain maximum nor the amount of a single assessment, to be paid to the beneficiary. This is not insurance, but relief work, to which the principles of insurance do not apply. If "fraternal insurance" had never been made to stand for anything else, it is probable that much of the confusion and many of the erroneous notions which prevail today could never have arisen. Many people seem to believe that there is one thing called "insurance" and another and a different thing known as "fraternal insurance." As a theory this is vicious; as practice it is criminal. Whatever the methods of organization employed, whether stock companies, mutuals or cooperative associations, assessment or stipulated-premium organizations, or any combination of these, ultimately all insurance, irrespective of external forms, must rest upon the same fundamental principles; if not, it is not insurance nor anything worthy of the prestige which this term has gained. "Insurance" which does not protect is no insurance at all. The old fraternal idea was chiefly remedial; insurance in the modern sense is primarily preventive.

While differences of opinion may exist with respect to the efficiency of legislation in bringing about reforms, there can be no question about the necessity of more adequate insurance legislation in general, and statutes relating to fraternal societies in particular. The inference should not be drawn that general insurance laws should not apply to fraternal societies. They should, in so far as these societies are insurance organizations; but because of their dual nature, uniform statutes relating to fraternal beneficiary societies exclusively should be enacted. Insurance legislation is in a chaotic state. The greatest diversities and antagonisms exist in law where conditions are essentially the same. The lack of uniformity is one of the greatest evils. The National Fraternal Congress has for a number of years recommended a uniform law, which has been enacted by the Congress of the United States for the District of Columbia, and which has also been adopted by the legislatures of several states. Only fifteen states have fairly complete legal provisions relating to fraternal societies, four of these having special laws governing the same. Six states are silent on the matter, and twenty others exempt fraternal societies from statutes regulating assessment societies, while four others require compliance with either the assessment or the regular insurance laws. Considering the magnitude of the interests involved, the urgent necessity of uniform general laws must be apparent. Either the United States Congress should establish a federal bureau for the national supervision of all fraternal and insurance organizations, or the states should bring about essential uniformity by voluntary cooperation. There exists much apathy among politicians toward this subject, for very few of them, it seems, have the moral courage to advocate measures which can bring about those radical reforms which are necessary in order to place fraternal beneficiary societies on a permanent footing. There are those in public life who believe that, because of the large membership of fraternal societies and the influence which they are capable of exerting, a man who would venture upon such an undertaking would thereafter be politically "dead." Many things in this "new world" of ours have to be borne vicariously, and this may be one of them; yet there are reasons for believing that any man in public life who would show the courage necessary to do this in a rational and fair-minded way would ultimately be the gainer thereby. Once let the illusion be thoroughly exposed, and a grateful public will remember its benefactors.

An excuse for the legislative neglect of fraternal beneficiary orders is found in the relative newness of the entire system. To be sure, a few orders count the period of their existence by centuries, but, with the exception of the three greatest fraternal orders and several smaller ones, the fraternal system, as it exists today, is but a quarter-century old. The fanciful connection between modern fraternities and medieval guilds has no significance from a social point of view, even if it could be established as a historic fact. The godfather of modern fraternal beneficiary societies is the Ancient Order of United Workmen, founded by "Father" Upchurch, a wage-earner at Meadville, Pa., in 1868. This society served as a model for the hundreds which have followed. Of 568 fraternal societies, the date of whose organization could be ascertained, 78 only were founded before 1880, 124 between 1880 and 1890, 136 between 1890 and 1895, and 230 since 1895. In other words, 86 per cent of the fraternal societies are only twenty years old, nearly one-fourth are between ages of five and ten, and over 40 per cent are either infants or children below five. The aggregate membership has risen from 3,707,947 in 1893 to 5,339,075 in 1900. The increase during the last five years has been 25 per cent., and during the past ten years it has doubled. The membership in two orders approximates one million each, and in two others it is about half a million each. There are a dozen societies with a hundred thousand or more members, ten which average over fifty thousand, and a second dozen with an average of about twenty-five thousand.

This large membership raises the question of the effect of fraternal societies upon modern life.

The "jiner" is a familiar character. Like some of the "poor" who puzzle charity workers, they distribute their fraternal affiliations in such a way as to secure the largest revenue. "Fraternity for revenue only" is their motto. They join one society to gain a *clientèle;* a second to secure customers; a third to win influence. If they do not join more, it is "because there is nothing in it." We need scarcely spend time with this abnormal type. It does not represent the "brother."

It has been asserted, however, that membership in a lodge frequently involves expenditures which should have taken another direction. Regalia and the like cost money, and the husband may spend five or ten dollars for a uniform while his wife must be satisfied with a cheap calico dress. Picnics and excursions and celebrations under the auspices of the lodge cost money, and money which, it is asserted, should in many instances be paid for better food and clothing and higher types of amusement and recreation. Whatever may be the ultimate truth in the matter, fraternal societies have here a problem which is worthy of their serious consideration. When membership in the lodge brings sorrow and pain into the family circle, the spirit of fraternity is violated at the very outset.

This applies chiefly, if not exclusively, to men. But women have also founded fraternal beneficiary societies. There are less than ten societies composed of women only, and about fifty admitting both men and women. Mixed societies may be passed over with the remark that their experience appears, on the whole, to be favorable. Women add an important social element, and seem to counteract that tendency toward "commercialism" which has made its way so far to the front in some of the newer societies. Fraternities composed entirely of women aim to accomplish pretty much the same thing which men's societies attempt. They operate systems of benefits and generally conduct their lodges in an analogous manner. The very rapid increase in the number of members of several women's societies is sufficient to show both some degree of success and of popular favor. In view of the fact that there are several millions of wage-earning women in the United States, the gradual extension of the fraternal system among women seems capable of accomplishing much good. Not only can these societies direct and cultivate the social habits of women, but they can maintain systems of benefits which will add security to woman's position in society. What has been said in an earlier paragraph in regard to protective features of fraternal societies applies also here. When multitudes of women are not only dependent upon themselves, but have also others dependent upon them, any system which adds certainty and stability to their status must be looked upon with favor. Even in far-off New Zealand, that experiment station of the world, women's fraternal societies, says the *Registrar of Friendly Societies,* "are growing in public favor." An important element in this problem is the matter of insurance risks. Extensive testimony brought before the National Fraternal Congress seems to indicate that on the whole women constitute as good insurance risks as men under the same climatic and industrial conditions, and that under certain circumstances the mortuary experience among women is even more favorable than among men. An extension of insurance among women is to be regarded as most desirable.

From a social point of view there are other important considerations which enter into the question of fraternal beneficiary societies. Whether meetings occur biweekly, as most of them do, or more or less frequently, the atmosphere of the lodge-room leaves its mark upon the brother. It is impossible for a person to visit year after year the same precincts, see and hear the same ritual, participate in the same unpretentious charitable work, hear the same gentle counsel, and be exhorted by the same lofty injunction, without being affected in his inmost soul. The very fiber of his being must show all this in its structure. Within the lodge-room all men are equal in both theory and practice. Questions of religion, politics, nationality, etc., are scrupulously avoided. Every brother must, it is true, believe in a supreme being; but he may worship where and how he pleases. A candidate is not admitted if he is addicted to drink, or if he is engaged in the manufacture or sale of liquor. Some are prohibitionists, but as a class fraternal societies stand for moderation rather than absolute prohibition. If a brother takes to drink after he has joined an order, he is privately admonished by his fellows. This unobtrusive personal work of fraternal societies is one of their greatest elements of strength. A brother has a definite place in the world. No matter what may befall him, he finds sympathy and assistance in the lodge, provided he does nothing contrary to the law. And even if he has seriously erred, his brothers will try to help him on his feet again and support him in his attempt to live an upright manly life. Many beautiful concrete illustrations could be cited to show this.

An important element in the fraternal beneficiary system of the United States is the National Fraternal Congress, organized at Washington, D.C., November 16, 1896. The congress started out with seventeen orders, representing 535,000 members, and carrying $1,200,000 benefits or insurance. At the close of 1899 the congress represented forty-seven orders, an aggregate membership of 2,668,649, and insurance risks amounting to $4,021,869,290. Last year the societies represented in the congress paid over thirty-eight millions in benefits.

The idea of such a congress originated in New York, in which state the fraternal orders had united in a similar way and had won much praise from the friends of the system by the able manner in which they had antagonized hostile legislation. It is a fact worthy of notice that the Ancient Order of United Workmen, which is the prototype of so many later societies, was also the promoter of the congress, for it was pursuant to a notice sent out by its supreme master-workman that the Washington meeting was held. In its organization the National Fraternal Congress presents no novel features. It has the usual set of officers and the customary methods of doing business. Its scope of work is indicated in the names of the standing committees on statutory legislation, medical examinations, statistics, and good of the order, and others. Along all of these lines it has done a large work. Much valuable statistical material has been gathered, which may ultimately serve as a basis for the insurance business of the orders. Reports have been made from year to year on legislation in the different states; and the discussions of the medical section have resulted in greater thoroughness and uniformity in examinations. Among the special committees which from time to time have been appointed, none has accomplished a better task than the committee on rates, to which reference was made in a preceding paragraph. The congress has done a great deal to clarify opinion among the orders in regard to their financial affairs. It has also brought together the fraternal press of some three hundred members and a total circulation of more than a million and a half. A similar body, the American Fraternal Congress, was organized at Omaha, in 1898, by the representatives of eighteen orders. The chief point of difference between the two congresses seems to be the reserve fund upon which the latter insists. This is significant as indicating a strong tendency toward the employment of well-established business methods. In one way or another, a number of societies have established a reserve fund, although, because of their dislike for old-line terms, it is usually called an "emergency fund." The federation of fraternal societies has given a strong impetus to reform.

Opposition to fraternal societies is based upon a number of different things. The imperfections of their benefit systems have called forth bitter attacks, which have only too often been justifiable. Those fraternal societies which do an insurance business on a sound basis do not seem to be able to control the system, and nothing but the most radical changes can prevent many others from moving steadily to certain destruction which has so often heretofore brought the whole system into disrepute. Secrecy is another source of opposition both on part of some churches and on part of private citizens. Attacks based upon this ground generally find much of their inspiration in the literature of the anti-masonic agitation following the abduction of Morgan, as anyone who will take the trouble to compare magazine articles of the last ten years with the pamphlets and articles of that period may convince himself. Some critics seem to assume that everything secret is bad and of the evil one, and everything open is of the light and good. "Disloyal oaths" even are mentioned. There is absolutely no evidence available anywhere which would even arouse the suspicion that secrecy as now practiced by fraternal societies is anything more than a prudent method of self-protection against imposters and designers. It is the most convenient and efficient method by which a person may establish his identity with a certain order in an unmistakable way in every part of the world. The oath, too, comes in for its share of the condemnation. The form in which some oaths are expressed is said to be barbarous and revolting. The investigations of history easily dispel such notions, by showing that these forms are survivals, and that all the oaths aim to accomplish is to impel every member to do his very utmost in living up to his obligations. No covenant is to be left unfulfilled so long as there is a single thing untried in the attempt to redeem a pledge once given. Some of the orthodox denominations object to the threefold count of secrecy, ritualism, and insurance. Ritualism is "counterfeit religion;" hence the church cannot tolerate it. "Insurance is against the first commandment, because it takes a man's trust from God and places it on the insurance company; it is against the eighth commandment, because by it the beneficiary gets something not paid for by him, therefore it is stolen; and it is against the tenth commandment, because the person who invests in life insurance is taught to covet something not his own . . . . Money procured through life insurance is obtained by good luck or a species of a game of chance." The church cannot be held responsible for the action of a particular synod; yet those high in the councils of the church can render a great service by disowning such arrant nonsense and enlightening their benighted brethren who are capable of passing such asinine resolutions.

The fraternal beneficiary system, then, like most institutions, embodies both elements of strength and of weakness. Its weaknesses are found chiefly in unsound financiering, the inimical possibilities of conviviality, undue multiplication of orders and the competition among them, encroachment upon family life by calling for large sacrifices in time and money, and in the utter lack of uniformity and the incompleteness of the statutes governing the orders. It is strong in its great relief work, its fraternal solicitude for members, its rules of equality, its unselfish and self-sacrificing acts of personal devotion, and in its teaching of right ideals, habits of thought and action. The first part of the duality constituting the system – fraternity - deserves unstinted praise; the second part – benefit - must be subjected to a process of metamorphosis (excepting, of course, individual societies) before it can meet the unqualified approval of thoughtful men. The fraternal beneficiary system of the United States deserves, as a whole, to be well thought of.

ENDNOTE

1. The investigation of which this paper is a by-product was conducted under the auspices of the Ethical Subcommittee of the committee of Fifty. This publication is by permission of that body.

Albert C. Stevens investigates the development of fraternal insurance at the end of the nineteenth century as an example of cooperative economic behavior. He indicates that millions of Americans received insurance benefits as the result of fraternal activity and did so at a cost that was significantly less than what was charged by commercial insurance companies. He argues that the lodge system of ritual is the "steel wire within the rope of brotherhood" which allowed the fraternal insurance organizations to function.

FRATERNAL INSURANCE
Albert Clark Stevens
1900
Review of Reviews 21 (1900): 59-66.

AT a time when two great industrial and commercial armies are concentrating under the form of combinations, or trusts, on one hand, and into trades unions on the other, it is more than ever important, in order to gauge our sociological progress, to note the degree of success attained in efforts which have been made for genuine cooperation.

Political economists and others during the latter half of the present century have recorded the attempts, the successes, and often the failures of cooperative movements; and one of the latest and most interesting books which refer to the subject points out, with conspicuous clearness, that cooperation as generally understood has not been entirely successful.

Col. Carroll D. Wright, in his "Outline of Practical Sociology," discusses the subject tersely and leaves little doubt that cooperative production has thus far been a failure. This is owing primarily to the worker's being obliged to wait indefinitely for the rewards of his labor— in other words, to the absence of the capitalist, who, as business is usually conducted, supplies the ready funds with which to promptly meet the wage account, to pay for raw material, rent, etc. Cooperative distribution, however, has been sporadically successful, and it is easy to recall English cooperative stores, and like ventures in this country which have not met with the prosperity which has attended similar enterprises abroad. Cooperative distribution, as is well known, is the distribution of goods by organizations the members of which expect to participate in the profits. A fault of the system, as has often been pointed out, is that it does not eliminate the evil of competition, except to those in immediate interest; and, as Colonel Wright says, is therefore "only a half measure as a remedy for defective distribution," lacking successful "cooperative production." This form of cooperation, in the opinion of the writer named, has not made much impression, in part owing to a lack of good business management and often because consumers prefer to pay a little more in order to be relieved of the task of being their own grocery men, their own dry goods merchants, and the like. It is also pointed out that cooperative distribution, in order to be complete, should include cooperative production and, of course, profit-sharing, which is a form of cooperative distribution itself, the latter serving to increase the rewards of both capital and labor and to raise the moral tone of all in interest.

There is, however, more notably in the United States than elsewhere, a highly successful form of cooperative insurance, more particularly that conducted by the so-called mutual beneficiary secret fraternities. This form of protection of the families of members of these organizations constitutes cooperation in the broadest sense of the word; and while many of the students of this sociological phenomenon are aware of it, the general public has been slow to appreciate the extent of the movement, the nature of its origin, its evolution, and the enormous proportions which it assumes to-day.

There are nearly 200 mutual beneficiary insurance organizations, conducted on what is called the "lodge system," surrounded by the attractions found in the mysticism, real or imaginary, which hedges about a secret society. It will have to be admitted that these attractions constitute one of the strongest features of such organizations, in that they form the steel wire within the rope of brotherhood which tends to hold the membership in line in spite of occasional drawbacks, disappointment in or failure of a particular system of insurance employed. For this reason the secret fraternal beneficiary insurance society, when conducted more or less successfully, is sometimes stronger than the open mutual assessment insurance society — that which does not employ the lodge system.

It would be too much to declare that the mutual beneficiary secret society, an organization of native inspiration and growth, has finally demonstrated the success and desirability of any particular system of paying life insurance by assessments, so as to meet all the requirements of the case and have enough left over for the actual cost of collecting and disbursing assessments. The rise and development of these fraternities have taken place within the last thirty years, and to the student of the subject something in relation to their origin and evolution, the characteristics of the societies themselves, their personnel and function, together with the degree of success which has been attained, cannot fail to be of interest.

In considering the subject it is necessary to keep in mind that so-called straight old-line life insurance itself has been a matter of experiment and gradual growth; that mortality tables and other records upon which such companies have based their risks required years to compile; and that discontinuances and failures incident to the development of the few enormously successful life insurance companies and more than forty prosperous smaller companies make up a long and gloomy list.

In a recently published work entitled "Facts for Fraternalists" (published by the Fraternal Monitor, Rochester, N. Y.) there are given the names of 775 old-line life insurance companies which, as stated, have disappeared and left no sign—this out of a total of 822 such companies recorded. The significance of this lies in the fact that the frequent mortality among mutual beneficiary secret societies has often been made the subject of special criticism.

It does not require much imagination to arrive at the conclusion that the germ of American insurance brotherhoods is discovered in the transplanted English friendly societies, of which the Independent Order of Odd Fellows, the Ancient Order of Foresters, and the United Ancient Order of Druids are the most important. The first named was introduced into the United States eighty years ago, the Druids sixty-five years ago, and the Ancient Order of Foresters was finally placed here thirty-five years ago. All of them are secret organizations, and by means of assessments or lodge funds otherwise acquired pay sick and disability benefits to members. All of them have imitators in this country, and shortly after the Civil War there were formed one or more non-secret beneficiary or purely cooperative assessment insurance societies, although only a few of them lived more than a year or two.

It was in 1868 that John Gordon Upchurch, a Freemason, founded at Meadville, Pa., the Ancient Order of United Workmen, a secret beneficiary society designed to pay stipulated sums to the surviving relatives of members at the deaths of the latter by means of assessments paid by surviving members. Mr. Upchurch had also been a member of what was known as the League of Friendship, Supreme Mechanical Order of the Sun, presumably a similar organization, but which for some reason had failed to give satisfaction to himself and others. The Ancient Order of United Workmen remains today practically the parent of all similar secret societies, of which there are perhaps 200, and more than one-half of which may be characterized as fairly successful. The membership of these organizations and the aggregate amount of insurance which they may be said to have obligated themselves to pay reach astonishingly large totals, fairly dividing interest with corresponding aggregates obtained from the records of old-line, or so-called regular, life insurance companies.

In a published list of 89 legal reserve life insurance companies reported as having failed in the last fifty years, 7 of them went down between 1849 and 1860, with assets amounting to $7,892,000, of which one company alone (the Knickerbocker Life of New York City) accounted for $7,232,000 of the assets in question, six of these companies evidently being small concerns. In the following decade — that in which the Civil War took place — there were reported 14 similar failures, with assets of $2,882,000, and between 1870 and 1880, a period which produced a panic and five years of depression in business, there were 64 reported failures of legal reserve life insurance companies, with assets amounting to $87,498,000. It was evidently in the 70s that many legal reserve life insurance companies found out their own weaknesses, for between 1880 and 1890 only 1 such failure is given in the list reported in "Facts for Fraternalists," while in the first half of the present decade only 3 are announced, with $2,748,000 of assets. In all, during the forty-five years 89 legal reserve old-line life insurance failures are reported, with assets amounting to $101,026,933, of which, as noted, 64, with assets of $87,498,000, took place between 1870 and 1880, and nearly one-sixth as many during or immediately following the Civil War.

It is no stretch of the imagination which attributes the incentive for the formation of mutual beneficiary assessment insurance societies, whether secret or not, to the extraordinary mortality among the legal reserve old-line insurance companies during the fifteen years following the Civil War, for that is the period during which were born the leading fraternal assessment benefit orders from which have sprung, directly or indirectly, nearly all which have since been organized.

Of the first five societies given in the following list (those organized between 1868 and 1879), the second, the Independent Order of Mechanics, was in all probability the offspring of the several secret or open benefit societies which, with suggestions from Freemasons and Odd Fellows, gave birth to the Ancient Older of United Workmen. St. Patrick's Alliance and the Catholic Benevolent Union were originally friendly societies, paying sick benefits and the like, but soon after organized beneficiary or insurance departments. A similar story may be told of the Order of the Star of Bethlehem, and from this beginning has been constructed the chain of organizations which have furnished the hundreds of thousands of opportunities for cooperative insurance which have followed. During the 70s, the period in which there were 64 reported failures of legal reserve old-line life insurance companies, with $87,498,000 of approximate assets, 29 assessment beneficiary secret societies made their appearance, all offspring of the Ancient Order of United Workmen, imitators of that society, or organizations inspired or stimulated by the successes of the latter. Some of them at the start were friendly societies paying sick benefits only or sums due on account of disabilities, either by assessments or from dues; but all of the 29 referred to, the names of which are given in the following list, sooner or later became assessment insurance organizations. The leading ones mentioned, those which have secured large memberships and which have attracted general attention, those which have given rise to similar organizations, directly or otherwise, or those which have been more than usually successful, in addition to those named, are the Knights of Honor, the Independent Order of Foresters, the Royal Arcanum, the American Legion of Honor, the Order of the Knights of the Maccabees, and the Order of Chosen Friends.

FORMED OR BECAME MUTUAL BENEFICIARY ORDERS BETWEEN 1868 AND 1879

Ancient Order of United Workmen.
Independent Order of Mechanics.

St. Patrick's Alliance of America.
Order of the Star of Bethlehem.
Irish Catholic Benevolent Union.
Knights of the Mystic Chain.
Artisans Order of Mutual Protection.
Knights of Birmingham.
Knights of Honor.
Knights of the Golden Eagle.
Independent Order of Foresters.
United Order of the Golden Cross.
Knights and Ladies of Honor.
Knights of Pythias (Endowment Rank).
Royal Arcanum.
Shield of Honor.
Catholic Knights of America.
Independent Order Sons of Benjamin.
American Legion of Honor.
Improved Order of Heptasophs.
Knights of the Maccabees.
Order of Mutual Protection.
Order of Scottish Clans.
Royal Templars of Temperance.
Knights of St. John and Malta.
Catholic Mutual Benefit Association.
Home Circle.
Iowa Legion of Honor.
Knights of the Golden Rule.
Order of Chosen Friends.
Order of the Red Cross.
Order of Sparta.
United Order of Pilgrim Fathers.
Massachusetts Catholic Order of Foresters.

Between 1880 and 1890 there were recorded the births of 36 similar organizations, a wholesome evidence of the force of the momentum in this direction due to the formation of the 34 fraternal beneficiary societies between 1868 and 1879. The list is as follows :

FORMED BETWEEN 1880 AND 1890

Modern Woodmen of America.
Order of Heptasophs or S. W. M.

Patriarchal Circle of America.
Golden Star Fraternity.
Loyal Knights and Ladies.
National Union.
Order of the Golden Chain.
Order of United Friends.
United States Benevolent Fraternity.
Catholic Benevolent Legion.
Knights of Columbus.
Royal Society of Good Fellows.
National Provident Union.
Royal League.
Catholic Order of Foresters of Illinois.
American Star Order.
Catholic Knights of Illinois.
Fraternal Mystic Circle.
Knights and Ladies of the Golden Star.
Northwestern Legion of Honor.
Legion of the Red Cross.
The Grand Fraternity.
Protected Home Circle.
Ladies of the Maccabees of Michigan.
Independent Order of Chosen Friends.
New England Order of Protection.
Improved Order of B'nai B'rith.
American Order of Druids.
Order of Select Friends.
Sexennial League.
Empire Knights of Relief.
Knights of the Globe.
National Aid Association.
Order of Unity.
United Fraternal League.
United Friends of Michigan.

Among the foregoing organizations which have secured relatively the greater prominence, in all instances to the credit of the societies in question, are the Modern Woodmen of America, the National Union, Catholic Knights of Columbus, the National Provident Union, the Grand Fraternity, the Protected Home Circle, the Empire Knights of Relief, and the National Aid Association.

If there remained any doubt of the popularity of this movement, it would only be necessary to give the following list of the most important societies which have appeared since 1890 — 74 in number. It does not include the names of several of quite recent date concerning which there is no reason to doubt the probability of their achieving a place in the world of fraternalism :

FORMED OR BECAME MUTUAL BENEFICIARY ORDERS BETWEEN 1890 AND 1899

American Guild.
Fraternal Aid Association.
Knights of Sobriety, Fidelity and Integrity.
Independent Order Free Sons of Judah.
Loyal Additional Benefit Association.
National Protective Legion.
United Commercial Travelers of America.
Woodmen of the World.
Fraternal Alliance.
Home Palladium.
Modern Knights Fidelity League.
National Protective League.
National Reserve Association.
Canadian Order of Chosen Friends.
Home Forum Benefit Order.
Iron Hall of Baltimore City.
Knights and Ladies of Security.
Loyal Mystic Legion of Honor.
Mystic Workers of the World.
Independent Order Sons of Abraham.
American Benefit Society.
Ladies of the Maccabees of the World.
Catholic Relief and Beneficiary Association.
Independent Order of B'nai B'rith.
Independent Order Free Sons of Israel.
Order of B'rith Abraham.
Kesher Shel Barzel.
National Fraternity.
The Eclectic Assembly.
Union Fraternal League.
Workmen's Benefit Association.
Knights and Ladies of Azar.
Family Protective Union.
Fraternal Aid Association.

Fraternities Accident Order.
American Fraternal Insurance Union.
Independent Order of American Israelites.
Order of Pendo.
Royal Tribe of Joseph.
Tribe of Ben Hur.
United Order of Foresters.
Ancient Order of the Pyramids.
Knights and Ladies of Columbia
Knights of the Loyal Guard.
Supreme Court of Honor.
Columbus League.
Fraternal Union of America.
Imperial Mystic Legion.
Order of Shepherds of Bethlehem.
Order of the Iroquois.
Royal Highlanders.
Sons and Daughters of Protection.
The International Congress.
The Royal Circle.
Order of Columbus.
Brotherhood of American Yeomen.
Columbian League.
Fraternal Brotherhood of the World.
Fraternal Tribunes.
Modern Brotherhood of America.
Mutual Protective League.
New Era Association.
Order of Americus.
Prudent Patricians of Pompeii.
United Moderns.
Business and Fraternal Association.
Continental Mutual Benefit Society.
Fraternal Army of America.
Knights of Aurora of the World.
Pioneer Reserve Association.
The Pathfinder.
Western Knights Protective Asociation.
Yeomen of America.
Ancient Order of the Red Cross.

Among these societies, those which have come most rapidly to the front for one or more of the reasons already specified are the

Woodmen of the World, the Independent Order of B'nai B'rith (which was organized prior to 1850 and was originally a friendly society, but which adopted the assessment beneficiary scheme in 1893), the Tribe of Ben Hur, the United Order of Foresters, and the Order of the Iroquois.

It was only natural that the system of assessment insurance originally adopted should be crude, and such was indeed the case, as is shown by its including the payment of $2,000 insurance at the death of a member by means of a uniform assessment of $1 per capita. But the experience of the earlier, larger, and better fraternal beneficiary secret organizations — the Ancient Order of United Workmen, the Royal Arcanum, Knights of Honor, American Legion of Honor, Independent Order of Foresters, and others — was such as to make plain the necessity for a system of assessments which should take cognizance of increasing age of members, whence arose the so-called step-rate assessment. In this the rate, instead of remaining uniform during the life of a member, increases gradually by periods of years. From this, however, the more progressive of the fraternal orders have graduated into a system by which assessments are graded according to age at joining, and it is in this group that we find classified 76 out of 87 of the more important among them.

As an evidence that the progress of evolution in determining the more efficient method of conducting organizations of this character has not ended, it is worth pointing out that two of the more prominent societies have gone still further and are making assessments which increase annually, according to the age of the member. Both the Knights of Honor and the National Union employ this method of accumulating sums due surviving relatives of deceased members, and the organizations named represent to that extent the degree to which these societies have progressed in solving the problem of how to insure the lives of members successfully during a prolonged period of years with only a minimum of cost for collecting and distributing assessments. Whether others, among which are many quite as successful as those just named, will imitate this example, remains to be seen, for it would not be safe to predict that the system of insurance employed by 76 out of 87 of these societies has reached perfection.

With few exceptions, the best types among the fraternal orders confine themselves to paying death benefits, although there are many (and a number of them are among the strongest of the organizations referred to) which furnish partial, total, or permanent disability benefits, in some instances a funeral, a burial plot, and a monument benefit; benefits designed to cover accidents and which will apply only in case of extreme old age ; a medical attendance benefit, and, in the instance of secret labor organizations which have mutual beneficiary features, a strike benefit, collected and distributed, of course, practically as similar funds are handled by straight-out trades unions. Most of these miscellaneous benefits have been or are paid by English and other friendly societies, and the adoption of such features by the modern American fraternal order is a recognition to that extent of the desirable characteristics of such organizations as the Odd Fellows, the Foresters, the Druids, their contemporaries and imitators.

Just as the old-line legal reserve life insurance policy of forty years ago has evolved from an almost entirely one-sided contract in favor of the companies into something very like a bond of the company, payable either at a specific date during the life of the holder or at the death of the latter, convertible, and having a surrender value for each year of its existence, so the fraternal orders have attempted to attract patrons, or rather members, by the special or particular benefits named.

While it may be humorously suggestive to point out that one of the most popular Western fraternal orders is that which announces that it will erect a hundred-dollar monument at the grave of each of its deceased members, its extraordinary rapid annual increase of membership, for this and other reasons, attests to the effectiveness of the plan by which, in part, it has attracted new blood.

The fraternal orders have also hedged themselves about with restrictions calculated to maintain a low death-rate, precisely after the manner of the more carefully managed old-line life insurance companies, by confining their field of operation and the solicitation for new members to the more healthful localities and to the country districts, and also by prohibiting membership to those who follow certain extra hazardous or even hazardous occupations.

A second variety of mutual assessment beneficiary secret societies is found among those having the short-term or endowment feature, those which have sought or are seeking to build up mutual life insurance on the tontine plan— those which agree to pay back to surviving members who shall have made certain payments, etc., for a certain number of years, the total amount of the assessments they have paid in, and in some instances with interest added thereto. Relatively few of the older short-term societies have survived. One of the best known is the Sexennial League, organized in 1888 "to enable all persistent members to have an opportunity to save small sums periodically, which, merging in a common fund, would produce large increase from safe investments, the benefit to be shared by the persistent members in proportion to the certificates held by them." The feature of this organization is the termination of membership at the end of six years, the plan contemplating each member, at the end of the sexennial period, rejoining, in order to continue to reap the harvests of maintained membership. It requires no special discernment to perceive that the success of this society is dependent on lapses of a proportion of its members. Those who are familiar with the subject are evidently aware of this, as shown by the use of the expression "persistent members."

Some idea of the financial importance of the operations of the leading fraternal orders not in the latter class may be gained from a reference to their transactions in recent years. Twelve out of 106 which furnish death benefits by means of mutual assessments included two-thirds of the membership of all of them for the calendar year 1897. Their names are as follows :

Ancient Order of United Workmen.
Modern Woodmen of America.
Knights of the Maccabees.
Royal Arcanum.
Independent Order of Foresters.
Woodmen of the World.
Knights of Honor.
Knights and Ladies of Honor.
Catholic Order of Foresters.
Knights of Pythias (Endowment Rank).
National Union.
Catholic Benevolent Legion.

That first named has a present membership far in excess of 350,000, while the Catholic Benevolent Legion, twelfth in order, possesses probably more than 50,000 members.

The largest annual increase in insurance written by fraternal orders in 1898 may or may not have been by the Ancient Order of United Workmen, totals for which have not been obtained. It is doubtful, however, whether the Workmen had more new business in 1898 than the Modern Woodmen of America, with two-thirds as large a membership, the latter reporting an increase in the amount of "insurance written," of death certificates issued, aggregating nearly $32,500,000, or about 5 per cent, of its total of death benefit certificates outstanding on December 31, 1898. The next largest increase was by the Woodmen of the World, $6,000,000. This society is the sixth largest of its kind, and its gain in the amount of death certificates issued in 1898 was nearly 4 per cent, of its certificates outstanding. The next largest gain was $4,400,000, by the Knights of the Maccabees, less than 3 per cent, of the total amount of death certificates. Relatively the largest increase, however, is that by the Ladies of the Maccabees of the World, a society which probably had few in excess of 30,000 members a year ago, but which issued $7,000,000 worth of death certificates in 1898 in excess of the like total in 1897, a gain of fully 25 per cent, over the total on December 31, 1897.

The total increase in the amount of certificates of the Modern Woodmen of America in force on December 31, 1898, as compared with one year before, shows a gain of $120,000,000, other conspicuous increases being as follows : Woodmen of the World, nearly $34,000,000; Independent Order of Foresters, nearly $24,000,000; Knights of the Maccabees, $19,000,000; the Modern Brotherhood of America, more than $9,000,000; Home Forum Benefit Order, a like sum; Tribe of Ben Hur, $5,000,000; Catholic Knights of Columbus and the Endowment Rank of the Knights of Pythias, each about $4,500,000; New England Order of Protection, $3,800,000; the Fraternal Union of America and the Canadian Order of Foresters, each about $3,500,000; and — a signal tribute to the energy and enterprise of women's mutual assessment beneficiary societies — Ladies of the Maccabees of the World, $11,500,000.

Of the 41 societies in the list from which these data are taken (organizations having each a total face value of certificates in force of $10,000,000 or more), three-fourths of them report increases in the expenses of management during 1898, a natural result, one which follows inevitably upon an increase in membership. The only gains of this which call for particular notice are in the instance of the Fraternal Union of America, where the expense doubled within a year; the Free Sons of Israel, where it more than trebled; the Independent Order of Foresters, where the gain was more than 45 per cent; the Brotherhood of America, where the expense of management in 1898 was three times that of the year before; the Royal Arcanum, with an increase of nearly one-fifth; and, last, but literally not least, an augmented disbursement for cost of management on the part of the Modern Woodmen of America of about 39 per cent. The enormously rapid growth in membership will account for a large proportion of this. The increase in the annual cost of management of the Woodmen of the World is, however, only a little more than 6 per cent.

This suggests a calculation of the expenses of management *per capita*. Among the six organizations the annual expenses of management of each of which were $100,000 or more in 1897, the lowest rate per capita was in the Royal Arcanum, 62 cents ; the next lowest the Modern Woodmen of America, 87 cents ; after which came the Knights of the Maccabees, the annual outlay for management of which was 94 cents per capita ; for the Knights of Honor, $1.23 ; and for the Independent Order of Foresters, which owns a magnificent building in Toronto and is presided over, at a large salary, by Oronhyatekha, M.D., the *per-capita* cost of management two years ago was, as appears, $1.56, or $195,650 expense for management with a total membership (1897) of about 125,000. The average cost of management *per capita* in 27 leading fraternities analyzed was about $1.65 in 1897, compared with a *per capita* cost of $1.48 about fifteen years before, when those societies averaged about three years of age.

In 30 societies the records of which are analyzed in the *Cyclopaedia of Fraternities*, the rate of mortality during the third year of existence of each averaged 4.10 per 1,000, while during the fiscal year 1897 (an average of from fifteen to eighteen years afterward) the death rate was 9.5 per 1,000.

It is of particular interest, in connection with the foregoing statement, to note that the average cost of $1,000 insurance, or benefits, in 28 of these societies in the third year of their existence was $5.04, while from fifteen to eighteen years later, in 1897, the average cost was $9.22 per $1,000 insurance. In these exhibits one finds the death-rate more than doubled and the cost of insurance per $1,000 almost doubled within the average period named, notwithstanding the increase in membership during that time. This may perhaps form the basis of the movement which has shown itself favoring fraternal orders providing for reserve funds, in which they practically follow old-line life insurance companies.

The rapid growth of membership in fraternal orders since 1870 has attracted attention and brought out severe criticism from State examiners and from representatives of old-line life companies. This has not been uniformly the case, for the fraternal or cooperative society has also found defenders among the class referred to. The most serious criticism is based on the lack of legislative provision for governing their incorporation and organization and for providing proper State supervision. The writer is aware that State supervision of the fraternal orders has met with violent opposition. But notwithstanding the existence of bonded treasurers, even in an organization in which only one assessment may be kept on hand with which to meet a death benefit, yet in as much as that one assessment may amount to a great many thousands of dollars and that legal reserves are now beginning to be provided, the institution becomes more than ever of a fiduciary character, and as it is generally managed by a very few officials, a requirement that the State Banking or the Insurance Department should supervise it would seem to be only in the line of reasonable precaution and propriety.

The Independent Order of Foresters, one of the more prosperous of these societies, finds no difficulty in meeting the requirements of the Canadian and British laws governing such bodies, and would probably be willing to meet like requirements on this side of the line. A similar argument should hold true with respect to all the fraternal orders.

As has been repeatedly pointed out in recent years, a successful old-line life insurance company — for that matter, any successful insurance company — must present three features : First, it must have an attractive plan; second, the payments of premiums must be so arranged as not to increase from year to year, which has not been the experience of assessment insurance societies, fraternal and otherwise, after having passed the period of youth ; third, the contract between the insured and insurer should be of such a nature as to be convertible, and possess a surrender value — that is, the insured must have the privilege of retiring at almost any time with something more than the recollection that he had been insured while he had kept up the payment of premiums.

The mere statement of the foregoing shows clearly some of the broadest differences between the fraternal order and the old-line insurance method. It may be granted, for sake of argument, that the old-line insurance companies and the fraternal orders both have attractive plans. It is easily within the power of the old-line companies to arrange the payments of premiums so that they will not increase from year to year, and this they have done. The experience in such companies is that lapses of policies decrease very rapidly after four years, while in the fraternal orders it has been shown that lapses tend to increase in time, in part because of changed circumstances of the insured or dissatisfaction on some personal ground, but more often because of increasing rates of assessments. The question, then, arises, What does the assessment insurance company possess which offsets this unfavorable feature?

The open assessment company — that is, the mere business arrangement between a certain number of thousand people to assess themselves to pay death benefits — often has little to offer, because interest in the organization may hang solely upon its ability to keep down the rate of assessments and to meet its obligations promptly. Not so with fraternal orders, which are veritable social centers, secret fraternities and sisterhoods, and about which hang the elements of permanence and strength over and above all question of life insurance. A secret bond of brotherhood, with all that the words imply, which in addition thereto proposes to confer certain benefits upon surviving relatives of deceased members, may with safety call upon its members for sacrifices to meet the obligations it has assumed, in many instances where the demand is such as would immediately disrupt an ordinary open mutual assessment society. Here, then, is the steel wire referred to which runs through the rope of brotherhood insurance, which has held and promises to maintain fraternal orders in spite of the difficulties attending an effort to solve the problem of mutual insurance.

Does any one for a moment suppose that a purely business association of, we will say, 40,000 men who have combined to assess themselves, for instance, on an average $2 apiece at the death of a member for the purpose of paying insurance to surviving relatives, would be able to hold itself together if, on finding the system faulty, a few representatives appointed with power promulgated a plan by which all its assessments were promptly doubled? In all probability hardly more than one or two such open assessment companies could, under such circumstances, prevent sudden disintegration. Yet that is exactly what the Royal Arcanum, one of the best and most prominent fraternal orders, has succeeded in doing within the past year. In no other society of this sort is the character of the membership higher, socially or otherwise, or has the spirit of fraternity and brotherly love been more strongly developed. No other leading fraternal order which has had to radically reorganize its plan of assessment — and most of them have had to do it — has succeeded in accomplishing it with so little friction and so immaterial a loss of membership as has the Royal Arcanum.

A prominent official of the Equitable Life Assurance Society said in his address before the National Insurance Convention at Milwaukee on September 14, 1898 : "It is quite possible for . . . a fraternal society to combine death-loss assessments with other elements of their constitution in so small a proportion that the dissatisfaction over assessments is counterbalanced by the cohesive power of the other features of the society." He adds that "those fraternal orders which furnish something desirable in addition to insurance — fraternity, a club, and social reunions — may struggle along with even a moderately imperfect system of assessments and so accomplish their purposes in some degree."

Here, then, we find, working side by side, two great influences for the amelioration of the condition of the human family. Each is striving to add to the sum total of human happiness by providing for the surviving relatives of members of fraternal orders or of policy holders in regular life insurance companies. The claim of the more argumentative members of some of the former organizations has been that the cost of insurance in the old-line companies is proportionately too high, and for proof a finger is pointed to the enormous surpluses which have been rolled up by the New York, the Equitable, and the Mutual Life. In the meanwhile each type of insurance society, the cooperative and that which really is not — the fraternal order and the old-line company — has been improving, strengthening, and developing its system. Probably neither claims to have reached perfection, although there is much to be said in favor of a policy in an old-line life company of high standing because of the security and permanence of the contract.

But true it is that without the fraternal order and its cooperative system of insurance, thousands upon thousands, in the event of their own deaths, would be unable to protect those nearest and dearest to them.

Here it is that the fraternal order is seen to be doing an enormous work for good and for happiness which the old-line companies have not been and are not able to perform. The mere statement that there were nearly 2,600,000 members of fraternal orders on December 31, 1898, compared with 2,106,274 policies in force in old line life companies reported to the New York State Insurance Department, will give some idea of the relative social importance of the two systems. On the date named there was about $5,700,000,000 worth of old-line life insurance in force in the United States, compared with $3,400,000,000 worth of benefit certificates in force issued by fraternal orders. It only remains to be added, to show clearly the point of view of the friends of cooperative life insurance, that the total expense of management of life insurance companies in 1898 was $71,898,501, while the corresponding item with reference to fraternal orders was $3,580,380. Thus we find two-thirds of the life insurance business of the country in the hands of about 46 old-line life companies and about one-third conducted on a cooperative basis by fewer than 200 fraternal orders. With one-third of the business the fraternal orders are carrying on their work of providing benefits for surviving relatives of deceased members at one-twentieth of the expense for cost of management reported by the old-line companies, a little less than 5 per cent, as much. This they have been doing with varying success, considerably more than less, for a quarter of a century, and the movement has always been one of progress. That they will so continue, that the system will be still further perfected, and that they will remain the source of life insurance or death benefits at a low cost per capita and per $1,000 of insurance, there is no possibility of doubt.

As a cooperative movement their success has fairly run away from the efforts at cooperative production and distribution. Were it not for the extraordinarily large number of fraternal orders which have appeared during the past eight or nine years, one might hope for consolidation rather than multiplication ; but, as someone has said, the desire for medals, brass buttons, gold lace, and for office and power continues as strong with some people as it does with others. Thus we frequently observe that when a fraternal order becomes large and powerful and develops rival candidates for office, a new order is promptly started, with high sounding titles, another ritual, with more grips and passwords and a ceremony of initiation which betrays the handiwork of those who have belonged to some of the older orders or who have delved deep into the descriptions of some of the so-called ancient mysteries.

Abb Landis provides an overview of fraternal insurance which includes a history of its development, tracing its roots to Great Britain's friendly societies. He argues that the fraternal orders greatly benefit society and that they are evolving institutions which have come a long way, but can still be improved. In contrasting them to commercial insurance companies, Landis asserts that the genius of the fraternals is that they are governed democratically by the very people who are insured. Ultimately, Landis suggests that the fraternal insurance companies might provide a model for future developments of the American economy in which mutual cooperation renders the capitalist unnecessary while workers run corporations for their own benefit.

LIFE INSURANCE BY FRATERNAL ORDERS
Abb Landis
1904
Annals of the American Academy of Political and Social Science. 24
(Nov. 1904), pp. 45-58.

ORGANIZATION for mutual assistance is of great antiquity and wide distribution. Societies of this kind have not always been as sharply differentiated as they are to-day. In common with other institutions they have emerged from a comparatively indefinite similarity to a comparatively definite heterogeneity, and have doubtless yet to undergo further development.

The first systematic effort at mutual co-operation along altruistic lines was in the formation of the great trade guilds of the Middle Ages. As the guilds degenerated and gradually outlived their usefulness, the need of substitute organizations became apparent. To the recognition of this need we may trace the rise of the Friendly Societies of Great Britain. Of these, it will suffice to consider a typical specimen, for which purpose I have selected the largest and strongest, the Manchester Unity, I.O.O.F. [Independent Order of Odd Fellows]

This great body, with a present membership of over a million, is composed of and governed by the laboring classes. Local lodges exist in all parts of the country and manage their own affairs in a thoroughly democratic manner. They are as independent as the New England town, being, like the latter, subordinate to a central body of strictly limited authority, to which they send representatives. In the local lodge itself one member is as good as another and discussion is perfectly free. The officers of the central governing body are elected annually, with the exception of the Secretary, whose tenure is permanent.

The founders of the Unity failed to appreciate the nature or magnitude of the financial problems involved in their undertaking. Although the plan of the society contemplated the payment of definite sickness and funeral benefits, no attempt was made to calculate adequate rates of contribution. Aside from the fact that such a calculation would have been impracticable for lack of a sufficient volume of reliable data, its importance was not recognized.

There existed in Great Britain the same feeling that we find so prevalent in our own country: namely, that "Fraternity" could be depended upon to overcome all the evil results of vicious business habits. That Fraternity is capable of accomplishing much can be doubted by no careful observer; but the tendency to regard it as a panacea is sure, soon or late, to lead to disaster. This the Unity learned in time by the teachings of bitter experience.

Organized in the year 1812, the Unity grew and flourished for several years, because its rates sufficed while the members were all young and mostly in good health. In fact, many of the lodges became burdened with accumulated funds, of which they proceeded to relieve themselves by exploiting the social virtues. They little realized that these very accumulations formed their only safeguard for the future when, on account of the increasing age and infirmity of their members, the claims should become too heavy to be easily satisfied from the proceeds of current collections.

After some thirty years of this loose, improvident operation, it became abundantly manifest to some of the more thoughtful members that the Unity had traveled far on the broad and pleasant road that leads to destruction. Then began an agitation which threatened the very existence of the society through the secession of individuals and entire lodges, but which resulted in a thorough investigation of its past experience and the formulation of adequate rate tables for future use. With the adoption of these tables in 1854, the Unity opened a new chapter in its history which thenceforth has been an uninterrupted record of growth and prosperity. One more reform needed to be, and was, instituted in the decade ending in 1870, by which year quinquennial valuations had become compulsory.

The record of the Unity demonstrates that it is quite within the capacity of the laboring classes to conduct a great business on democratic principles. It is an object lesson which justifies a most optimistic attitude toward future industrial conditions. As such, it has attracted the favorable attention of the actuaries, economists and legislators of Great Britain, all of whom seem to have recognized the fact that they were confronted with a phenomenon of most hopeful import. It is regrettable that a similar movement in this country has received far less sympathetic treatment from experts and officials. Some reasons for this difference of attitude will be given later.

Before leaving the subject of Friendly Societies, of which the Manchester Unity was selected as a type, some mention should be made of the exhaustive investigation of their plans and circumstances which was conducted between the years 1870 and 1875 by a royal commission. The report of this commission is in every respect a model document, and the recommendations therein contained were not only eminently practical, but were admirably calculated to assure safety and permanence to institutions which had accomplished a vast amount of good and had sinned chiefly for want of light. In 1875 the recommendations of the commission were incorporated in an act of parliament which places the stamp of government approval on such societies as take advantage of its provisions and comply with its requirements.

In the United States, prior to 1868, there were no organizations closely resembling the British Friendly Societies. It is true that secret societies, such as the Freemasons and Odd Fellows, and trade unions were accustomed to assist distressed members, but such work was more or less incidental and not the main object of their existence. Furthermore, the help so extended partook of the nature of charity; that is, it was dictated by sympathy or fraternity instead of by contract.

In 1868, however, John J. Upchurch, a Pennsylvania working-man, founded the Ancient Order of United Workmen, in the plan of which mutual insurance was dominant, although the features characteristic of secret societies in general were by no means ignored. In various centers in the State were organized local, self-governing lodges which were entitled to send delegates to the grand lodge at Meadville, the central legislative body, the elected officers of which managed the financial affairs of the society and compelled obedience to the by-laws on the part of the local bodies. In fact, the grand lodge, although a representative assembly, was the real source of authority, the self-government of the local lodge being based on sufferance rather than on right.

As the society spread into adjacent States and additional grand lodges resulted, the supreme lodge was organized at Meadville [PA] in 1871, for the purpose of harmonizing the work. Its function is advisory, rather than authoritative, the grand lodges having declined to surrender their independence and having reserved the right to repudiate their allegiance to the supreme body. The rapid growth of the Workmen, indicating that it met a popular want, of course inspired imitation, and to-day there are in the entire country upwards of two hundred fraternal beneficiary societies. They all have representative government, the lodge system and ritualistic ceremonies; in fact, these features are required by the statutes of most of the States. In respect of benefits offered and rates charged, they exhibit all the picturesque variety of which the untrammeled human fancy is capable. That there need be any particular relation between the respective values of the benefits promised and of the contributions charged never seemed to occur to the founders of these societies. In fact, all suggestions of that nature were brushed aside as smacking of theory and, therefore, unworthy of consideration by practical men who had competition to meet and could guess just as clearly as their rivals.

In the seventies, a great impetus was given to the formation of fraternal beneficiary societies by the failures of old-line life companies and the startling disclosures as to the methods followed by some of the most prominent among them. A description of these methods will be unnecessary. They are fully set out in the reports of the Insurance Departments of Massachusetts and New York, published in the decade 1865-1875. Extravagance and mismanagement ran riot; self-interest dominated official conduct and utter recklessness characterized the investment of funds. There was a repetition in this country of the methods adopted in England which disgraced and demoralized the British Life Insurance business. In *Martin Chuzzlewit* they have been depicted for all time by the master hand of Charles Dickens. Suffice it to say that the exposures, principally by the New York and Massachusetts Insurance Departments, so seriously affected public confidence in the life companies in America that the business of the latter remained subnormal for years thereafter. In fact, it did not regain its former proportions until after the passage of stringent inspection laws by several of the State legislatures.

The full tontine policy, now prohibited, but once common, by which the lapsing member forfeited all surplus payments made to the company over insurance cost and expense of management, was productive of great dissatisfaction amongst those who had been compelled by adverse circumstances to discontinue policies which had often been kept in force for years, and to the credit of which there were substantial reserve accumulations, to say nothing of deferred dividends. To these disgruntled victims of old-line methods, the siren voice of the fraternal beneficiary society was sweet indeed. Within the sacred precincts of the lodge room they could denounce to a sympathetic audience the "outrageous treatment" to which they had been subjected by a "soulless corporation" and could resolve to demonstrate to the world the possibility of combining the business of mutual insurance with the practical exemplification of the golden rule. The idea was a noble one, albeit somewhat too elevated for present-day human nature and insufficiently enlightened by a knowledge of the cost of insurance. To fraternalists the mathematical reserve on life policies has always been a more or less unholy mystery. Having, in the old tontine days, seen this accumulation confiscated in the case of lapsing members, it was a natural inference that a similar course was followed in respect of the dead. Obviously these millions of reserve bore a sinister aspect and represented an unnecessary burden on the helpless policy holder. Thus originated the popular battle cry of "Keep your reserve in your pocket."

For many years the societies remained true to their principles and seduously avoided accumulation and only with the utmost reluctance did they begin to abandon the practice under the irresistible pressure of experience.

In the oldest societies, such as the Workmen, business principles were at first completely subordinated to the demands of fraternity. No discrimination was allowed because of age, occupation, residence or physical condition—all members were on a perfect equality. That such methods did not wreck the society before it was fairly launched is conclusive proof that the fraternal tie is more than an empty sentiment.

Slowly, but none the less surely, the faulty system of the Workmen has been mended until now the supreme lodge urges with all the force at its command the adoption of a plan prepared under the guidance of a competent actuary. In other words, here, as in Great Britain, the common people have demonstrated their capacity to manage large enterprises on democratic lines. To one who has the welfare of humanity at heart, few signs could be more encouraging.

Few societies have imitated the Workmen's original example of a uniform rate of assessment at all ages. We find the vast majority adopting the system of rates graded to admission ages and remaining level thereafter. Within a few years, a society so operated would find itself composed of groups, corresponding to entrance ages, each containing members of various ages paying the same rate. In short, a compound Workmen plan had been substituted for the original simple device, with little or no practical advantage.

Of one society, the National Union, special mention should be made, because of the fact that it started on the step-rate principle, the rates being graded by ages and each member being required to pay the rate corresponding to his attained age. This plan was defective because of the fact that the rate schedule stopped abruptly at age 65, no adequate provision having been made for members who should pass that point. It is particularly gratifying to be able to say that this weakness has now been overcome through the efforts and upon the initiative of the members themselves.

In course of time, the older societies began to experience difficulties. In spite of their most strenuous efforts, they found themselves compelled to levy assessments more and more frequently, with the result that they were unable to compete on equal terms with their younger rivals. The latter, having learned something from the experience of their predecessors, endeavored to prevent their own future decay by every fantastic device that the wit of man could conceive. Some of these were actually patented, which fact would indicate that their inventors at least believed them to be effective. A study of these various schemes to secure the advantages of a mathematical reserve, without accumulating it, will convince any unprejudiced mind that the ingenuity of ignorance is still in active operation. Fortunately, the older societies do not find these vagaries attractive, but manifest a tendency to readjust along scientific lines, with the assistance of expert advice.

An important distinction between the British friendly and the American fraternal beneficiary societies should not be forgotten. The main purpose of the former was and is the payment of sickness and funeral benefits, and, although some of them offer ordinary life insurance, the maximum risk assumed on any one life is 200 pounds. The American societies are essentially mutual life insurance organizations, although some of them pay limited sickness and accident benefits. The most popular certificates have a face value of $1000 or $2000, but not infrequently they are written for $5000. The foregoing distinction may help to explain why in the one country the attitude of the actuaries is tolerant or sympathetic, while in the other it is hostile. Practically all of these gentlemen are or have been, connected with old-line companies, and have thus become somewhat biased, perhaps unconsciously.

The British societies occupy a field of their own, their competition with the business corporations being hardly perceptible. The American societies, on the other hand, are active and most successful competitors of life companies. Furthermore, the founders of the fraternal societies provoked the experts by sneering at them and ignoring their sometimes disinterested advice. At first glance the situation would seem to be unfortunate, but the indications are that it may result in the development of a new generation of actuaries, unfettered by traditions.

The fraternal beneficiary system is now in its thirty-sixth year and its amazing vigor is a source of perennial grief and astonishment to its old-line enemies who regarded it at first with the kind of intolerant contempt that Alexieff used to display toward the Japanese. It seems impossible for men to learn that there are more things in heaven and earth than are dreamt of in their philosophy. The Ancient Order of United Workmen which, by all the rules of orthodoxy, ought to have perished years ago, had, at the end of the year 1903, a membership of 435,015, carrying insurance to the amount of $745,928,000. Only one society exceeds it in size.

It is evident that we are here confronted with a phenomenon that defies mathematical analysis. The plans of the fraternal beneficiary societies may be simultaneously abhorrent to mathematics and acceptable to human nature.

The policy holders of an old-line company, even though it be the mutual variety, are practically impotent to affect its management, being without organization or knowledge of one another's ideas. As few of them can attend the annual meetings, they usually designate as proxies men of whom they never before heard, and of whose opinions they are blissfully ignorant. They feel and are as helpless as the depositors in a bank who place their trust in the honesty and sagacity of the officers and hope for the best. This is business, pure and simple, and to it business principles apply in all strictness.

The members of a fraternal beneficiary society are organized in numerous local lodges which hold meetings at least once a month and sometimes every week. Here the members become acquainted and here they discuss every detail of their co-operative enterprises. As the time approaches for the regular annual or periodical meeting of the supreme body, they elect thereto trusted representatives, whom they may instruct if they so desire. There develops in these members a very active feeling of proprietorship in their society and of loyalty to its interests. It is, so to speak, their child, and they will endure no inconsiderable sacrifices to conserve its existence. To such a condition, business rules and principles are inadequate, as they ignore the most vital feature of the phenomenon.

That the foregoing is the true explanation of the failure of facts to verify actuarial predictions is indicated by another striking circumstance. About the time that the fraternal beneficiary movement originated there were organized on the same faulty plans, but with government similar to that of the old-line companies, a number of so-called assessment associations. Although their officers were, as a rule, more keenly sensitive than those of the fraternals to approaching dangers, yet, with a single exception, due to peculiar conditions, every one of these associations has disappeared or has been transformed into a legal reserve or stipulated premium company. As Carlyle would have said, "This is significant of much."

As a direct result of the lodge system, the societies minimize the expense of field work. The members become voluntary solicitors, without pay. They love and take pride in their organizations, and believe that they render a genuine service to their friends by persuading them to join. A comparison of the respective costs of management of the business companies and the fraternals is highly enlightening. Thus, for the former, it is annually between eight and nine dollars for each $1000 of insurance in force; while, for the latter, it is less than one dollar.

If it be argued that lodge dues have been ignored in the comparison, the answer is that their main object is to pay for fraternal features for which there is no counterpart in an old-line company. Nor are these features imaginary. We find them sufficiently powerful to hold together vast societies like the Masons and Odd Fellows, which do not pretend to conduct an insurance business. Millions have been paid by the local lodges for the relief of members who were sick, injured or out of employment. Other millions have been expended in social entertainment, which is a feature not to be over-looked when estimating what has been accomplished by these bodies. I have noted, in many publications, slurs cast at this latter kind of expenditure. Those who belittle the social feature evince ignorance of one of the strongest points in favor of mutual insurance under the lodge system. Life insurance, *per se*, is taken and carried for the protection of dependents. No benefit is realized until the death of the insured, and, consequently, he who carries and pays for the insurance has no other satisfaction from it than that derived from the consciousness that he has provided for loved ones in the event of his death. Of itself, such a performance indicates a high and noble purpose. Man owes a duty to himself, and when this can be combined with that owed to his family, much has been accomplished toward the consummation of a perfect system of social organization. The lodge meetings not only provides the ordinary pleasures of social intercourse, but under the influence of the teachings of the ritual, they are an inspiration to higher ideals, and beget the altruism that turns the mind outward and makes men wish to live for others beside their own immediate families. This social feature of the fraternities has saved thousands from drunkenness and other forms of dissipation into which they otherwise would have plunged in their blind quest of pleasure. Many of these societies accept members of both sexes, and most of them absolutely bar alcoholic liquors from their lodge rooms.

The combination of life insurance operation along with fraternal and social relations is one that appeals to reason and sentiment and tends to popularize co-operative effort for mutual protection. The life companies have recognized this fact and have undertaken to minimize its effect by representing that they sold policies under which the insured did not "have to die to win."

The not unnatural desire of the policyholder to derive some personal benefit has been met by the business companies in the form of investment or endowment insurance, as well as by the promise of dividends, the latter being simply such portion of his excess payment as the company sees fit to return. Of endowment insurance it may be said that it is an excellent refuge for the man who cannot trust himself to make provision for his old age. The exceedingly wasteful character of this form of investment has been by no one more scathingly exposed than by President Greene, of the Connecticut Mutual Life Insurance Company, a man who believes that the union of insurance and investment is unsanctioned by nature.

In order to add to the attractiveness of dividend estimates and, at the same time, to provide a huge fund to be used at discretion, the business companies devised the semi-tontine or accumulation policy, by which those who live to the end of the accumulation period are to get magnificent returns, according to the estimates. Unfortunately, actual results have always fallen far short of the estimates, because, with so much money at their disposal, the companies could not resist the temptation to indulge in extravagance. It is always pleasant to spend the money of others, if one does not have to account for it.

An important difference between the old-line and fraternal systems is in respect of elasticity. The life company is rigid, the contract being definite as to both benefits and contributions. For the sake of safety, the company is, consequently, obliged to overcharge. Some of this excess doubtless returns to the policy holders in the shape of dividends, but as these are seldom guaranteed, the opportunity for extravagance is obvious. Whether or not it is utilized may be inferred from the fact that the companies make little or no effort to sell non-participating policies, the premiums on which are only moderately loaded for expenses. Some do not sell them at all. One prominent stock company, which used to confine itself to the non-participating form of policy has recently abandoned the practice. Another large company, with a most enviable reputation for conservative and economical management, has of this kind of premium-paying insurance in force only about $4,000,000 out of more than three hundred millions.

In the fraternals the amount that a member will be required to pay from year to year is seldom entirely definite. His assessment rate may be established in the by-laws, but almost invariably these are subject to amendment by the supreme legislative body. In most of the societies the number of assessments that may be levied in a year is limited only by the needs of the organization. Furthermore, it is not unusual to find a provision whereby no claim can exceed the proceeds of one assessment on the entire membership. As the provision for expense of management is generally quite definite, there results not only the ability to collect each year the exact cost of protection, but a most effectual discouragement of extravagance. The members have never shown a disposition to endorse the doctrine that the services of some men are worth from fifty to a hundred times as much as those of the average citizen, and, as a consequence, salaries above $5000 are rare. Strange as it may seem to those conversant with old-line conditions, capable officers are secured without difficulty, in spite of the uncertain tenure of their position. The wisest selections may not always be made, but, on the other hand, the unfit do not survive.

Democratic government naturally involves politics, and from the latter it must be confessed that the fraternals are not exempt. That this circumstance is to their detriment is by no means certain. Political aspirations are distinctly honorable when not tainted with graft. From suspicion of graft, the administration of the societies has been singularly free. Although large sums of money have been handled, the losses that have occurred have been due almost exclusively to faulty judgment. Even such losses have been inconsiderable. In fact, in respect of both honesty and economy of management, the fratemals can well stand the test of comparison with old-line companies.

Although enough has been said to indicate that the fraternal beneficiary system is in harmony with existing conditions in the United States, it will be useful to investigate its prospect of permanence. In the first place, let it be premised that the failure of individual societies proves nothing against the principle upon which they were founded if other adequate causes are known to exist. The whole movement is still in the experimental stage, for which reason alone uninterrupted success would be little short of miraculous.

Representative government has not in every instance proved equal to the tasks imposed upon it, but it has shown an ability to profit by experience. With few exceptions, the recent history of the societies under consideration has been most encouraging. There is every indication that the great majority of them will, through their own efforts and without compulsion, so reform their faulty plans as to assure their financial stability.

Unfortunately, the paternalistic tendency, which is becoming more and more apparent in both State and Federal governments, has so affected the various commissioners of insurance that they are not content to let well enough alone, but must break the shell to let the chicken out. Verily, a little knowledge is indeed a dangerous thing when the possessor thereof is a public official. At their 1903 convention, held in Baltimore, Md., the commissioners agreed upon measures which, if carried into effect, would almost certainly destroy the fraternal beneficiary system. It is difficult to avoid the conclusion that they were influenced by either hostility or ignorance. In this connection, how unfavorably do they compare with the sympathetic, painstaking members of the royal commission that investigated the British friendly societies.

On this subject I speak feelingly, because I believe that the fraternals are beginning to solve one of the most important of industrial problems and that their defeat through ill-advised legislation would be little short of a public calamity. They should be required to exhibit their financial condition in a more scientific manner than has been customary, so that the accusation of deception may be deprived of its plausibility, but we should hesitate to take from them the right to establish such rate schedules as they wish. The members are neither children nor imbeciles, and do not need the fatherly care of insurance commissioners or State legislators. They enjoy the advantages of representative government and have demonstrated their ability to modify their plans when the latter have proven unsatisfactory. They are attempting to provide cheap protection for their families and they are accomplishing their design, not perfectly it is true, but with really amazing success. A single one of these societies has since its organization paid in death claims not less than $135,000,000. This enormous sum of money has gone to the widows and orphans of men who would have carried far less insurance or none at all had it not been for the existence of the fraternals.

In the face of this fact there are not wanting critics with the effrontery to assert that the societies are vicious institutions, because, forsooth, they may fail some day or they may become too expensive for old men who no longer have any excuse for being insured. Suppose they do fail, as in the case of the American Legion of Honor. The downfall of that society has hurt a mere handful as compared to the numbers that have been benefited by its existence. As fraternals have usually been operated, their failure does not involve the loss of large accumulation, for these they do not possess. It does involve, however, a very serious hardship to those members who can no longer gain admission to other societies because of age or infirmity.

Popular government has been sufficiently tested to justify my belief that the fraternal orders will not fail, in the long run, if let alone. They can be killed, doubtless, and against this danger the only safeguard is eternal vigilance. Their success, as I have already intimated, means much to the cause of humanity.

No thoughtful observer can regard our present industrial regime as final. With its remittent warfare between capital and labor, it is obviously a temporary condition. By what is it to be succeeded? Shall it be the deadly stagnation of socialism, or shall opportunity be left for the development of individualism which has played so prominent a part in the history of the human race? Perhaps, if the great business of life insurance can be successfully conducted on democratic lines, the outlines of the answer may become discernible. Possibly capitalists, as a distinct class, may become as unnecessary as an hereditary aristocracy.

One may be permitted to indulge the dream that some day capitalist and labor may be combined in the same person, and that great industries may be competently managed by officers elected by the whole body of the workers. There is nothing incredible in the supposition, which is, on the contrary, in line with the course of human evolution. Such a condition would allow free play to individual ambition, while abolishing strikes and the existing abnormal contrasts of wealth and social position.

Since reforms are inaugurated by movement of the masses, and since five millions of the wage-earners and breadwinners in the United States and ten millions in Great Britain are taking lessons in economical science from the best of all teachers, *Experience*, is it beyond reason to anticipate development of the mutual and co-operative principle underlying fraternal society management in the business relations between producers and consumers, the great majority of whom are the wage-earners and breadwinners of the country.

To be more definite, let me call attention to the fact that the *insurers* and the *insured* are the same persons in a fraternal Beneficiary society. The officials and managers are strictly and truly the agents of the members from whom the contributions are collected and to the beneficiaries of whom they are distributed. No capitalist stands between the contributing members and the dependents of deceased members. Only a central office, with competent agents in charge, is needed for the collection of millions from the many and the distribution of the same in the payment of promised benefits. Why is it not possible to extend this principle of mutual cooperation and entirely eliminate the capitalist and forever be rid of his exploitation of labor with its attendants of friction and ferment? Will not the masses, some day, learn the general application of this principle?

The fraternal beneficiary system has a profound significance; it is symptomatic of the times, and what it needs is intelligent direction with a minimum of State interference. Any institution that has distributed to widows and orphans, within three decades, the enormous sum of more than seven hundred millions of dollars, $63,000,000 of which was paid out in 1903, is certainly entitled to serious consideration by those who make a study of political and social science. One hundred and fifty of the existing societies have promised to pay death benefits amounting to more than six thousand millions of dollars. The ability to fulfill their promises means much in more than four million of American homes. Penury, misery and crime will result from inability to carry out their contracts of insurance.

Nichols offers a less salutary view of fraternal insurance than Abb Landis. He indicates that there is a niche for it within the American economy, but also suggests its limitations. Nichols' depiction of what he terms the "popular delusions" embraced by fraternalists comprise the most compelling aspect of his argument. He indicates that actuarial realities differ from the generous and romantic vision upon which many organizations were founded.

FRATERNAL INSURANCE ITS CHARACTER, VIRTUES AND DEFECTS
Walter S. Nichols
1904

Yale Insurance Lectures Vol. 1 (New Haven: Yale Alumni Weekly, 1904), 162- 183.

MORE than four millions of American citizens are to-day looking to fraternal societies like the Knights of Honor, the Ancient Order of United Workmen, the Independent Order of Foresters and others whose name is legion for protection to their families in case of death. The distinguishing feature of these societies is that they are associations whose members are banded together through a spirit of charity or fraternity for mutual assistance and protection. They are wholly outside the line of our ordinary life insurance companies, which deal in insurance for the general public on a business basis. Their membership is chiefly made up from those of limited means who are seeking insurance at the smallest outlay. Over one-fourth of the population of this country may be said to be directly or indirectly interested in these societies. A knowledge of their principles and of the character of the insurance which they offer is a matter which concerns every American citizen regardless of his interest in insurance as a profession.

Nearly all our existing, fraternal societies have started within the past thirty or forty years, but they have a long line of predecessors extending back through centuries. Their proper understanding requires a glance at their historic relations. To the student of sociology as well as of economics a peculiar interest attaches both to their origin and history. As a race we are communal as well as social in our very instincts and in those instincts are the fundamental impulses that have developed all our political and social organizations. To the evolutionist they are the inherited traits of a remote ancestry which man shares with lower forms of life. We find the social organism in its simplest type in the ruminants, which herd together for mere association or protection. We find its fuller developments in the more strictly communal animals and insects. The beaver lodges join their forces to build the common dam for the benefit of all, but when the dam is built each separate lodge confines its attention to its own affairs. In the ants and bees we find this communal instinct in its extreme development. The female bee surrenders her maternal functions to a single queen and becomes a mere worker, to build and provision the common hive and care for the offspring. The ant marshals its warriors to guard the common nest or enslave its neighbors. Thus do we find the germs of those social and political organizations which characterize our twentieth century civilization implanted in the lower orders of creation.

It may seem a far away thought from the habits of the insect and mammalian world to the subject of the present lecture. But there is a deep significance in the fact that the fundamental principles which underlie fraternal insurance are thus operative in the lower orders of life. The fraternal society must be studied not as the mere artificial product of an advanced civilization, but as an organization whose roots and tendrils are implanted deep down in our common humanity. Civilized communities have no monopoly in this spirit of fraternalism. It was the active force at work in primitive days when the family relationship grew into the patriarchal form of government and this in turn expanded into the tribal state. As tribes solidified into nations this social evolution moved along lines so familiar in the physical world. The homogeneous pursuits of the tribesman became the heterogeneous occupations of the civilized state. Each occupation had its separate corps of workers, who banded together in a society for their common interest and protection in the economic struggle which followed the barter and trade between the groups. Thus was evolved the early benevolent or fraternal societies that are met with in so many of the nations of antiquity.

We find them in the ancient Roman empire as numerous and influential as now. Rome had her trade unions, and her religious confraternities devoted to the service of her gods, and her social clubs, and was compelled to legislate for their regulation.

Contribution to a common fund for the assistance or burial of their needy members was then as now a familiar feature. The downfall of Rome scarcely interrupts the story. Phoenix-like, they arose out of the ashes of her empire when her distant provinces developed into the industrial states of Modern Europe. In Great Britain, to which our own fraternal societies directly trace their origin, they were known as guilds and during medieval times when agricultural serfdom was being broken up and when centres of trade and manufacture were developing, these trade societies wielded a strong political influence. Along with them too were religious fraternities, which were the foundation of some of England's most important schools of learning. Aid to their needy members in ways more or less crude was a common feature of these associations.

As the power and influence of the guilds declined they were succeeded by the modern British friendly societies, from which our own have been so largely patterned. Members chiefly from the working classes united for mutual aid in sickness and for funeral benefits, through contributions to a common fund. They recognized the distinctly insurance character of their work and sought to frame scales of moneyed contributions which would be adequate. But they knew little of the principles of insurance, and their frequent and disastrous failures at last attracted the attention of the British Parliament. Investigations by that body aided by leading British actuaries disclosed the total inadequacy of their rates and the mismanagement which characterized their affairs. Attempted legal reforms were strongly resisted for a while by the members, and it has required nearly a century of legislation to place the friendly society system of Great Britain on the comparatively sound basis where it now rests. Under the existing laws in that country, such societies are induced to register and to accumulate reserve funds and charge rates which, like those of ordinary life companies, will be adequate to meet their future obligations. When registered they are required to have expert valuations periodically made of their resources and liabilities and proper balance sheets published of their affairs. The knowledge of their condition thus furnished to their members and to the public is relied on to check mismanagement. The law makes no attempt at further interference.

The strength of the system in that country lies in the fraternal ties which bind the members to their societies. It was this which enabled reforms to be successfully introduced into many of them which, according to any commercial standard, were already bankrupt. The strength of the system in any country must depend on the fraternal character of the society in fact as well as in name. The chief weakness of the system lies in the temptation to divorce its two-fold functions of benevolence and insurance, to regard the society either as a mere insurance organization for business purposes, or else as a brotherhood whose ties are strong enough to outweigh any defects in its insurance methods. When the fraternal spirit among the members is wanting, its work, to be a success, must be carried on along the business lines which characterize the ordinary insurance office. Such a change has actually taken place on a magnificent scale in the more recent development of these societies. It was from the fraternal society both here and in Great Britain that industrial insurance was evolved. It was just fifty years ago that the managers of such a society in London conceived a plan for abandoning its fraternal features and furnishing insurance to the poor on a strictly business basis. This was the origin of the famous British Prudential Insurance Company, whose policies are now found in the home of almost every working man in that country. Such was the origin too some twenty years later of the Prudential Insurance Company of America, which started as a friendly society in New Jersey and whose policies along with those of its later competitors are to be found in millions of American homes.

The experience of Great Britain is being repeated in America. A similar insufficiency in the rates and ignorance of sound insurance principles have resulted in numerous failures and now threaten the solvency of many of our American societies. Similar efforts are now being earnestly made both by the more intelligent of the members and by state authorities to place fraternal insurance on a sounder basis.

With this preliminary historic review, I enter at once on the discussion of the more technical features of fraternal insurance. First let us examine the structure and legal character of these associations. They generally consist of one parent society with its constitution and by-laws and having numerous subordinate local branch societies termed lodges. These local societies are created by the parent, from which they receive their charters or right to exist. They are governed by its constitution and the laws which it lays down. In all questions of dispute the parent society has final jurisdiction. In a word, the local lodge, while it has separate existence as a society itself, and may within the limits allowed regulate its own affairs, remains subject to the parent society of which it is a part. This parent society is known as the grand lodge and is made up of representatives chosen by the local lodges. Sometimes a further subdivision is made and the parent society or supreme lodge is made up of representatives from a number of grand lodges each with its local lodges.

The membership of the society as a whole is thus made up of the members of these various local lodges. The government is purely democratic. Every member is entitled to a vote in his own local society and thus has a voice in the selection of the rulers and in making the laws for the whole. Initiatory rites and ceremonials are a common feature. Unlike the British societies, in which sick relief is a prominent feature, most of our American associations confine their insurance work to the payment of death and disability benefits. The funds required for this purpose are collected in the form of assessments by the local lodges and turned over to the officers of the parent society, by whom the insurance business of the whole is managed. Sick benefits when allowed are usually paid by the local lodges to their members out of their own separate funds. Expenses are generally met by dues and initiation fees. These local lodges thus act both as separate societies in the management of their own affairs and as agents of the parent society in collecting the common insurance funds and in securing the membership.

It will thus be seen that in their constitutions these societies resemble in many ways the ordinary social club and for certain purposes the law so regards them. The active fraternal or benevolent features of the society apart from its insurance work are chiefly confined to the local societies, where the individual members meet for business and social purposes and where the spirit of fraternity is fostered. They resemble too in certain respects some of our church organizations, with which the law frequently compares them. We have our individual church societies with their social and benevolent activities governed by representative bodies from the various churches and the whole united under one denominational form of government. These correspond to the local and grand lodges.

These societies are sometimes organized under corporate charters granted by the state, sometimes like the ordinary club they are mere voluntary associations. Most of our states now have general laws prescribing how these societies may be formed and carried on. When so formed the law itself becomes their constitution. Sometimes the parent society is thus incorporated while the inferior lodges remain voluntary associations. Sometimes it is the reverse. But in all laws regarding their formation their character as benevolent societies is insisted on. They are not allowed like ordinary companies to carry on insurance business for profit, and its benefits are usually limited to the relatives or dependents of the members. There are some important legal distinctions between those societies which are incorporated and those which are not, especially as to property rights, upon which I have not the time to enter. The courts endeavor in either case so far as the law allows to enforce the rules which they have made for themselves if they are fair and reasonable. Nearly all these societies have their own judicatories for determining the standing and rights of their members, by whose decision the members must abide. These the courts will refuse to interfere with so long as they act honestly and fairly within their legitimate province. They are mutual societies in which like churches the members are expected to abide by the form of government to which they have subscribed. A local lodge may be cut off from affiliation with the parent society or may cut itself loose just as a church may cut loose from its denominational connection. In neither case is the society itself dissolved. It simply loses the rights which belonged to it as a member of the parent society and must surrender whatever is in its possession belonging to the parent. If it has a charter from the state, the state laws governing it as a corporation are superior to any rules of the association itself.

On one point however, whether incorporated or not, the courts are insistent, that is, no rule or action of the society can deprive a local lodge or a member of insurance or other property interests which are already vested, that is in which an unconditional ownership has been established. Where they are incorporated, like other corporations they are regarded by the law as artificial persons acting through their officers as their agents and with no personal liability on the part of the members except those imposed by the rules of the society itself. Where they are not incorporated their legal character is not so easy to define. They are often regarded as a peculiar kind of partnership qualified by the special purposes for which they were organized.

It will be seen from this brief sketch that these societies in their constitution and structure are strongly analogous to the ordinary social club or religious society, and bear all the ear marks of their historic origin.

But they also have another aspect in the eyes of the law. In respect to their insurance features they are regarded as business associations furnishing a peculiar type of insurance under contracts or agreements which are governed by the ordinary principles of the law of contracts. This leads us at once to the insurance features of these societies. As insurance associations they are treated as mutual companies regulated of course by their charter and by-laws, with which every member is assumed to be familiar. An application, much like that of the ordinary company, setting forth the age and health and other details regarding his desired insurance is usually required of the applicant for membership. Instead of the ordinary policy he usually receives what is called a certificate of membership, reciting that he is a member of the society and entitled to its privileges, and to share up to a specified amount in its beneficiary fund, subject however, to the laws and rules of the order, and conditioned on his compliance with them. This certificate in connection with the laws of the society is his insurance contract. It will be noted that unlike the ordinary insurance policy, which is a mere business agreement between the company and the purchaser for a specified consideration, these certificates are simply a recognition of the rights of the member which flow through his membership, to share in the benevolent fund. Unlike the ordinary policy which becomes the property of the beneficiary named in it, no matter who secured it or paid the premium, these certificates remain the property of the member, who can usually change the beneficiary at will.

The conditions on which those rights are to be enjoyed are not, as in the case of the policy, set out in the certificate itself but are to be found in the rules of the society. Thus the mutual and fraternal idea of this insurance is adhered to. More than this, it is not allowed under the laws of most of the states to be a cold business agreement for the payment of a fixed sum of money for a definite premium. Either the amount must be capable of modification and adjustment according to the actual ability of the society to pay, or it must reserve the right to assess its members for enough to make up the required benefit. The societies are thus relieved from the obligation imposed on ordinary life companies to create and maintain a reserve fund which will be mathematically sufficient to pay their insurance obligations. In theory they can never become insolvent because never obliged to pay more than they are able or than that they can collect from their members. As a matter of fact, they have failed disastrously at times because they had neither the requisite fund nor could collect the needed assessments.

Until very recent years it has been the almost universal practice to limit the actual funds of the society to the smallest amount which was deemed necessary to meet special emergencies. The constant inflow of new members, it was argued, would prevent serious deficiencies, and the fraternal spirit of the members would do the rest. The prime object aimed at was to give the insurance at the least possible outlay to the members in a work which was assumed to be benevolent in its character and not conducted for profit. The fallacy of these views is now being generally recognized, as we shall shortly see.

The payments made by the members are not, as in ordinary life insurance, premiums paid for the purchase of a pure business contract but are generally of two kinds, initiation fees and dues, used as in ordinary clubs for the expenses of the society, and assessments levied on its members as contributions to its insurance fund, and are provided for in the rules of the society itself.

In the earlier days of the societies these assessments were generally alike in amount regardless of age and were collected only on the death of a member for the payment of his benefit, thus, as you observe, carrying out still further the idea of fraternity. But as the societies grew older the fallacies of this method were taught the members by a hard experience. By simply dropping his insurance which he had already enjoyed a member could escape paying his share of the death losses. As the members grew older and the death losses increased, those that were younger were not long in discovering that they were contributing more than their share to the death losses, which were chiefly among the old. As a result these dropped their membership and joined younger societies. New recruits to fill their places could not be obtained. The average age of those that were left continued to increase and the assessments to grow heavier. This in turn increased the withdrawals, until at last few remained except the sick and aged. Assessments for losses could no longer be collected, and the society would dissolve, leaving a body of old and infirm deprived of the benefits for which they had so long contributed. This has been the story of scores of these societies in the past, and where otherwise honestly managed has been the cause of the numerous failures in this class of insurance. In spite of all the efforts to place assessment rates on a sounder basis, their inadequacy and inequity as between the younger and older ages still continues to threaten the permanence of a large proportion of our fraternal societies. As we have stated, most of the existing societies are less than thirty years old. In many of them the members have only within recent years reached the ages where these dangers in a serious form began to be felt. The members themselves were generally unfamiliar with the principles of insurance. The favorite argument was that a society of this kind was like any village community where the young continually take the place of the old and the community as a whole grows no older. Hence it was said that a scale of assessments which were sufficient for the early years of such a society would continue so. I emphasize this point. It has been in one shape or another the favorite argument and popular delusion among the members of these societies which more than any other has been, and continues to be, perhaps the greatest obstacle in the way of reform. To this day, when the need of larger contributions on the part of older members is urged, some veteran will bring forward the old simile of the village or town community whose average age is no greater to-day than it was a score of years ago, and insist that all which the society needs is to increase its membership by securing new applicants in order to bring down the death rate and make the rates sufficient.

Let us see why this is not true, for it is a vital question in this business. The average ages of a village community remain unchanged only after that community has reached a normal average age and only so long as there are neither removals from or to the village and the birth rate just keeps pace with the death rate. But any change in these conditions will alter that average age of the inhabitants until a new normal age is reached. If the average age of the inhabitants is thirty years and the births should exceed the deaths, it would begin to drop to some lower age. On the contrary, if there should be an excess of deaths the average age would begin to go up. The removal from or to the village of younger members would have the same effect. Throughout New England you will find scores of towns made up almost entirely of elderly people. The young folks have emigrated and the children are missing. On the contrary, in the great west are hundreds of settlements made up chiefly of young settlers and their children, whose average will increase in the way described until a normal age is reached as the settlement itself grows older.

The process in these societies is the same. When first organized they are chiefly made up of younger members among whom the deaths are comparatively few. Rates may be charged that are not only enough to pay the claims as they arise but to create a surplus in the hands of the society. This further helps to mislead the members, who point to the surplus as a proof of the soundness of the association. But gradually these members grow older and the deaths increase. For a time new members who are young can be procured to take their places. But the whole group is still young and unless the new additions are largely in excess of the death losses and withdrawals, the average age in such a society, and with it the death losses, will continue to increase until as in the village community a normal average age is reached. If the average age of the members in a new society was thirty, for instance, it might gradually increase to forty, although a new young member was added for each member that was lost. But this is not all. As the members of such a society grow older the death rate increases faster than the age. At forty it may be only one in a hundred. At sixty it will be three times as great. So that while enough new members may have been taken in to keep the average age in such a society down to the original figures, the actual losses will continue to roll up through the increasing deaths of these older members.

As the assessments for these losses grow heavier the difficulty of procuring new members will increase, and those who have already joined will continue to drop off and hasten on the ruin in the way already described. The society may really be likened to one of those western village communities whose inhabitants are all young at the start but from which the young and healthy are gradually drawn away to more attractive settlements elsewhere until the whole becomes like a New England village. As the membership dwindles the average age continues to increase indefinitely.

When the members of such a society have reached a certain age the cost of insurance becomes too heavy to be borne by themselves unless aided by younger members. It has been found that the average member who has passed much beyond the age of sixty can no longer afford to pay the heavy cost of his own insurance.

In practice, these societies start with a limited membership which they increase year by year. The births as it were at first far outnumber the deaths and as a consequence for a while there will be no noticeable increase in the death rate. This growth may be rapid enough to conceal the real conditions for years. But there is another peculiar feature here. In order to keep down the death rate, not only must the society grow but the number of new members added must each year become greater. Now there is a limit to this rate of growth even under favorable circumstances. When it is reached, be it sooner or later, then the trouble begins. This is why some of the larger societies have gone on year after year with apparent success while their small competitors were in distress. They were able to increase their new membership at a faster rate than the others. And what is worse, this long continued success makes the members skeptical about the insufficiency of their rates when the assessments finally become inadequate to meet their claims. They simply rely on their past experience.

It has been a favorite argument too on the part of these societies that the spirit of fraternity should be strong enough to overcome any feeling of injustice among the members and to induce them to make good deficiencies. In truly benevolent organizations this fraternal feeling has proved a valuable aid in sustaining societies that were financially embarrassed. Both in Great Britain and America, associations which, measured by ordinary mercantile standards, would be pronounced hopelessly insolvent, have been carried along for years through the loyal support of their members. Such was in fact the condition of many of those British associations which were finally rescued and placed on a sound basis through the adoption of correct principles.

And just here I wish to speak of a class of associations in this country which are often confounded with the fraternal society and whose disastrous records in the past have done much to bring reproach on these associations. I refer to a certain class of assessment companies, organized on somewhat similar lines, whose premiums were collected in the shape of assessments, but which were in reality nothing more than ordinary life companies, carried on for profit on the assessment principle. There were no real fraternal features in their make-up nor fraternal feelings among their members, who were solicited and joined solely for the purpose of securing insurance on what was claimed to be cheaper terms. Many of them were conducted in an honest belief that the principle was sound. As business institutions their history has been so replete with failures, that they have evoked the severest condemnation on the part of state officials and called forth restrictive legislation. Their system has since been admitted to be fallacious by its most intelligent former supporters, and those of them which remain have for the most part abandoned or altered their assessment methods.

It is almost needless to say that they are not included in the subject of the present lecture. I refer to them chiefly as illustrations that the assessment methods of the fraternal society have proved fallacious when applied to mere business companies in which the principles of fraternalism were absent.

Another favorite argument has been that inequalities between the members on account of differences in age would in a measure correct themselves as each member in turn passed through the successive ages. But this is assuming that each entered at the same age and survived and retained his membership to the end, none of which are true. Experience has shown that ordinary selfish business instincts influence the members even in the most fraternal of these associations, and that new members can neither be procured nor existing members retained after finding that it is to their interest to drop their connection.

Various plans have been proposed or adopted by the societies from time to time in order to remedy these conditions. Assessments monthly or at other fixed periods have now been substituted for assessments on the death of a member. Emergency and mortuary funds have been accumulated to meet deficiencies, but generally wholly inadequate for the purpose. Diminishing benefits at the older ages have been proposed. Assessments graded according to the age at entry but remaining fixed thereafter have been tried, and this is the present method adopted by a large number of these societies. Assessments increasing with each age attained by the member have been proposed. As a compromise, assessments increasing with each ten years, known as the step-rate plan, have been recommended, as have assessments increasing with each age attained by the member and covering the cost of his insurance for that year, known as the natural premium plan, but the trouble with this last is that the cost becomes too heavy for the older members to carry. A few have actually accepted the better class of British friendly societies as their models and have undertaken, like the regular companies, to charge a level assessment rate fixed according to the age at entry and which will be large enough to accumulate a reserve that will meet the increased cost of insurance at the older ages or that modified form of the same referred to as the step-rate plan.

This is the plan now advocated both by the most intelligent advisers of these societies and by state officials. It is the plan which many of the best of these societies are considering or proposing to adopt. It would seem to be the only true solution of the difficulty. Their insurance business in order to be permanent must be conducted on the same mathematical principles as that of ordinary life companies. This does not mean that it must in all respects conform to the methods applicable to the latter. The business of the ordinary company is carried on for profit. Its policy-holders are like the creditors of any other corporation. The contract is a rigid one and the premiums are fixed; its commercial security demands that both the premium payments and reserve funds shall be in excess of the probable needs, in order to meet the uncertainties of the future.

With the fraternal society the case is different. The insurance which it promises is either simply a maximum sum whose actual amount may be reduced by inability to pay, or additional assessments may be levied to make good the deficiency. The conditions which would make an ordinary life company commercially insolvent and lead to its closing, may simply cause increased assessments or reduced benefits in the case of the friendly society. The fraternal ties of the members help to hold them together in case of adversity.

The great aim of these societies is to furnish insurance at the least possible immediate outlay to their members, and to avoid the expenses incident to insurance as a business. Hence their paid officers and agents are as few as possible. The salaries needed for expert talent are usually wanting. The work is largely carried on through the members themselves and their lodge system. Their equipment for conducting the society as a financial business corporation is limited. Surplus in the sense of business profits is regarded as foreign to their character and the accumulation of funds beyond what is absolutely needed is discouraged as a temptation to extravagance as well as an additional tax on the members.

Dividends of surplus profits to the members are not allowed. Any supposed excess of funds is met by reducing the assessments and any interest which a member might have in those funds is lost on his withdrawal. He has no right to claim a surrender value as in the ordinary company on giving up his certificate.

You note how in all these features the idea of fraternalism distinguishes these societies from ordinary life companies. They enter directly into the question of the proper remedies for their defects. The failure on the part of many officials and life insurance experts to properly appreciate them has been one of the difficulties in the way of reform. A premium rate adequate to the risk and a reserve adequate for future deficiencies in the life insurance sense would seem to be essentials if they are to furnish anything more than mere temporary or term insurance. But it does not follow that this rate must be computed on a table of mortality heavier than their own experience nor that it must be loaded with a margin for contingencies and expenses like that of the ordinary life companies. Nor does it follow that their reserve funds as in the case of ordinary companies should be in excess of their obvious needs. It would seem essential too that, as in the case of our ordinary companies, official valuations of their assets and liabilities and balance sheets of their accounts should be required. It does not follow, however, that the same measure of supervision and control over their affairs should be exercised by the state authorities, since they are not ordinary business corporations nor subject to commercial insolvency in the strict sense of the word. It is held by many that the functions of the state are ended when, as in Great Britain, such valuations and balance sheets are published and the members are left with a knowledge of the facts to deal with their societies as they will. These are all controverted questions on which I hesitate to express any decided opinion. When, however, a society has become so mismanaged or its affairs have become so hopelessly involved that its ruin is inevitable, the state should at least have power to prevent a further increase of its membership.

In new societies the needed reforms are comparatively easy. But many of these societies have been years in existence. The increase of their rates to an adequate figure at the older ages means a heavy burden on their older members which some would be unable to bear. Hence these members are apt to favor the inequalities of present methods. Otherwise, they say, we shall be driven out. On the other hand, the young member argues that the societies are for the benefit of those with dependent families. The families of the old are no longer dependent and the young should not be forced to pay for their insurance.

Most of the reforms thus far attempted have been a compromise between these two views. The rates have from time to time been increased, especially at the older ages when deficiencies arose that actually compelled it, but never to an adequate figure, and as the ages continued to increase new revisions were made. In some of the older societies such a system of compromise may be the only solution of the problem unless their old members are to be driven out or their ability to secure new members is to cease and the society is allowed to collapse. But even then the difficulty will be to so regulate the inequality between the groups that additions to the young membership can be kept up until such time as the rates can step by step be finally raised to an adequate basis.

The hardest task of all has been to educate the members up to these needed reforms, which mean to them heavier assessments and an insurance more costly than was promised when they joined. The insurance officials of our various states and the best representative men of these societies themselves are now earnestly striving both through legislation and through the education of the membership to solve the difficult problem. The laws regarding these societies to-day are little else then mere rules for their organization and management. No provisions for securing their permanent solvency are made as in the case of our ordinary life companies. In most of the states they are left to run their own course. Their members as a body are exceedingly jealous of attempts by legislation to increase the cost of the insurance which they offer or in any way to reduce their popularity or their freedom of action. Through the ballot box they stand ready by their numbers to defeat any attempted laws which they believe to be inspired by a spirit of antagonism. Any attempted legislation for the regulation of these societies to be successful must be framed in a friendly attitude with a recognition of their rights as mutual clubs to regulate their own affairs within proper limits.

Now a few words in conclusion concerning the character of the insurance offered by these societies. In essential respects it is widely different from that furnished by our regular companies. In the first place it is strictly benevolent in its character and limited to the members and their dependents. It aims to relieve the necessities of these in a way more effectual than the random charitable assistance furnished by ancient associations. It needs for its success that the members should be bound by a spirit of real fraternity to their association, and not use their membership as a mere cloak for ordinary insurance purposes. It needs that the members should be actively interested in the affairs of the society and should be ready to bear their share of the burdens in case of errors in its management. Their fraternal bonds are the chief substitute for the commercial security required of an ordinary business corporation.

To that large class in the community whose instincts and tastes lead them to seek insurance protection from such societies they aim to offer that protection at the smallest immediate cost. The work is done chiefly by the members. Expenses are reduced to a minimum. No dividends are provided for and the assessment rates are reduced to the lowest figures. These are the strong points urged by its advocates. Fraudulent claims too are less likely where the members take a personal interest and for that reason these societies, in theory at least, should be peculiarly adapted to deal with sick and accident risks where fraud is a special danger.

On the other hand, this insurance must of necessity lack those elements of commercial security which attach to the ordinary life company as a business institution conducted by experts protected by large cash accumulations and regulated by laws enacted with a view to permanent solvency. Until at least the reforms referred to have been carried out, this insurance can hardly be regarded as of more than a temporary character covering the younger and more productive years of life, with the contingency that the cost at old age may prove too heavy to be borne or that inability to keep up its membership may cause default. In view of the fact that the whole machinery of these societies is organized on a benevolent rather than a business basis, it has been seriously questioned how far they should attempt to grant endowments or large life insurance benefits which involve investments of capital for the beneficiaries rather than a simple relief from misfortune.

I believe that their work should be confined within their legitimate sphere and that associations, whether incorporated or not, should not be permitted to organize and conduct their affairs as benevolent societies while they are merely seeking through this device to sell ordinary life insurance to the public. Those who wish to purchase life insurance policies as they would purchase ordinary stocks or bonds as a pure business investment, who desire insurance contracts which shall be commercial and marketable in their character and who care nothing for the institution which may furnish them, should seek their protection from the ordinary companies that deal with insurance simply as a business.

The numerous failures among these societies in the past and the disappointments resulting from the errors in their management have called forth severe criticism and even condemnation of the system itself from many quarters. This has been largely aided by the disastrous operations of organizations which were in reality life companies carried on for mere business purposes but employing the methods of the fraternal associations. Despite the failures it must be remembered they have furnished temporary protection to millions of families and have distributed hundreds of millions among the needy dependents of their members. It should be said too that, carrying small accumulated funds, the actual moneyed losses have been small compared with the failures. The gravest loss has been the disappointment of those whose protection failed at an age when they could no longer afford to purchase fresh insurance.

Despite their defects these societies are doing a great and responsible work among those who prefer the form of protection which they offer. The communal spirit which created the ancient clubs of Rome and the guilds of more modern Europe has been strengthened by the antagonistic spirit of selfish individualism which characterizes our commercial age. Fraternal insurance should be dealt with as an evolution of these more primitive societies that is here to stay, backed by the votes, if need be, of the millions who support it; but calling as in Great Britain for beneficent laws and the intelligent cooperation of its membership to remedy its defects.

Walter Page, the Editor of The World's Work, *a popular early-twentieth century magazine, offered his readers a dire warning concerning fraternal insurance. In very plain language, he suggested that the endeavor could not continue as it had developed. The low rates offered by fraternal organizations were insufficient to support the benefits offered. The rates must be raised, he claimed, or the companies inevitably will fail. From his vantage outside of the bonds of brotherhood, Page argues that fraternal ideals are praiseworthy, but that they are valueless unless undergirded by solid business principles which are simultaneously subject to government regulation. At base, Page argued that American consumers required protection from their own lack of business acumen and from the unwarranted optimism of fraternal leaders.*

INSURANCE THAT DOES NOT INSURE
Walter H. Page
1911
The World's Work 21 (5) (March 1911): 14083-14085.

THIS is an extract from a letter received by the *Readers' Service* a few weeks ago:

> *I have paid my rates on the life-insurance policy in the Knights of Pythias for nearly a quarter of a century.*
> *Now I am seventy-five years old and can work no more. A little time ago a message came from the Society telling me that hereafter my rate will be more than five times as much as it has been through all these years. I cannot pay this new rate. It would take more than half of our scanty income.*
> *What can I do to escape from this trap? Is there no law to protect us?*

The reply to that question was brief. It was that the bulk of the legal decisions in this matter indicates that the fraternal associations have the right to raise their rates to an adequate level. There are one or two decisions that favor policyholders who have objected to the raising of the rates, but these decisions seem based on special clauses in the policy itself.

He must pay the increased rate, or he must drop the policy. To drop it means a total loss of all that he has paid in. There is no surrender value, no extended insurance, no loan value — nothing but an empty piece of paper.

It would be unkind and unjust to publish a letter which names the Knights of Pythias, if I should go on to draw the moral that this fraternal order is weak and ought to be avoided. The Knights of Pythias is one of the oldest, one of the largest, and, I should say, one of the cleanest of the fraternal orders that write insurance.

Its action in raising the rates, however much one may criticize the sudden and abrupt manner in which it is done, is a sign of courage rather than of weakness. The one and only thing it could do is to raise the rates. If it did not raise them, it would go into bankruptcy within a very few years — and then, indeed, all would be lost.

It is well to look the facts in the face. There are in the United States, more than 7,000,000 fraternal insurance policies and the total amount of so-called insurance under them is more than $7,000,000,000. Scarcely a dollar of all that total is signed by a company that is entitled to respect, judged by the standards of the insurance laws in any well-regulated state.

Not long ago I had an acrimonious correspondence with the head of one of the newer orders. I had warned an intending buyer of its policy that the rates were ridiculous; and that, so sure as rain follows sunshine, the rates must go up or the association must go down. The letter was turned over to the association. It brought about a deluge of argument. The gist of it was that the rates were high enough. The basis of this belief was about like this:

"We cannot help but grow constantly. The young men who come in will be a constant flood. The ever-increasing amount of premiums will be adequate to meet all the payments due."

It is pitiful to see men taking out insurance on such a ground as that. That order, at that time, was gaining thousands of members. To every one of them was presented a statement showing that the rates *had been* adequate, during the short life of the company, to pay all death losses, to pay expenses, and to put aside certain special funds. I venture to say that not one out of every hundred of those new members looked forward twenty years. All hoped to live that long; but none tried to judge the association far into the future.

However one may pity the old men of the orders, forced to give up all the protection that they have, or to meet heavy payments in the lean and bitter years of whitened head and weakened hand, the thing is inevitable. Last year, in 1910, for the first time in their history, the fraternal orders practically went on record to the effect that all fraternal rates must be raised. Conventions all over the country, in the summer of 1910, endorsed resolutions calling upon all honest men to cooperate with State Insurance Departments, looking to the regulation of fraternal insurance by the skilled hands of the State's departments.

And, at all these conventions, strong, clean men, officers and makers of fraternal orders, proclaimed to the world the absolute necessity of sweeping reformation that would raise the fraternal rates and put the fraternal insurance of the country on a basis where it could live.

I venture to say that by the year 1917 there will be hardly a member of a fraternal order in this country who will not be paying rates on his insurance that, if not really adequate, are at least far and away above the rates he has paid in the past. Thousands of old men, like my Knight of Pythias, will have to make their bitter choice between dropping the insurance and beggaring themselves to pay the new rates. More than half will drop the policies. Nearly all of these will go on down the path without protection.

It is a cruel thing to contemplate, yet it is inevitable. If rates are not raised, practically the whole of this $7,000,000,000 of insurance must be swept away, and not more than half of it would ever be worth a cent. In fact, if the fraternal-insurance associations of the country were to stop writing insurance to-morrow, the policies of all the members below the average age would be worth little more than the paper on which they are written.

What the result of it all will be is hard to guess. If it be humanly possible, the best result would be that the fraternal societies should continue to live and to carry on their beneficent work, but under conditions far removed from the present. Their rates should be adequate to make it absolutely certain that all the insurance they ever sell will be sound. Yet the fraternal idea should remain. They would eliminate the inordinate cost of getting new business and of carrying it on — cost which marks the last decade in regular insurance. They should be properly regulated by the state in which they do business. They should be inspected, audited, and reported just as other insurance companies are.

Of course, no one may hope that such a result can be obtained in full. The rise of the rates will drive thousands away from the fraternals. There will be great failures, bitter distress, much suffering of mind and body, particularly among the older men who cannot get insurance in any other form and cannot afford to pay the high costs. There will be bitter dissensions, splitting of counsels, dividing of fair minds. In many cases, there will be disruption and upheaval.

The man who contemplates the taking of insurance for the protection of his future will stop and figure before he turns to the fraternals. His friend, who would persuade him to take out a policy, will have to answer many questions. In the past, the very low rates have been the main argument. As time goes on, those low rates will become immediately an adequate cause for just suspicion. "Something for nothing" is always suspicious. In insurance it is worse than suspicious. It almost carries conviction in its very name.

It is no time to take a chance. If you are in a sound fraternal order and can find out exactly where you stand, stay there; but, whatever you do, supplement your protection in some other way. Either invest money against the future or take out more insurance of the soundest kind that you can get.

The member of a fraternal order who does not set to work to study and find out where he and his order stand to-day, will probably be pleading for pity to-morrow. He will get it; but he won't deserve it, for he is of those who have eyes but will not see.

Charles Knight, writing in 1927, provides an overview of the impact that business reforms had upon the fraternal organizations offering insurance. As these groups sought "actuarial solvency," they found that they could no longer compete financially with more traditional insurance providers and their members simultaneously lost enthusiasm. As they commercialized and thus became more financially stable, the fraternal organizations lost the institutional characteristics which had formed the basis of their appeal. Enthusiastic fraternalists were replaced with trained actuaries and professional salesmen, and the fraternal organizations essentially became businesses.

FRATERNAL LIFE INSURANCE
Charles K. Knight,
1927
Annals of the American Academy of Political and Social Sciences 130
(Mar. 1927), 97-102.

THE past decade has witnessed an actual decline in the total number of dollars of fraternal insurance in force in this country. Thus at the close of 1916 there was approximately $11,000,000,000 in force with the fraternal societies, whereas there is but approximately $10,300,000,000 on their books at the present time. When one considers the decline in the purchasing power of the monetary unit and the increase in population during this period, the significance of these figures is even greater than it is when one considers merely the sums themselves. Meanwhile, life insurance granted by the so-called old-line or legal-reserve companies has been increasing by leaps and bounds, the totals in force on the above-mentioned dates being $25,000,000,000 and $79,000,000,000, respectively. Furthermore, during the period from 1910 to 1920, the societies wrote about thirty-three per cent of the total amount of life insurance written in this country, whereas of late years they wrote but fifteen per cent of it. It is clear, therefore, that the decline in fraternal insurance has not been due to a lowering of the demand of the people of this country for life insurance, but to conditions within the fraternal system itself.

Fraternal insurance societies sell insurance for the protection of the insured person's dependents in event of his death. They also offer old-age insurance, health and accident insurance, and juvenile insurance. All of these forms except juvenile insurance have been offered for many years, the first fraternal benefit society having been formed in this country in 1868. Down to about fifteen years ago, the rates charged by most societies were inadequate to meet the benefits promised. As a result, many of such organizations passed out of existence, and others were forced to readjust their insurance to an adequate-rate basis.

This necessary readjustment has been a serious matter for most fraternal societies that have attempted it. The older method of accomplishing it was simply to pass a by-law requiring higher assessments, or the reduction of benefits. Such a procedure resulted in heavy withdrawals of healthy members, whereas the unhealthy ones remained with the society. More recently it has been learned that greater success attends the efforts at readjustment when expert salesmen are employed for the purpose of securing the consent of each member to the conversion of his certificate to the adequate-rate class. The conversion is made by issuing a preliminary term certificate at the member's attained age. The salesman receives a substantial proportion of the first twelve monthly premiums. Special "service" corporations have arisen to train salesmen for this work. By such a process, enough healthy lives can be transferred to offset the tendency toward adverse selection.[1] A society in the process of readjustment, however, finds it difficult to secure new members, as well as to hold all of its old ones. The immediate result of readjustment, or of an attempt at readjustment, has nearly always been a smaller membership as well as a smaller amount of insurance in force. Furthermore, the process tends to destroy the prestige of the society, particularly with those who do not understand the necessity of the higher rates.

Failure on the part of some societies, then, and the necessity of readjustment on the part of others, has resulted in greatly weakening public confidence in the institution of fraternal insurance generally. Before the societies can hope to make much progress in the future, they must re-establish that confidence. In other words, fraternal insurance must be resold to the public.

It is a fairly safe prediction, however, that fraternal insurance on the old inadequate-rate plan can never again be sold in any considerable amounts to the American public. The public has learned that this plan, though furnishing cheap protection during a society's early years when most of its members are young, is unsatisfactory in the society's later years when the advancing age and death rate of its members render failure or readjustment inevitable. The beneficiaries, relatives and friends of those members who die early enough to have the face amounts of their certificates paid in full, are quite well satisfied with the inadequate-rate plan. A large majority of the members of such a society, however, live to the time when increased rates or a reduction of benefits is absolutely necessary. These members, together with their relatives and friends, are prone to voice their disappointment and disapproval of the plan. This disapproval has not been minimized by those interested in increasing the amount of sound protection. These are the chief reasons for believing that the public could not be induced to purchase any considerable amount of unsound protection.

ACTUARIAL SOLVENCY

The principal efforts of the fraternal societies during the past decade have centered around the question of adequate rates, or, stated differently, the question of actuarial solvency. A society, or indeed any other life insurance organization, is said to be actuarially solvent when it will be able to pay all of its promised benefits without increasing the rates of assessments or premiums paid by its members. A life insurance organization will be able to meet its claims without such an increase when it has funds which, together with the present value of assessments or premiums payable to it in the future, equal the present value of the benefits promised, all calculations being made on a conservative mortality and interest basis. The determination of the amount of these necessary funds is called valuation -- the funds themselves, reserves, reserve funds, or funds to meet the reserve liability. Life insurance companies, speaking generally, are required by law to maintain funds to meet a reserve liability determined according to the American Experience Table of Mortality with interest at three and one-half per cent compounded annually. Companies may elect full-premium valuation, or some modification of it that will yield lower reserves than it would yield, such as the preliminary term method modified according to the Illinois standard, or some other standard.

For the societies, again speaking generally, the National Fraternal Congress Table of Mortality with interest at four per cent compounded annually has been established. This basis yields lower reserves than those required of commercial companies, but they are high enough for practical purposes.

Fraternal societies of sufficient size may use a mortality table constructed from their own experience. Recently there has been considerable discussion of a table described by Mr. Edward B. Fackler in a paper read to the Fraternal Actuarial Association in February, 1926.

Legislation compelling actuarial solvency on the part of fraternal benefit societies by setting up legal minimum standards of valuation has met with but varying success in this country. The so-called Mobile Bill, agreed upon in 1910 by a committee composed of state insurance commissioners and representatives of the National Fraternal Congress and the Associated Fraternities of America, was thought to be too severe when put in practice in a few instances. For it was substituted a bill drawn by a similar committee in 1912, and known as the New York Conference Bill. This bill, with modifications and additions, has been adopted as the fraternal insurance code of many states. The code, as it exists today in most states, allows a wide latitude to the societies in the way of actuarial solvency.

The situation at the present time is that some of the societies are on an actuarially solvent basis as regards all members, others place new members in the adequate-rate class, and still others are in need of further readjustment. A valuable aid to the person who is considering the advisability of entering a particular fraternal benefit society would consist in a frank and simple statement of the ratio of reserve funds held by it compared to those required to meet all of its claims. The Wisconsin Insurance Reports contain tables showing the important results of valuation in that state including the ratio of actual assets to required reserves, and the ratio of assets (actual and contingent) to liabilities (actual and contingent). A copy of the important tables appears in the August issue of *Best's Insurance News*, published by the Alfred M. Best Company of New York.

JUVENILE MEMBERSHIP

Aside from the struggle toward actuarial solvency, and aside from legislative matters, the fraternal benefit societies have been interested during the past decade in several other problems that have confronted them. In the first place, it was realized during this period that some measure should be taken to enable societies to accept children for membership, so that members need not have recourse to the so-called old-line or legal-reserve companies in order to insure all of the members of their families. Facilities for offering such protection have been provided by legislation in many states, and a number of societies have attempted to sell insurance on the lives of juveniles. Considerable success has attended their efforts, probably as much as $70,000,000 being now in force on approximately 300,000 lives. The mortality rate experienced thus far on juvenile risks has been very favorable. During a recent year the actual deaths were only forty-eight per cent of those expected, according to the Standard Industrial Table of Mortality, which is the table commonly used by commercial life companies for industrial insurance. The funds necessary for conducting the juvenile department of a society are segregated from its other funds.

Originally it was provided that only children of members could be insured in a society's juvenile department, but more recently the law has been amended in many states so that children of non-members as well as those of members may be insured. It is hoped by fraternalists that insurance on the lives of juveniles will result in training them to believe in, and to continue, this form of protection upon attaining the required age for entering the adult class, and that parents who are not members of a society will be attracted to the fraternal plan. There seems to be little doubt but that juvenile insurance can be written by the fraternal societies in sparsely settled regions where the weekly house-to-house visitation of the industrial agent would be impracticable. In such regions, however, the head of the household is likely to receive his income at irregular intervals, such as at the marketing of important crops, and would therefore be more likely to purchase annual premium insurance than to make regular weekly or monthly payments of either industrial premiums or fraternal assessments.

As pointed out by the writer in his *Advanced Life Insurance*, Chapter XX, fraternalists admit that the cost of mortality is not likely to differ much in one large group of well-selected lives from that in another and similar group. Some fraternalists maintain, however, that the economy of management resulting from the democratic form of government renders the overhead expenses of fraternal insurance less than that of commercial insurance; and that, as a result, the total cost to the fraternal certificate-holder is less than the cost to the old-line policyholder.

OVERHEAD EXPENSES

As regards overhead expenses, it may be stated that during a recent year the societies belonging to the National Fraternal Congress of America spent almost $18 for each $1000 of new insurance written. The lapses were so numerous, however, that the net cost of new business to the societies was probably twice as great as this. Thus in that year the societies paid out over $11,000,000 for new business, and yet ended the year with over 200,000 fewer members and more than $200,000,000 less insurance than they had at its beginning. New business expenses, though preponderant, do not, of course, constitute all of the expenses over and above mortality costs.

COMMERCIAL VS. FRATERNAL INSURANCE

Taking up the question of cost to the insured person, it is difficult to make an accurate comparison of fraternal insurance with commercial policies. The current method of determining the average annual payment of the commercial policyholder is discussed quite fully in the author's book, *Advanced Life Insurance*, pp. 209-20. Local dues and payments made by fraternal certificate-holders for purposes other than insurance should be eliminated to arrive at the fraternalist's average annual payment. In a paper read before a recent meeting of the National Fraternal Congress of America, Dr. George W. Hoglan[2] states that he made a comparison of the yearly cost, without local lodge dues, of ten representative fraternal societies operating on an adequate-rate basis, with the cost of ten representative old-line companies. He selected age thirty, and, though he did not state his method of determining the costs, it seems probable that he used the usual methods, and chose non-participating premium rates for policies without double indemnity or disability provisions. His conclusions were that the fraternal societies' average cost to those entering at age thirty was $20.81 per $1000 of insurance per year; whereas the companies' average cost to those entering them at that age was only $18.29, or $2.52 per $1000 per year less than the cost with the societies. He further pointed out that the lowest old-line rate was $3.62 lower than the average rate for the ten societies, without local lodge dues, and that if these dues were included in the cost to members, the average cost of the ten fraternal societies would exceed the cost of this old-line company by $6.62, or by nearly thirty-eight per cent.

REASON FOR INCREASED COST

In view of the fact that, until very recent years, fraternal insurance has been looked upon as much cheaper than old-line or commercial insurance, these figures are indeed startling. The increase in the cost of this form of protection has been brought about chiefly by the efforts of the societies to accomplish two objects. The first of these was the attainment of actuarial solvency by re-adjusting their business to an adequate-rate basis, and the second one was to resell the plan of fraternal insurance to the public.

It should be understood that cheap fraternal insurance on an inadequate-rate basis still exists, the most recent Wisconsin report showing a grand total ratio per cent of actual assets to required reserves of but 56.2 per cent for all societies operating in that state. Readjustment has been discussed previously in this article.

Reselling the fraternal insurance plan to the public has involved a large increase in the remuneration of fraternal deputies or special representatives who act as agents of a society in much the same manner as do the agents of a commercial company act for it. In former years, societies grew because of the efforts of members -- old ones bringing in new ones. This method of increasing membership is no longer effective since so many old members lost enthusiasm for the plan when readjustments were necessary, and new business must now be secured in the same manner as that of commercial companies. When faced with this change in conditions, the societies found themselves without an organized sales force to do the work formerly done by members. So-called service companies have trained salesmen to help the societies, for a substantial commission, to resell the plan, especially on readjustment. Sales forces have now been developed by the societies and by these companies to such an extent that considerable fraternal insurance can be, and is being, sold, but after it is sold a second difficulty presents itself. Most of the members pay in but a small fee on joining a society. They are then supposed to be held in the society by the local secretary or collector, who is often given little or nothing for his work. The result is that from one-third to one-half of the new business written lapses within a year. It is thus seen that fraternal insurance has commercialized its field work to the extent that the cost of securing new business at least equals, and indeed it often exceeds, the cost of obtaining new business for the commercial companies. Yet to date the societies have been unable to obtain the same efficiency, economy, stability, and confidence that characterizes the business of the companies. In fact, the most progressive societies that are maintaining, or striving successfully towards, actuarial solvency, are repeating, in large measure, the early experience of the companies.

FRATERNAL BENEFITS

Another phase in the recent development of this business has to do with the provisions of the fraternal benefit certificate. In addition to juvenile insurance, one may now purchase insurance covering the whole of life, or only a term of it. Whole-life certificates may be purchased on either the level-premium or the step-rate-premium plan. In the case of whole-life insurance on the step-rate-premium plan, the premium becomes a level one after attaining some specified age such as sixty or sixty-five. If the insured person wishes to do so he may pay an extra premium, over and above the step-rates, during the step-rate period, the accumulation of extra premiums being used to reduce the level premium that begins late in life below what it otherwise would be. One may also purchase endowments of different durations, or limited-payment life insurance. In fact the life benefits promised in fraternal benefit certificates are quite similar to those guaranteed by the contracts of commercial companies. It is also not uncommon to provide an accident and sickness benefit in fraternal certificates.

It should be noted, however, that the fraternal benefit certificate is not a closed contract, but includes the by-laws of the society, and any amendments of them that may be made. Furthermore, the society is required by law to reserve the right to levy additional or increased assessments, and if these are not paid, it may reduce the amount of insurance. A commercial company cannot increase the premium rate on policies that have been issued beyond the gross rate stipulated in the contract.

IN SUMMARY

To summarize the principal occurrences in the field of fraternal life insurance during the past decade, which covers the time elapsing since the publication of the last volume of *The Annals* of the American Academy of Political and Social Science, devoted to insurance,[3] we may state that the fraternal system has made substantial progress toward placing its business upon sound and enduring plans. Assets have increased and a higher percentage of solvency than that prevailing a decade ago has been attained. As a whole, the societies have steadily advanced towards an adequate-rate basis. They have adopted more businesslike methods and plans for conducting most of their activities than those previously employed. In the matter of selling their insurance and keeping it in force, they have not yet succeeded in perfecting an organization that functions efficiently. The cost of securing new business has greatly increased until it now seems very high compared to former costs. In fact, this increase has been so great that we have numerous instances in which sound fraternal insurance costs the insured person more than does the sound commercial insurance issued by old-line or legal-reserve companies.

ENDNOTES

1. See the author's *Advanced Life Insurance*, pp. 370-91. New York: John Wiley & Sons, 1926.

2. See *Proceedings*, 1923, pp. 393 et seq..

3. See *The Annals* for March, 1917, on "Modern Insurance Problems."

CONTRIBUTING AUTHORS

David Brion Davis, Ph.D., (1927- Present) is the Sterling Professor of History Emeritus at Yale University. A Past President of the Organization of American Historians, he is a Pulitzer Prize recipient for *The Problem of Slavery in Western Culture* published in 1967.

John Mitchell Foster (1850-1928), the author of books including *Christ the King, The Basis of Moral Reformation,* and *Reformation Principles Stated and Applied,* served as the Pastor of the Second Reformed Presbyterian Church in Boston, Massachusetts. He received an A.B. from Indiana University in 1871.

Noel P. Gist, Ph.D., (1899 - 1983) earned his Ph.D. from Northwestern University. A prolific writer of articles and influential sociology textbooks, Gist taught at both the University of Kansas and the University of Missouri.

Charles Moreau Harger (1863-1955) served as a reporter and editor for the *Abilene Daily Reflector* for 25 years and contributed articles concerning western business and financial affairs to *The Century, Harper's, Scribner's, The Atlantic,* and many others. He also served as the director and first lecturer for the Department of Journalism at the University of Kansas from 1905 to 1910.

William Sumner Harwood (1857-1908) was a prolific journalist and author of *New Creation in Plant Life: An Authoritative Account of the Life of Luther Burbank* and *The New Earth,* among other works.

Walter B. Hill, A.M., L.L.D., (1851-1905) served as the Chancellor of the University of Georgia from 1899-1905. A respected lawyer, jurist, and writer, he was a leader in the movement in support of prohibition and an activist for improved education for African-Americans.

Charles K. Knight, Ph.D. (1890-1982) served as Professor of Insurance at the Wharton School of Business at the University of Pennsylvania for forty-two years. He was the author of several books on insurance.

Abb Landis (1856-1927) was a lawyer and owner of the *Nashville Banner*. He authored several books on the fraternal insurance system and argued important fraternal cases in the courts as well as constructing the National Fraternal Congress's *Table of Mortality*.

Milton Lehman (1917-1966) was a free-lance writer who contributed nearly 250 articles to national magazines including *The Saturday Evening Post, Life, McCall's,* among others. In 1963, he authored a biography of rocket scientist Robert Goddard.

Charles Merz (1893-1977) was a writer and managing editor of the *New York Times* from 1938 to 1961. He began his career at *Harper's Weekly* and subsequently served as the Washington Correspondent for *The New Republic*. His books include *Centerville, U.S.A., The Great American Bandwagon,* and *The Dry Decade*.

Balthasar Henry Meyer, Ph.D., (1866-1954) was a professor of Political Economy at the University of Wisconsin. He also served as the chairman of the Wisconsin Railroad Commission from 1907 to 1911. From 1911 to 1930 he served on the Interstate Commerce Commission.

Walter H. Page (1855-1918) began his career as a journalist and rose to become editor of *The Atlantic Monthly*. Later he was Vice President of Doubleday, Page & Company, before serving as the U.S. Ambassador to the United Kingdom from 1913 to 1918.

Walter Smith Nichols (1841-1921) was the editor-in-chief of *The Insurance Monitor* and *The Insurance Law Journal*.

Arthur M. Schlesinger, Sr., (1888-1965) was a prominent and influential American historian. Trained at Ohio State University and Columbia, Schlesinger championed the introduction of social and cultural materials into historical discourse. The author of many books, he served as Francis Lee Higginson Professor of History at Harvard University from 1931 to 1954.

Georg Simmel, Ph.D., (1858-1918), was an influential early sociologist at the University of Berlin. He authored more than fifteen major works in the fields of philosophy, ethics, sociology, and cultural criticism.

Albert Clark Stevens (1854-1919) was a journalist and editor of *Bradstreets*, the *New York Commerical*, the *Patterson Guardian*, and the *Newark News*. An active Freemason, Stevens compiled the seminal *Cyclopedia of Fraternities*.

Hugh C. Weir (1884-1934) was a newspaper reporter, magazine editor, author, and screenwriter. Having written his first screenplay for Universal Studios at the age of 20, he subsequently authored at least 300 screenplays and numerous short stories and articles.

Index

Odd Fellows, Manchester Unity,
233-235
office-holding, 11, 25, 30
Oklahoma Masonic Charity
Foundation, xi
Oklahoma State University, xi
Olive Leaf Circles, 80
Omladina, 152
Orange Institution, Loyal, 194, 196
Orangemen, 170
ordeal, ceremonial, 178-180
ordeals, burlesque, 180
organizational structure, 194-196,
200, 250-251
Orioles , 51, 53
Oronhyatekha , 227
Owls, Order of, 51, 194

Page, Walter, 264, 278
password, 177
Pathfinder, The, 222
patriotism, 187
Patriarchal Circle of America ,
220
Patricians of Pompeii, Prudent, 222
Patriots of America, 52
penalties, fraternal, 21, 57
Pendo, Order of, 222
perversity, sexual, 107, 111
Phi Alpha Phi, 189
Philip of France, 42
Phythian-Adams, W. J., 183
Pilgrim Fathers, United Order of, 4,
219
Pioneer Reserve Association, 222
Pocahontas, Degree of, 57, 62
political influence, 9
politicians, 207

polygamy, 107, 110
Populist Party, 86
Princeton University Press, viii
professional associations, 82, 86-87
Prophets of the Enchanted Realm,
Mystic Order of Veiled, 51, 56,
189
Protected Home Circle, 220
Protection, Sons and Daughters of,
222
Prudential Insurance Company of
America, 250
publications, reform, 80
Putnam, Robert, x
Putnam, Rufus, 74
Pyramids, Ancient Order of the, 222
Pythagorians, 41, 149
Pythias, Chevaliers of , 52
Pythias, Knights of, vii, 2, 4, 38, 44,
51, 176, 187, 189, 194, 195, 203,
219, 225, 226, 264-265
Pythias of North and South
America, Europe, Asia, and
Africa, Knights of, 190

racial discrimination within
fraternal groups, 190
Rainbow, Order of the, 178, 190
Rameses, Order of, 189
rates, benefit, 204, 234, 265
Rebekah, Daughters of, 46, 51
Rechabites, Independent Order of, 5,
196
Reconstruction, 92
Red Cross, Ancient Order of the, 222
Red Cross, Legion of the, 220
Red Cross, Order of the, 219

CPSIA information can be obtained at www.ICGtesting.com
Printed in the USA
LVOW041557051211

257920LV00006B/42/P